GANG DELINQUENCY
AND DELINQUENT SUBCULTURES

Readers in Social Problems

DONALD R. CRESSEY, CONSULTING EDITOR
UNIVERSITY OF CALIFORNIA, SANTA BARBARA

GANG DELINQUENCY AND DELINQUENT SUBCULTURES

EDITED BY

JAMES F. SHORT, JR.

WASHINGTON STATE UNIVERSITY

HARPER & ROW

Publishers

NEW YORK, EVANSTON, AND LONDON

Contents

our language

PART II / THEORIES AND DATA
CONCERNING DELINQUENT SUBCULTURES

Preface

EDITING A COLLECTION of readings can be an onerous task, indeed, if one seeks merely to cull the literature for representative pieces concerning a subject matter area. It can be exciting and informative, however, if one has a hand in the development of a literature. In the fall of 1965 I had agreed to aid in the organization and editing of a special issue of the *Journal of Research in Crime and Delinquency* (Vol. 4, January, 1967), to be devoted to the subject of gangs. In the process of recruiting papers for this issue I "discovered" projects and articles of which I had not previously been aware. This volume is the beneficiary of the *JRCD* issue. Three articles are reprinted from it, and readers are referred to others which discuss topics not covered here. In particular, excellent articles trace the history of empirical inquiry in this area,[1] focus on important theoretical and empirical issues,[2] report on study of gang phenomena in other cultures,[3] and on a unique—and hopeful in its findings—attempt to evaluate the effectiveness of a detached worker program.[4]

---

[1] Dale G. Hardman, "Historical Perspective of Gang Research."

[2] LaMar T. Empey, "Delinquency Theory and Recent Research"; and Muzafer Sherif and Carolyn W. Sherif, "Group Process and Collective Interaction in Delinquent Activities."

[3] Jean Monod, "Juvenile Gangs in Paris: Toward a Structural Analysis"; and Lois B. DeFleur, "Delinquent Gangs in Cross-Cultural Perspective: The Case of Cordoba."

[4] Stuart Adams, "A Cost Approach to the Assessment of Gang Rehabilitation Techniques."

Selection of articles for this collection has not been easy. Exciting theoretical formulations and provocative essays have appeared with increasing frequency in recent years. We have chosen to emphasize contemporary and empirical research, and the vital and creative interplay between theory and the findings of such research. Present levels of activity of this type are such that the speculations and empirical probes which so largely comprise this volume are likely, in the not too distant future, to be replaced with a more firm foundation of knowledge.[5]

As editor, it is a pleasure to acknowledge the aid and co-operation of all my coauthors in this enterprise. My thanks, also, to series editor Donald R. Cressey for his encouragement and to Mrs. Bernice Dayton and Rita Rastorfer, secretaries extraordinaire, for their good offices in getting the project "off the ground."

JAMES F. SHORT, JR.

August, 1967

---

[5] Impressive beginnings are evident in the reports of the President's Commission on Law Enforcement and Administration of Justice. See, especially, *Juvenile Delinquency and Youth Crime,* containing reports of the Task Force on Juvenile Delinquency (Washington, D.C.: U.S. Government Printing Office, 1967).

Introduction:
On Gang Delinquency
and the
Nature of Subcultures

INTRODUCTION

IT IS generally agreed among behavior scientists and professionals concerned with problems of juvenile delinquency, that focus upon different *patterns of behavior*, as contrasted with juvenile delinquency in general, will lead to greater knowledge and control of the illusive phenomena so loosely grouped under this rubric. This book deals with several such patterns of behavior. They have in common a *collective* character, in the sense that they exist by virtue of the fact that groups of youngsters (sometimes referred to as gangs) are responsible for them, and they appear to be subcultural in nature; that is, they have become traditional among these and other groups which give them support.

THE GROUP NATURE OF DELINQUENCY

The focus on gang delinquency and delinquent subcultures stems from several bodies of sociological research and theory. There is, first of all, the common observation that delinquency tends to be a group phenomenon. From 60 percent to more than 90 percent of the offenses committed by youngsters have been reported in a variety of studies to have occurred in groups.[1] Most of these groups are quite small, consisting of two to four youngsters, though these often are

All footnotes appear in the Notes section, grouped by article, at the end of this book.

found to be part of still larger groups, or gangs. Gangs tend to be relatively small, however, popular reports of unusual and sensational episodes of gang violence notwithstanding. Thrasher reported that more than a quarter of the 895 gangs on which he had such data had 10 or fewer members, and nearly three-quarters had no more than 25 members.[2] At the other extreme, 4.2 percent had more than 100 members. Thrasher noted that the larger "gangs" tended to be "conventionalized" and less delinquent.

A recent investigation which studied intensively 16 of Chicago's more delinquent gangs found that gang membership fluctuated considerably from time to time, with only four gangs having more than 50 active members at any one time (the most was 68).[3] Rarely were more than 20 members of a gang gathered at any one time and place except when specific events were planned for or by the gang or in times of crisis for the gang, as in the case of impending conflict. Jansyn has noted among the Chicago gang he observed for more than a year that estimates by the boys of group size "varied from a very few 'good members' to over a hundred whom they could 'get together' if they wanted to." Estimates became particularly large when the boys felt they were being pushed around and a fight seemed imminent.[4]

Yablonsky has noted that the violent gangs he studied were characterized by "diffuse role definitions, limited cohesion, impermanence, minimal consensus on norms, shifting membership, disturbed leadership, and limited definitions of membership expectations."[5] These matters vary from group to group, of course, and there is some evidence to suggest that the gang leaders may be less "disturbed" than other gang members.[6] Yablonsky's observations confirm the reports of others, however, that many—and probably most—gangs are not as cohesive as popular accounts would have us believe.

While definitive evidence is lacking, the extent to which delinquent behavior occurs in groups apparently varies a great deal by age, sex, social class, and type of offense. Gang behavior is particularly a phenomenon of adolescence, of males, and of the lower socioeconomic classes, where the one-sex peer group is traditionally an important aspect of social organization. The latter is by no means exclusive to the lower classes, however.[7]

Early studies found stealing, especially, to be a group offense, but recent attention has focused particularly on the depredations of gangs in conflict with one another and on drug use among groups of young people. Most of the studies—and most of the problems—concern groups of young men, but females are not immune. In the selections chosen for this book, descriptive studies bearing on three hypothesized delinquent subcultures are reported. In Part I we have focused on conflict, criminal, and drug-use patterns. Others, entailing delinquent behavior of many sorts in varying degrees, might be discussed, e.g., the Hell's Angels motorcycle group and various "beat" and "hippy" groups, or the riotous behavior associated with the appearance of popular rock and roll idols in the United States and in other countries.[8] The latter appear to be more a function of the collective excitement involved in crowd behavior than of subcultural or "traditional" behavior, but there is almost no systematic evidence on the point.[9]

William Foote Whyte's classic description of "corner boys" and "college boys" makes an important contribution to a typology of adjustment to the human condition of the slum.[10] Here two groups of young men growing up in an ethnic slum of a large city are described as having adopted very different patterns of behavior, or styles of life, in relation to their class, ethnic, and community background. The college boys are upwardly mobile, ambitious, oriented toward education as a means of self-betterment. The corner boys, on the other hand, have accepted their lower-class life and are content to remain in this station of life with its familiar patterns. The delinquent gang, Cohen has hypothesized, is different from both of these, for the gang member chooses life with the gang rather then either the college boy or the stable corner boy adjustment.[11] His is a life devoted to the pursuits of the gang and whatever rewards it may bring. The nature of these re-

wards and of the behavior patterns associated with them has
been the subject of much speculation and no little research
effort.

ON FEMALE PARTICIPATION IN
DELINQUENT SUBCULTURES

The gang world is dominated largely by males, as reports
emphasize from Thrasher, and earlier, to the present. But
girls are important, too, for many reasons: as sex objects,
hustles to be exploited, sources of prestige among the boys
with whom they are associated, and in their own right.
"Female auxiliary" groups are not uncommon, and when
they exist they perform many functions for boys' gangs and
enjoy a degree of autonomy among themselves. Their names
characteristically suggest their association with boys' gangs,
e.g., Vice Queens (associated with the Vice Kings), Egyptian
Cobrettes (associated with the Egyptian Cobras), and Lady
Racketeers (associated with the Racketeers).

Salisbury's description of the girls in the "Shook-up Generation" suggests that patterns similar to those described for
boys by Whyte and Cohen may be found also among girls.[12]

I think that only one among the young people in the candy store
that night had a reasonable chance of breaking the pattern. This
was Maureen, a tall mature brunette of eighteen. She talked very
frankly and looked you in the eye as she talked. She was in her
last year of parochial high school. She wanted to go to college.
"But not with the sisters, thank you," she laughed. "I've had twelve
years with them. They are very nice and all that but enough is
enough. I'm going upstate. To a teachers' college."

The girl sitting next to Maureen was called Flora. She was a
blonde with wide blue eyes and heavily painted lips. She didn't
pay any attention to Maureen's talk. There was a bridge of
freckles over her nose and traces of a tan. Flora had only been
back home two weeks from Florida. She went there with a married
man who kept her a month and then put her on a bus for home.
No one thought the worse of Flora for this. She had come right
back to the candy store. If a boy wanted to take her out in
his car that was fine. If another boy wanted her when they got
back that was okay, too. She was just sitting around, waiting for

something to turn up. Maybe another man who would like to take her to Florida. Or possibly California. It didn't really make any difference.

Maureen did not disapprove of Flora. If Flora wanted to go with men that was Flora's business. It just wasn't Maureen's style, that was all. Nor was Maureen like Annabella, the dark-haired Italian girl with ruby cheeks who sat across from her. Annabella had a single-track mind. She wanted a boy to go steady with, a boy who had a job and who wanted to get married. Annabella wanted to get married. Nothing else made the slightest difference. When she went out with boys she didn't let them fool around. Not unless they wanted to get married. Some girls said she was foolish. That wasn't the way to get a boy. Let him make love. Get pregnant. When the baby was coming he would have to marry you. Maybe the girls were right. So far Annabella wasn't sure. If she didn't get a boy this year maybe she would change her tactics. She would see.

Maureen laughed at Annabella.

"Go steady if you want to," she said. "Go ahead and get married. Have your babies. As for me, I'm not going steady. There's not a boy in the world I would go steady with. First, I'm going to college. Maybe I'll meet somebody there. One thing I'll tell you, I'm going to get out of this dump. And never come back."

It will take a year or two to test Maureen's determination. But she had a better chance of success than the boys. Her parents were backing her. Her father earned enough money on the docks to send her to school. He was not a heavy drinker. Maureen was a strong, tough girl. If a boy used filthy language, and the boys liked to use obscenity before girls, Maureen told him off in the same words. She knew them all. If a boy got rough with her she knew where to hit him so it would hurt most.

I did not meet many youngsters of Maureen's tenacity but I did not meet a single gang leader who did not say that he wanted to break out of the pattern of street life. I think the boys are sincere in this. The difficulty lies in their ignorance of how to go about it and their lack of strength to cope with stubborn reality.

Flora apparently was not a member of a gang, but her orientation toward life appears otherwise similar. Being a member of a gang provides another dimension to problems of status management, and to other problems. If the gang is a female auxiliary of a gang of boys, these problems and their solutions are very much colored by this fact.[13]

Delinquent subcultures in which females participate are as varied as any. Participation of girls in drug-use subcultures, for example, is extensive.[14] A common theme in much of the literature relative to female delinquency which is subculturally supported concerns the lack of social skills and "normal" boy-girl relations among the girls studied. The drug users seem especially caught up in a vicious cycle of unsatisfactory interpersonal relations, particularly with males, isolation from "respectable" society, addiction, and prostitution. Even the nondrug-users, however, appear to be swept along by limited social and other abilities, and experiences which limit opportunities to acquire these skills or to exercise them if acquired.

The major questions, of course, have to do with how patterns of behavior come about and why. Part II presents several selections which attempt in various ways to answer these questions. Broadly, they are couched in terms of three theoretical perspectives, emphasizing respectively (1) the impact of socialization in cultures associated with one's local community and social-class membership, (2) *reactions to* one's position in the social order, in terms of opportunities for achievement of economic and status rewards by legitimate or illegitimate means, and (3) processes in the ongoing life of peer and other groups within the context of the local community.

THE ECOLOGICAL BACKGROUND

Much of the early sociological concern with the gang was associated with the "old Chicago School" of urban sociology, with its emphasis upon urban structure and processes of city development. Here the focus was on location of gangs in the ecology of the city. Gangs were discovered to be concentrated in slum areas—in the "zone in transition" of Burgess' sketch of urban growth.[15] These were residential areas which were being encroached upon by the commercial and industrial expansion of the city. Sociologists studying these areas found overcrowded and substandard housing conditions, low income and education levels, and unstable residential populations (as commercial and industrial land use increased). Recent research demonstrates the continued association of a great variety of social ills, including juvenile delinquency, with these same factors. There is a difference in the old studies and the new, however, for while the earlier studies found delinquency to be a common problem among the foreign born, recent data find the problem to be especially acute among unassimilated native-born groups, particularly Negroes.[16] As was true of other ethnic groups in the past, delinquency rates of Negroes vary a great deal from place to place, in association with the same types of community conditions to which the rates of other groups are closely related, especially economic status and the adequacy of community institutions. And, as Shaw and McKay have reminded us, while Negro rates

. . . are higher than the rates for white boys . . . it cannot be said that they are higher than rates for white boys in comparable areas, since it is impossible to reproduce in white communities the circumstances under which Negro children live. Even if it were possible to parallel the low economic status and the inadequacy of institutions in the white community, it would not be possible to reproduce the effects of segregation and the barriers to upward mobility.[17]

McKay's continued research in the tradition of the earlier studies has produced new findings concerning community factors related to delinquency and its control.[18] The *trends* of officially recorded delinquency for Chicago's 79 community areas, from 1927-1962, reveal that both the communities with the most pronounced *upward* trends and those with the steepest *downward* trends are Negro communities. A most significant difference between these communities is the fact that the communities with the most rapidly rising rates have experienced *recent* settlement by Negroes, while those with the most rapidly falling rates experienced Negro "invasion" before the beginning of the period under study, or during the very early years. The inference seems clear: residential shifts involving the invasion of communities by socially and economically disadvantaged groups is disorganizing for traditional institutions of social control, weakening the ability of communities to control the behavior of their constituents. Thus, delinquency and other social problems increase during the early years of such population shifts. (For example, Mc-Kay finds that truancy and mental illness rates behave in much the same manner as delinquency rates.) When (and if) these communities stabilize in population, however, institutions of social control apparently stabilize and become more effective. The process of disorganization is likely to be especially acute when the transition in population is rapid, and the displacement of white by Negro populations customarily occurs rapidly as a result of the extreme pressures placed on Negroes by housing restrictions and the reactions of whites who flee to the suburbs and to other "all-white" housing areas once Negro invasion has begun. Problems of social control are also aggravated for Negro communities, because they have lacked traditions of indigenous leadership and urban community organization, both important factors in the adjustment of other migrant populations. Nevertheless, organization does develop and apparently becomes increasingly effective with stability. Precisely how this occurs, and why, are important matters for research as yet unaccomplished. There is evidence of change in these respects in the civil rights movement of recent years, and in increased political activity of Negroes, individually and collectively.

Those who have stressed social disorganization in relation to various social problems in the urban slum have tended to ignore, or view simply as pathological, forms of organization which they found in slum communities. In recent years a body of literature has developed which documents the existence of organizational forms in slum communities which are fundamental to the structure of these communities and which embody many of the cultural values to be found in them. These forms include some which are nonconventional, such as the gang, various forms of illegal enterprise, e.g., gambling and prostitution, "quarter parties," and neighborhood taverns. They include, also, conventional institutions, which are related to these less conventional forms, or at least are influenced by them, e.g., political organizations, the police, churches, and various ethnic ("old country," in the case of immigrant groups) organizations.[19]

As we have written elsewhere,

> The point is not so much that all communities are organized, but that the nature and degree of social organization varies from community to community and that these variations are related in important ways to the behavior of residents of these communities. It is the case that in many communities the traditional, conventional institutions of socialization and social control are ineffective. It appears, also, that some of the forms of organization which arise in such communities are conducive to behavior which is illegal and disturbing to the larger community and, in many instances, to local residents. This is particularly true of episodes of violence which result in serious injury, robbery, or property damage, and of predatory activities such as purse-snatching and burglary. No community condones these activities—even those who participate in them wish to be protected against victimization by others.[20]

The answer to why gang delinquency exists—in its predatory, violent, and retreatist forms—resolves into questions concerning the nature of the groups in which it is found, of the individuals comprising them, and of interaction within them. Important consideration must be given the subcultures carried by these groups—including delinquent subcultures, specifically, and subcultures of youth[21] and of segments of youth, generally, such as those bounded by social class, ethnicity, and local community.

ON SUBCULTURES

It is important to distinguish between gangs and subcultures, for most subcultures are not carried solely by a particular group, and what happens within any one group is a function not only of the values of the particular subculture which binds the members of a group together. Indeed, the character of *conflict* gangs depends to a considerable extent upon their relationships with other conflict gangs—as allies or enemies—and their reputations among these gangs. By way of contrast, the *criminal* orientation of some cliques or gangs is likely to be influenced by their relations with adult role models and intermediaries, such as fences, with those who are their customers, and with law enforcement officials to a greater extent than by their contacts with other gangs. Similarly, *gang* identification tends to decrease and often to disappear among drug users, particularly addicts; the physical and subcultural demands of drug use become virtually consuming of the time and energy of its carriers.

The universe of gang members is one of largely unknown dimensions, and no census of gangs is likely to be complete for any length of time, so variable are the definitions and so shifting in character are these phenomena. It is clear that public definition, e.g., by the mass media, and definition by those who are closer to the "action," e.g., detached workers and youngsters who participate in gangs, differ a great deal. Yablonsky, Jansyn, and others have demonstrated that there is much difference of opinion even among gang participants.[22] A recent study of young people in a random sample of New York City's Lower East Side[23]—regarded by many as a hotbed of gang activity—finds that less than 10 percent of the boys interviewed identified themselves with a named group when asked, "Who do you usually go around with?" The group of two or three boys was most commonly reported among all age groups. A "regular group," more than a triad, was reported by about one-third of the boys, though this percentage reached nearly 50 percent for the 14- to 15-year-olds, tapering off to 30 percent among 16- to 19-year-olds. This same study finds evidence of shared, collective deviance, both officially in the form of police records, and unofficially as based on self-reports of the respondents. A high incidence of police contact was found for boys high in a subcultural typology, based on knowledge of bopping and drug argot and shared deviant values. Except for boys in the highest category of the typology, however, most respondents indicated that most of the illegal acts they reported had been committed while they were alone. Forty-three percent of those highest on the subcultural typology reported they were with one or two others, 38 percent were by themselves, and 13 percent were with a regular group. The extent to which these responses are typical of a general adolescent population is, of course, unknown. To what extent responses may have been distorted by boys who were unwilling to confide in the interviewers is also unknown. Even known gang members have been found to report that they usually go around with one or two others rather than with the gang, and field observation confirms that they do. Gang identity and participation are greatly influenced by situational variables, some of which are discussed in the selections which follow.

It is clear, from these findings and from studies which have directed attention specifically to gangs, that in most cases gangs and subcultures are not coterminous and that among gang boys most delinquencies do not involve the total group. That the gang is an important referent for many youngsters is equally clear, however. Both social or interactional components and subcultural components must be recognized in behavior causation; and the behavior of gang members is a function not only of participation in the subculture of the gang, but of other subcultures as well, e.g., social class and ethnicity associated with neighborhood residence.

Subcultures are patterns of values, norms, and behavior which have become traditional among certain groups. These groups may be of many types, including occupational and ethnic groups, social classes, occupants of "closed institutions" and of various age grades. In the case of gang delinquency, particular gangs may change subcultural orientations over time—or they may remain very much the same over different "generations" of gang boys—and these are important aspects of gang delinquency for study and explanation.[24] Subcultures are, in any case, important frames of reference through which individuals and groups see the world and interpret it. We need to know a great deal more about the nature of subcultures, how and why they develop, change, and die, or are maintained over time.

Albert K. Cohen has set forth a general theory of subcultures which illuminates their nature and the manner in which they develop.[25] Cohen begins with the psychological assumption that behavior is problem solving; that is, whenever people act, they do so in response to some problem or set of problems, ranging from the most trivial and habitually solved to the most difficult and demanding. Choices among behavior alternatives, Cohen reminds us, depend upon the nature of the problems, and this in part is dependent upon the nature of the individuals involved and the situations in which they find themselves.

The nature of human problems and situations are never matters simply of objective conditions. The extent to which an objective condition is a problem—whether it be the job a person has, his automobile, place of residence, or any other aspect of the human condition—depends to a considerable extent upon how he interprets this condition and whether he defines it as a problem. This, in turn, is determined by a host of influences from early childhood to the present. But these influences are not randomly distributed. They are patterned for the individual in important ways. We say that a person comes to "see the world" as a male or female, as a member of a particular racial or ethnic group, as a Russian or an American. We mean by this that these groups serve as important referents for the individual as he interprets the world in which he lives.

The influences of particular subcultures on an individual's behavior depends, to a considerable extent, on the nature of his relations with other carriers of these subcultures. The member of an ethnic group, for example, may associate almost entirely with other members of this group—they may, in other words, constitute a most important reference group for him—or he may disavow his ethnic identity, choose to live and associate with those who do not belong to his ethnic group, in which case his ethnic group may be important as a reference group in a negative sense, as something to be avoided.

The influence of reference groups and the subcultures they represent depends upon many factors, e.g., the frequency, priority, duration, and intensity of one's association with them, to employ Sutherland's terminology,[26] the degree of freedom of the individual to associate or disassociate himself with them, and important situational elements. It is easier for most Caucasian ethnics to dissociate themselves from their ethnic identity than it is for most Negroes, for example. One may avoid the influence of some occupational subcultures more easily than others, though occupation tends to have an important influence on most individuals.

Age, sex, and class status have been given particular attention in theories of delinquency. We know that young persons bulk large in the proportion of persons arrested, as reported by the FBI. In 1965, for example, the largest number of persons arrested for all crimes were 16 years of age, followed by 17-, 18-, and 15-year-olds in that order.[27] Bloch and Niederhoffer argue that for some youngsters gang delinquency serves as a substitute for the *rites de passage* which marked the transition from childhood to adulthood for adolescents in primitive societies.[28]

While sex ratios among youngsters who come to the attention of juvenile courts have decreased considerably in recent decades, there still are between four and five boys to every girl making a court appearance. Sex ratios vary greatly for different offenses, boys coming to official attention primarily for stealing and property destruction or general mischief, girls most often for offenses involving sex behavior, directly or indirectly. Further, it appears that when boys and girls steal, they do so for different reasons. Grosser found that the girls he studied most often engaged in stealing behavior which was role *supportive,* i.e., objects which could facilitate performance of feminine roles, such as cosmetics and clothing.[29]

These age and sex differences reflect, in part, subcultures which develop in response to problems which are associated with childhood, adolescence, and with being male or female. It is with reference to social class, however, that social scientists have been most concerned in subcultural theories of delinquency. It has long been known that official delinquency is distributed in the familiar ecological pattern discussed above. In large cities, data gathered by means of field observation and self-reports confirm official records suggesting that lower-class children are more likely than children from more favored economic circumstances to become involved in delinquency.[30] Studies conducted in smaller cities and towns do not find this relationship.[31] All of these studies find that delinquents associate largely with one another, however, and that they share certain ways of looking at the world. Thus, both social and cultural bases for delinquency are confirmed, though a convincing rationale for their existence remains undemonstrated.

The most thoughtful effort to interpret class differences in delinquent behavior is found, again, in the work of Albert Cohen. Cohen takes as his point of departure the importance for the youngster of growing up in a class system, and he proceeds to identify common problems of adjustment of working-class boys which he feels are relevant to explain the delinquent character of the response of some of these youngsters. The argument, greatly condensed, is as follows:[32]

. . . the delinquent subculture is a response to status problems associated primarily with the male working-class role—*male* because "being somebody" is for males, more than for females, dependent upon personal achievement; *working class* because persons in this stratum face problems not encountered by those above them. There is, apparently, no single set of criteria by which young people are evaluated in our society, and one must, therefore, be guarded in his generalizations. However, in the United States, where the value of upward mobility pervades all segments of the population, an important set of criteria is that which emphasizes those personal qualities and achievements that facilitate upward mobility and which is applied by those segments of the population that control the gateways to "getting ahead," such as teachers, business and professional people, ministers, and civic leaders. Cohen calls this set of criteria the *middle-class* criteria of status, not because they are peculiarly middle class but because they are subscribed to by middle-class people more consistently and with less ambivalence than by other classes.

These criteria include the following: ambition; a pattern of deferred gratification, that is, a capacity for sustained effort, involving the subordination of immediate satisfactions in the interest of achieving long-run goals; a sense of personal responsibility for one's failures and achievements, the possession of skills of potential academic, economic, and occupational value; the rational cultivation of manners, courtesy, and personableness, which involves patience, self-discipline, and the control of emotional expression, physical aggression, and violence.

Socialization in working-class homes is less likely to produce young people with the ability to do well in terms of these criteria than is middle-class socialization. Many working-class children thus appear rough, uncouth, ill-bred, undisciplined, and lacking in ambition, ability, and drive. In school they are ill-equipped, lacking the background and the habits that would help them to master academic subjects and to perform acceptably in other ways. Furthermore, the "democratic" ethos allows and even encourages working-class children to "better themselves" and to compete for status with middle-class children, and holds that they are entitled to the same rewards if deserving. By the same token, however, it subjects children of differing backgrounds to evaluation by the same set of standards, the "middle-class measuring rod." Thus, working-class children are systematically disadvantaged in the competitive pursuit of status and are likely to find themselves repeatedly "at the bottom of the heap" with their self-respect damaged.

This is true, however, only so long as the working-class child accepts the validity of the middle-class definitions and expectations of the child role, or, in different words, if he elects to play the game and seek the prizes under the rules as defined by the dominant, middle-class culture. It is not true if the child can successfully repudiate the validity of those rules and can convince himself that the game is unworthy of his participation. To do this, however, he still needs support from others and alternative sources of status. As it happens, he is not unique. There are many "in the same boat" and for the same reasons. These individuals, says Cohen, tend to draw together and, through their sympathetic interaction, develop social systems of their own and their own rules of the game and criteria of status. The new status system, according to the theory, is fully intelligible only as a reaction to the conventional status system. Virtue comes to consist in flouting and defying middle-class morality. Orderliness, amenability to adult supervision and guidance, respect for property, polite speech and manners, the preference of diplomacy to violence—these are contemptuously spurned by the new, jointly supported way of life, the delinquent subculture. It is to be noted that this conception of delinquency as behavior in accordance with a subculture tailored to certain socially structured problems of adjustment of working-class boys make sense only as a group response.

Cohen's thesis has provoked much discussion and theoretical controversy and, more recently, considerable research effort. Research does not support the hypothesis that members of delinquent gangs reject middle-class values or those who administer the "middle class measuring rod."[33] It is found, however, that the gang discourages expression of conventional values, and that values which are given active support within the context of gang interaction, e.g., toughness and sexual prowess, are not conducive to conventional types of achievement.

Other theories have been proposed to account for variations in delinquent subcultures and for behavior within the context of gangs. To the extent that these have received systematic empirical attention, they, too, have been dealt with less than kindly by the data. There is evidence that these theoretical efforts are beginning to pay off, however, in revision and synthesis, in experimental action programs to control gang delinquency and delinquent subcultures, and in more comprehensive research efforts. The selections brought together here offer both historical and contemporary relevance, a sampling of responsible theoretical concern and of empirical assessment. While it is clear that not all the data are in—they can never be for such complex and changing phenomena—the prospect for better knowledge and control is encouraging and exciting, indeed. The scientific literature concerning delinquency control is as vast, and growing as rapidly, as that devoted to etiology—so much so that its treatment in this volume regrettably has proved impossible.

Part I

Variations Among Delinquent Gangs and Subcultures

Conflict Gangs
and Subcultures

GANG conflict, for the most part, is a combination of "cold" and "guerrilla" warfare rather than sustained and carefully planned conflict between well-organized groups. Extensive reports from New York City,[1] Los Angeles,[2] and Chicago[3] testify to this fact in these cities, and observations from smaller communities suggest that such conflict as occurs in these settings is even more situationally determined.[4] In Part III of this book, particularly in the articles concerning "group process," some of the *dimensions* of situations which bring about conflict and their parameters are discussed.

It is probably true, also, that most aggressive behavior on the part of even the most conflict-oriented gangs takes place within the gang rather than between gangs. Body-punching, wrestling, and aggressive verbal exchanges involved in "signifying" are pervasive activities among these groups; in effect they are means of *interacting* with one another. At times these activities help to establish a "pecking order" of status; at times they appear rather to *reflect* such a pecking order.

Despite the intragroup and situational character of most aggressive behavior, the notion of a *conflict subculture* appears to have merit. Gangs differ in the nature of their *shared perspectives* concerning status-giving activities, the nature of their groups, and how it and they relate to the world about them. For some gangs, conflict with other gangs is a major focus of group attention, even though little actual gang fighting may take place. Fighting prowess is especially status giving, individually and collectively. Such gangs are heavily invested in their fighting reputation. The relevant "others" for this "rep" are not clear. We know it includes other fighting gangs, but there is evidence, also, that it includes a much broader public. Members of such gangs often evidence great pride when the mass media take note of their activities, even though the notices usually are derogatory. A prominent member of one such gang in Chicago compiled a scrapbook filled with newspaper articles featuring his gang.[5] The scrapbook was embellished with "art work" featuring guns, dynamite, "brass knucks," money, a skull and crossed pool cues (!), and a motto—"Lords of Lovers." The names of the gang and of individual members were underlined whenever they appeared in the articles. Gang boys at first are suspicious and ambivalent about having newsmen follow them around in search of a story, as occasionally they do; but to the best of our knowledge reporters never experience prolonged difficulty and willing informants are usually at hand.

Conflict gangs create roles expressive of their conflict orientation, thus differing in structure from other gangs. Such positions as "war counselor" and "armorer" are jealously guarded, even though the duties and privileges of office rarely are defined in a formal way. These roles serve as a focus of ceremonial deference within the group, and they provide still another basis for individual status and for group identity.

The most important status universe for boys in conflict gangs appears to be other conflict-oriented gang boys, individually and collectively. The degree to which a particular group is included in this status universe appears to be primarily a function of that group's rep for fighting and the immediacy of involvement of one's own gang with any other gang. A status hierarchy of conflict gangs is created in which a gang's past reputation for conflict and its present conflict activity largely determine the position of that gang vis-à-vis other gangs. Groups which are *not* good fighters are downgraded in this status hierarchy.

The Junior Potentates, a powerful conflict-oriented gang which had diminished its conflict activity, apparently under the influence of a detached worker assigned by the YMCA program, lost some newly-recruited members because they were not engaging sufficiently in fighting activity. These new recruits had joined the Juniors when they came out of a state institution for the treatment of delinquents "because we heard they were the best fighting gang on the West Side." They left with the observation that "the Juniors don't fight no more" and they joined still another group whose "rep" was built upon *present* rather than *past* fighting exploits. The Junior Potentates shortly thereafter disbanded, with the exception of a segment which retained its identity, devoting most of its energies to drinking and smoking marijuana. This clique became known within the conflict-oriented subculture as "a bunch of wine heads"—a very low-status designation.[6]

It is also the case that gangs *use* each other in building a rep. Thus, in 1962 a newly formed housing project gang attempted to incite to conflict the virtually defunct Egyptian Cobras in Chicago because the latter had a formidable rep even though they had been inactive as a fighting gang for several months.[7] Engaging the Egyptian Cobras in "humbugging" activity would have gained considerable prestige for the new gang.

We know from study of numerous incidents that not all members of conflict gangs participate in conflict, even when they are on the scene. Why this should be the case is not entirely clear, but it appears that boys who are most likely to be involved at any time are those who are heavily committed to the gang at the moment, usually gang leaders or other boys who aspire to prominence in the gang. Outstanding performance on such occasions is one of the few available avenues to achievement in gangs such as these.[8]

Two selections illuminate various aspects of gang conflict and aggressive behavior, in general, by gang boys. The first, from New York City, is a narrative account of episodes involving gang conflict and related activities. It illustrates very well the situational aspects of much conflict, and some of the status and normative considerations associated with it. Similar cases from Chicago are discussed in the article "Why Gangs Fight" by Short and Strodtbeck, on pages 231 to 240. The second article is a more systematic analysis of aggressive behavior by a gang in the Boston area. Each, in its own way, documents the nature of gang conflict. There is much in common among conflict gangs in these and in other cities.

THE CHERUBS ARE RUMBLING

+ Stompers

Walter Bernstein

ONE Saturday night a few weeks ago, I attended a dance at
a Y.M.C.A. in Brooklyn given by the Cherubs, a street gang
with about thirty-five members, all between the ages of fourteen and seventeen. The Cherubs are not good boys. They
regard the police as their natural enemies, and most policemen who have come to know them reciprocate this attitude—
with some justification. The Cherubs fight other gangs, using knives, baseball bats, and guns; they have been known
to steal; they occasionally commit rape, though usually of
the statutory kind; many of them are truants; a few of them
take dope; and while they fear the law, they do not admire
or respect it. The prospect that the Cherubs, if left to themselves, will grow into model citizens is not at all bright. Their
normal activity, though organized, is rarely social, and for
this reason I was interested to learn that they were about to
give an organized social dance. I heard about it from a friend
of mine named Vincent Riccio, who knows the Cherubs well.
He lives in their neighborhood and teaches physical education
at Manual Training High School, in South Brooklyn, where
some of them are reluctant students. Before becoming a
teacher, in 1955, Riccio spent five years as a street-club
worker for the New York City Youth Board, an agency dealing
with problems of juvenile delinquency. His job was to go
into a neighborhood that had a street gang known for particularly vicious habits, try to win the confidence of its members,
and then, if possible, guide them in the direction of healthier
pursuits. He is generally considered to have been the most

successful street-club worker the Youth Board has ever had. "In his day, the Youth Board in Brooklyn *was* Riccio," a present Youth Board worker told me. Riccio has almost total empathy with young people—especially the delinquent kind—and they trust him. He speaks their language without patronizing them. Like most of the delinquents he has worked with, he comes from a rough, semi-slum background; his parents were immigrant Italians, and they had twenty-one children, six of whom have survived. As a boy, he did his share of gang fighting and thievery, though he claims to have been interested in stealing food rather than money. His specialty was looting the Mrs. Wagner pie trucks. His youthful experiences have convinced him that, except for the relatively rare psychotic cases, no delinquents are beyond help—that all are responsive to anyone they feel really cares for them. Riccio cares very deeply; he may even care too much. He had good reasons for switching to teaching as a career—among other things, he had a family to support—but he has a strong sense of guilt about having quit the Youth Board, and feels that it was a betrayal of the boys he had been working with.

For all practical purposes, Riccio hasn't quit. He has a name among the young people in his part of Brooklyn, and they are still likely to come to him for help with their problems, seeking him out either at home or at the school. He takes pride in this, and does what he can for them. He was particularly enthusiastic about the Cherubs' dance—as I could see when he asked if I'd like to attend it with him—because one of the gangs he had worked with when he was employed by the Youth Board was the forerunner of the Cherubs. That gang was also called the Cherubs, while the gang now known as the Cherubs was called the Cherub Midgets. Today, although a few of Riccio's former charges are in jail, most of them are respectable young men, gainfully employed and, in some cases, married. They are no longer bound together in a gang, but, Riccio explained, they take a collective avuncular interest in the current lot. In fact, they had helped organize the dance, and some of them were to act as chaperons. "They're trying to steer the kids straight," he said. "Show them they can get status by doing something besides breaking heads."

Riccio had asked me to meet him in front of the Y.M.C.A. at about nine o'clock on the night of the dance, and when I arrived he was already there, looking like an American Indian in a Brooks Brothers suit. A swarthy, handsome man of thirty-eight, he has a sharply angular face, with a prominent hooked nose and high cheekbones. He is not tall but he is very broad; his neck is so thick that his head seems small for his body, and his muscular development is awesome. He used to be a weight lifter, and still has a tendency to approach people as though they were bar bells. Whenever I shake hands with him, I have an uneasy feeling that I will find myself being raised slowly to the level of his chest and then, with a jerk and press, lifted effortlessly over his head. Actually, Riccio's handshake, like that of many strong men, is soft and polite. He is essentially a polite man, anxious to please, and he has a quick, warm smile and a trust in people that might seem naive in a less experienced person. I shook hands with him warily, then followed him inside the building and into an elevator. "The kids were lucky to get this place," he said as the door slid closed. "The last club dance held here broke up in a riot." We got out at the fourth floor and walked into a solid mass of music. It roared at us like water from a burst dam, and the elevator man hastily closed his door and plunged down again before he was flooded. A table stood by the elevator door. Seated importantly behind it was a boy of about sixteen, with long black hair carefully combed back in the style known as a ducktail and wearing a wide-shouldered double-breasted blue suit. He was a good-looking boy, with regular features, and he had an innocent look that did not seem 'quite genuine. His face lit up when he saw Riccio.

"Man, look who's here!" he said. "It's Rick!"

Riccio smiled and walked over to the table.

"Man, where you been keeping yourself?" the boy asked.

"You come to school once in a while, Benny, you'd know," Riccio said. He introduced me as his friend, and I felt for my wallet to pay the admission fee of a dollar that was announced on a piece of paper tacked to the table.

Benny reached across and put his hand on mine. "You're a friend of Rick's," he said reprovingly.

Riccio asked Benny how the dance was going. "Man, it's *crazy!*" the boy replied. "We got two hundred people here. We got Red Hook, Gowanus, the Tigers, the Dragons." He counted them on his fingers. "We got the Gremlins. We got a pack from Sands Street. We even got a couple of the Stompers."

"I thought the Stompers and Red Hook were rumbling," Riccio said.

"They called it off," Benny said. "The cops were busting them all over the place. They were getting *killed.*" He laughed. "Man, the law busted more heads than they did."

"Well, I'm glad it's off," Riccio said. "Whatever the reason, it's better off than on. Nobody gets hurt that way."

"It'll be on again," Benny said. "You don't have to worry about *that.* Soon as the cops lay off, they'll swing again."

Leaving Benny, we went through a door into the room where the dance was being held. I was astonished to see that all the music came from four boys, about fifteen years old, who were seated on a bandstand at one end of the room. They were small but they looked fierce. They were playing trumpet, guitar, piano, and drums, and the room rocked to their efforts. It was a large room, gaily decorated with balloons and strips of crepe paper. Tables and chairs ringed a dance floor that was crowded with teen-age boys and girls—including a few Negroes and Puerto Ricans—all wearing the same wise, sharp city expression. The usual complement of stags, most of them dressed in windbreakers or athletic jackets, stood self-consciously on the sidelines, pretending indifference.

I followed Riccio over to one corner, where two boys were selling sandwiches and soft drinks through an opening in the wall. Business appeared to be outstripping their ability to make change. As we came up, one of them bellowed to a customer, "Shut up a minute, or I'll bust you right in the mouth!" Watching all this tolerantly were two husky young men—in their early twenties, I guessed—who greeted Riccio with delight. He introduced them to me as Cherub alumni, who were helping chaperon the dance. One was called Louie, and the other, who limped, was called Gimpy. The boys at the refreshment window saw Riccio and immediately yelled to him for help. He went over to them, and I stayed with Louie and Gimpy. Louie, it developed, had been a paratrooper in the Army until only a few days before, and was nervous about resuming civilian life. He said he would never have been able to get into the Army if it had not been for Riccio. He had been on probation when he decided to enlist, and Riccio had persuaded the probation officer to let him sign up.

"Believe me," Gimpy said, "we owe a lot to that Riccio."

I asked what else Riccio had done for them, and Gimpy said, "Well, he was looking out for us. We needed a job, he'd try to get us a job. He'd try to keep us out of trouble."

"It ain't exactly what he did," Louie said. "We just didn't want to louse him up."

"Well, he did a lot, too," Gimpy said. "A kid might be sleeping in the subway, scared to go home. He'd be scared maybe his old man would beat him up, like Mousy was that time. Well, Rick fixed it so Mousy could go home and his old man wouldn't beat him up."

"Oh, he did a lot," Louie said. "That's what I mean. A guy that's doing a lot for you, you don't want to louse him up. I mean, we'd start thinking of something to do. What are we going to do today? Break a few heads? Steal a few hubcaps? We'd be talking about it, and then somebody would say, 'What about Rick? What's Rick going to think about this?' So then we wouldn't do it." He stopped, looked over at the refreshment window, where Riccio was helping the two boys make change, and added, "Well, a lot of the time we wouldn't do it."

A small boy came up to Louie and whispered in his ear. "Excuse me," Louie said, and headed determinedly toward the door.

Riccio returned, and we stood watching the dancers, who

were doing the cha-cha. He seemed pleased with what he saw. "Notice the Negro kids and the Puerto Ricans?" he said. "Two years ago, they wouldn't have dared come here. They'd have had their heads broken. Now when a club throws a dance any kid in the neighborhood can come—provided he can pay for a ticket." A pretty little girl of about twelve danced by with a tall boy. "She's Ellie Hanlon," Riccio told me, nodding in her direction. "Her older brother was a Cherub—Tommy Hanlon. He was on narcotics, and I could never get him off. I was just starting to reach him when I left the Youth Board. Two weeks later, he was dead from an overdose. Seventeen years old." Riccio had told me about Tommy Hanlon once before, and I had suspected that, in some way, he felt responsible for the boy's death.

The Hanlon girl saw Riccio and stopped dancing to run over to him. He picked her up and kissed her on the forehead. As soon as he had put her down, she started to pull him out onto the dance floor. "Hey, I'm too old for that kind of jazz," Riccio said, but he allowed himself to be pulled. He turned out to be an excellent dancer—graceful and light on his feet. When the dance ended, he returned the girl to her partner and came back, panting a little. "Man, am I out of shape!" he said.

Louie rejoined us, shaking his head. "Look what I took away from a kid at the door," he said. He showed us a blackjack.

"You know the kid?" Riccio asked.

Louie said he thought it was one of the Sands Street boys.

"That's a rough crew—Sands Street," Riccio said.

The demon band was really sending now. The trumpet player had put on a straw sombrero that came down to the bridge of his nose. He looked as though he had lost the top part of his face, but it didn't hamper his playing. The notes shrieked from his horn, desperate to escape. The boy on the drums seemed to be going out of his mind. On the floor, the dancers spun and twisted and shuffled and bounced in a tireless frenzy. "Man, I get pooped just looking," Riccio said.

Benny, the boy who had been collecting admissions, pushed his way through the crowd to us, his eyes wide with excitement. "Hey, Louie!" he said. "The Gremlins are smoking pot in the toilet."

"Excuse me," Louie said, and hurried away to deal with the pot, or marijuana, smokers.

"Them stinking Gremlins!" Benny said. "They're going to ruin our dance. We ought to bust their heads for them."

"Then you'd really ruin your dance," Riccio told him. "I thought you guys were smart. You start bopping, they'll throw you right out of here."

"Well, them Gremlins better not ruin our dance," Benny said.

I asked Riccio if many of the boys he knew smoked marijuana. He said that he guessed quite a few of them did, and added that he was more concerned about those who were on heroin. One trouble, he explained, is that dope pushers flock to neighborhoods where two gangs are at war, knowing they will find buyers among members of the gangs who are so keyed up that they welcome any kind of relaxation or who are just plain afraid. "You take a kid who's scared to fight," Riccio said. "He may start taking narcotics because he knows the rest of the gang won't want him around when he's on dope. He'd be considered too undependable in a fight. So that way he can get out of it." He paused, and then added, "You find pushers around after a fight, too, when the kids are let down but still looking for kicks." Riccio nodded toward a boy across the floor and said, "See that kid? He's on dope." The boy was standing against the wall, staring vacantly at the dancers, his face fixed in a gentle, faraway smile. Every few seconds, he would wipe his nose with the back of his hand.

"Man, that Jo-Jo!" Benny said. "He's stoned *all* the time."

"What's he on—horse?" Riccio asked, meaning heroin.

"Who knows with that creep?" Benny said.

I asked Benny if any special kind of boy went in for dope.

"The creeps," he said. "You know, the goofballs." He searched for a word. "The *weak* kids. Like Jo-Jo. There ain't nothing the guys can't do to him. Last week, we took his pants off and made him run right in the middle of the street without them."

"You wouldn't do that to Dutch," Riccio said.

"Man, Dutch *kicked* the habit," Benny said. "We told the guy he didn't kick the habit, he was out of the crew. We were *through* with him. So he kicked it. Cold turkey."

Louie returned, and Riccio asked him what he had done about the offending Gremlins. Louie said he had chased them the hell out of the men's room.

I kept watching Jo-Jo. He never once moved from his position. The music beat against him, but his mind seemed to be on his own music, played softly and in very slow motion, and only for him.

As the dance continued, Louie and Gimpy and several other chaperons policed the room with unobtrusive menace, and there was no further trouble; everyone seemed to be having a good time. At eleven-thirty, Riccio said to me, "Now is when you sweat it out." He explained that the last half hour of a gang dance is apt to be tricky. Boys who have smuggled in liquor suddenly find themselves drunk; disputes break out over which boy is going to leave with which girl; many of the boys simply don't want to go home. But that evening the crucial minutes passed and it appeared that all was going well.

A few minutes before midnight, the musicians played their last set, and proudly packed their instruments. The trumpet player took off his sombrero, and I saw that he already had the pale and sunken face of a jazz musician. As the crowd thinned out, Riccio said, with some relief, "It turned out O.K." We waited until the room was almost empty, and then walked to the doorway. Benny was standing at the entrance of a make-shift checkroom near the elevator. "Good dance, Ben," Riccio said, "You guys did a fine job." Benny grinned with pleasure.

Just then, a boy came out of the checkroom. He seemed to be agitated. Riccio said, "Hi ya, Mickey," but the boy paid no attention to him, and said to Benny, "I want my raincoat. I checked it here, it ain't here."

"Man, you checked it, it's here," Benny said.

"It ain't here," Mickey repeated. Benny sighed and went into the checkroom, and Mickey turned to Riccio. He was a small boy with a great mop of black hair that shook when he talked.

"I paid eighteen bucks for that raincoat," he said. "You can wear it inside and out."

"You'll get it back," Riccio said.

"It's a Crawford," Mickey said.

Benny came out of the checkroom and said, "Somebody must have took it by mistake. We'll get it back for you tomorrow."

"I don't want it tomorrow," Mickey said.

"Man, you'll get it tomorrow," Benny said patiently.

"I want my raincoat," Mickey said, his voice rising. Some of the boys who had been waiting for the elevator came over to see what was happening.

"You're making too much noise," Benny said. "I don't want you making so much noise, man. You'll ruin the *dance*."

"There ain't no more dance," Mickey said, "The dance is over. I want my raincoat."

More boys were crowding around, trying to quiet Mickey, but he was adamant. Finally, Riccio pulled Benny aside and whispered in his ear. Benny nodded, and called to Mickey, in a conciliatory tone, "Listen, Mick, we don't find the raincoat tomorrow, we'll *give* you the eighteen bucks."

"Where the hell have you got eighteen bucks?" Mickey asked suspiciously.

"From what we made on the dance," Benny told him. "You can buy a whole new coat, man. O.K. You satisfied? You'll shut up now and go home?"

"I don't want the eighteen bucks," Mickey said.

"Oh, the hell with him," one of the other boys said, and turned away.

"I want my raincoat," Mickey said. "It's a Crawford."

"You can buy another Crawford!" Benny shouted at him, suddenly enraged. "What are you—some kind of a wise guy? You trying to put on an act just because Rick's here? What do you think you are—some kind of a wheel?"

"I want my raincoat," Mickey said.

"And I don't want you cursing in here!" Benny shouted. "You're in the Y.M.C.A.!"

"Who's cursing?" Micked asked.

"Don't *curse*," Benny said grimly, and walked away. The

other boys stood about uncertainly, not knowing what to do next. In a moment the elevator arrived, and Riccio asked the operator to wait. He went over to Mickey and spoke a few soothing words to him, then came back, and the two of us got into the elevator. Two boys from the crowd got in with us.

"What do you think of that creep, Rick?" one of them asked.

"Well, it's his coat," Riccio said. "He's got a right to want it back."

"I think he stole the coat in the first place," the boy said as the elevator reached the ground floor.

Riccio and I walked through the lobby, already dimmed for the night, and out into the street, where he saw Louie and Gimpy getting into a car. They offered us a lift, but Riccio said he had brought his own car, so they waved and drove off. At that instant, a couple of boys dashed out of the building, looked wildly around, and then dashed back in. "Now what?" Riccio said.

We followed them in, and found perhaps a dozen boys bunched near the entrance. I could see Mickey in the middle, red-faced and angry and talking loudly. Benny, who was standing on the edge of the group, told us, "Now he says one of the Stompers took his coat. Man, he's *weird!*" He waved at Mickey in disgust and went outside.

Riccio pushed his way into the center of the crowd and separated Mickey from several boys who were arguing with him heatedly. A few of these wore jackets with the name "Stompers" stitched across the back. "Come on, now," Riccio said to Mickey. "We got to get out of here."

"He says we robbed his lousy coat, Mr. Riccio," one of the Stompers said.

"It's a Crawford!" Mickey yelled at him.

"The coat was probably taken by mistake," Riccio said calmly. "You'll get it back tomorrow, Mickey. If you don't get it back, you'll get the money and you can buy a new one. You had a good time, didn't you?" He was speaking to all of them now, his arm around Mickey's shoulder as he guided the boy gently toward the door. "You ought to be proud, running such a dance. You want to spoil it now? Hey?"

Mickey was about to say something when a boy burst in through the door, shouting, "Hey, Benny and one of the Stompers are having it out!"

Everyone rushed for the door. When I got outside, I saw Benny and another boy swinging desperately at each other on the sidewalk. Benny hit the boy on the cheek, the boy fell against a car, and Benny moved in and swung again. The boy went into a clinch, and the two of them wrestled against the car. I heard a click near me and turned to see one of the Stompers holding a switch-blade knife in his hand, but before he or any of the other boys could join in, Riccio was down the steps and between the fighters, holding them apart. The boy with the knife turned suddenly and went back into the building, and then I saw what he must have seen—a policeman walking slowly across the street toward us. Riccio saw him, too. "Cut out!" he said, in a low voice, talking to the whole crowd. "Here comes the law!" Cut out!" He pushed the fighters farther apart as two of the Stompers ranged themselves alongside Benny's opponent. "Beat it!". Riccio said, in the same low voice. "You want to end up in the can? Cut out!" The Stompers turned and started to walk away, but the rest of the boys continued to stand around the steps of the Y. The policeman, now at the curb, looked curiously at Riccio and Benny, and then at the boys. Everyone appeared casual, but the air was heavy with tension. The policeman hesitated a moment, and then went on down the block.

"All right," Riccio said, with a tone of finality.

"He started to rank me," Benny said, meaning that the Stomper had been taunting him.

"Now, forget it," Riccio told him. "You want a ride home?"

Benny shook his head. "I'll grab a bus," he said, looking up the street, where the Stompers could still be seen walking away. Then he turned back to Riccio and said defiantly, "Man, what did you *want* me to do? Punk out?" He straightened his jacket, ran his fingers through his hair, and set off across the street with several other Cherubs. We watched them until they got to the corner. The other Cherubs kept walking straight ahead, but Benny turned down the side street. "You see how it can start?" Riccio said. "One minute they're having a dance, and the next minute they're having a war."

We went down the block to where Riccio's car was parked. I got in beside him, and he drove to the corner, where he stopped for a red light. I found that my hands were shaking. The light changed, but Riccio did not move. "I got a feeling," he said reflectively. "If you don't mind, I want to go back for a minute." He drove around the block until we were in front of the Y again, and then he turned the corner where Benny had left the others. And there was Benny, caught in the glare of our headlights, held down on his knees in the middle of the street by two boys while a third boy savagely hit his bowed head. The headlights fixed the scene like a movie gone suddenly too real—Benny kneeling there and the boy's arm rising and falling—and then Riccio had slammed on the brakes and we were out of the car, running toward them. By the time we reached Benny, the other boys were gone, lost in the dark; all that was left was the echo of their footsteps as they ran off into the night, and then there was not even that —no sound at all except the soft, steady ticking of the motor in Riccio's car. Benny was getting slowly to his feet. "You O.K.?" Riccio asked helping him up. Benny nodded, and rubbed his neck. "I figured something like this," Riccio said to me, and then, turning back to Benny, he asked, "You sure you're all right? Maybe we ought to stop by the hospital."

"Man, I'm all right," Benny said. "They didn't hit me hard."

After looking the boy over, Riccio took him by the arm and led him back to the car, and the three of us got into the front seat. We drove in silence to a housing project near the waterfront, where Benny got out, still without speaking. We watched him enter one of the buildings, and then Riccio drove me to a subway station. "Now you know about these kids," he said as we shook hands. "They can blow up while you're look-ing at them." Riding home, I kept thinking of Benny as he had knelt there in the street, his head bent as though in prayer.

One afternoon a few weeks later, I got a telephone call from Riccio. "I thought you might be interested," he said. "The Cherubs are rumbling. They just put Jerry Larkin, from

the Stompers, in the hospital. Caught him out of his neighborhood and left him for dead. He'll be all right, but they
beat him up pretty bad. I think they worked him over with
one of those iron tire chains." He said that there was now a
full-scale war between the Cherubs and the Stompers, and
that he had been talking with members of both gangs, trying
to get them to call it off. Then he told me he was going to try
to mediate again that night, and asked if I would like to go
along. I said I would, and we arranged to meet at his house at
seven o'clock.

Riccio lives in a small apartment on the top floor of an old
brownstone in the Park Slope section of Brooklyn, with his
wife and two children—a girl of eight and a boy of eleven.
From the steps of the house, one can see the Statue of Liberty,
like a toy in the harbor. When I arrived, the children were
watching a Western movie on television. Riccio and his wife,
an attractive blonde named Evelyn have fixed up their apartment with modern furniture and abstract paintings, some of
the latter the work of Riccio himself. He has done a lot of
painting, and once considered a career as a commercial artist,
but decided that it would be too insecure. As we were about
to leave, Mrs. Riccio came out of the kitchen with a dish
towel over her arm, and her husband kissed her goodbye. She
looked worried. I recalled that one reason Riccio had quit the
Youth Board was his wife's fear that he might be beaten up
himself. But now she just told him not to stay out late, because he had to get up early the next morning.

"There's a lot going on tonight," Riccio said as he and I
walked downstairs. "Some kid shot another kid with a zip
gun, and the heat's on." He went on to explain that this shooting had nothing to do with the rumble between the Cherubs
and the Stompers. The boy who was shot had not belonged
to any gang; he had simply not wanted to go to school, and
had asked a friend to shoot him in the arm, so he would have
a good excuse to stay home. The friend had obliged, using a
homemade gun, but the wound had been a little deeper than
planned. The injured boy's parents had taken him to a hospital, where the bullet was removed. The police were notified,

as a matter of routine, and now they were searching for the friend and the gun, both having disappeared.

We got into Riccio's car, and he started to drive slowly through the neighborhood. "We ought to find some of the Stompers hanging around these corners," he said. At first, no boys were to be seen. The part of Brooklyn we were riding through was not quite a slum. The streets were lined with old and ugly brownstones, but they seemed in good repair. The whole effect was dispirited, rather than poor; it was a neighborhood without cheer. As night fell, the houses retreated gradually into shadow, but they lost none of their ugliness. The street lamps came on, casting pools of dirty-yellow light. "The Stompers used to have a Youth Board worker assigned to them," Riccio said. "But he was pulled off the job and sent up to the Bronx when all that trouble broke up there. I guess these kids won't get another worker until they kill somebody." He said this without rancor, but I knew he felt strongly that the best times to do any real good with a gang are before it starts fighting and after it stops.

Ahead of us, a boy appeared from around a corner and walked rapidly in our direction. "One of the Stompers," Riccio said, and drew over to the curb. He called out to the boy, and when the latter paid no attention, he called louder. "Hey, Eddie, it's me! Riccio!" The boy stopped and looked at us warily, and then, reassured, came over to the car. His face was bruised and he had a lump under his left eye. "What happened?" Riccio asked. "You get jumped?"

"The cops busted me," Eddie said. He was about fifteen, and he was wearing a leather jacket with spangles on the cuffs that glittered in the light from a street lamp. His hair was blond and wavy and long. "They just let me out of the God-damned station house," he added

"Why'd they pick you up?" Riccio asked.

"For nothing!" Eddie said indignantly. "We was just standing around, and they picked us all up. We wasn't doing a thing." He paused, but Riccio didn't say anything, and after a moment he went on, "You know *them*. They wanted to know did we have zip guns like what shot that stupid kid. I

told them I didn't have no gun. So they banged me around."
He laughed. "You think they banged *me* around. You should
have seen what they done to Ralphie." Riccio asked where
the other Stompers were now, and Eddie replied that he
thought they were hanging around a nearby grammar school.
"But not me," he said. "I'm going home."

"Good idea," Riccio said.

"I got to get my gun out of the house," Eddie said, "I don't
want them coming around and finding it."

"Why don't you give it to me?" Riccio said.

"No, sir," Eddie said. "I paid three bucks for that piece.
I'm going to leave it over at my uncle's house. Maybe I'll see
you later." He waved and walked off.

I asked Riccio how teen-agers could buy guns for three
dollars, or any amount. He shrugged wearily and told me
that salesmen of second-hand weapons periodically canvass
sections where gangs are known to be active. A good revolver,
he said, costs about ten dollars, but an inferior one can be
bought for considerably less.

"Well, anyway, now I know Eddie's got a gun," Riccio said
as we started up again, heading for the grammar school.
"That's important—that he told me about it. Every time a
kid tells you he's got a gun or he's going to do something bad,
like break heads or pull a score—a robbery, I mean—he's
telling you for a reason. First, he wants your attention. Maybe
nobody has been giving him attention. You know—at home or
in school or with the gang. He knows the way to get it is to
do something real bizarre. And when he tells you, he knows
this is one way to get you to stop and listen to him. You know
—talk to him, pay him a little attention. But at the same
time he's saying to you, 'Show me how I don't have to do it.
Show me a way out.' But it's got to be a way that will let him
save face. That's the big thing. It's all a question of status.
Show him a healthy way out, in terms of his social setup, not
yours—show him a way out that will make it possible for him
to preserve his status with his friends—and he'll grab it in a
minute. But first you've got to reach him. If you haven't
reached him, he won't listen to your way out. Some of them
you can reach, and some of them you can't reach. Some of

them you know you ought to be able to reach, but then you find you just can't." He paused, and I imagined that he was again thinking of the Hanlon boy's death from an overdose of drugs. "You try, but you can't really reach them. They're too disturbed, or you're not going about it right. So you give up on them. You turn your back, and they go down the drain." I remarked that he could hardly hope to help them all, but he said, as if he hadn't heard me, "You can't turn your back on them."

In a minute or two, the grammar school loomed up before us in the darkness with a solid, medieval look, and we saw a group of boys lounging under a street light—hands in pockets, feet apart, and, as they talked, moving about in a street-corner pattern as firmly fixed as that of the solar system. Riccio parked the car, and we got out and walked over to them. They froze instantly. Then one of them said, "It's Rick," and they relaxed. Riccio introduced me, and I shook hands with each of them; their handshakes were limp, like those of prize-fighters. There were eight of the boys—all with long hair and wise little faces. They said they had been picked up, like Eddie, and questioned about the recent shooting, and they laughed about their experiences at the station house, taking for granted their relationship with the law—the obligation of the police to hunt them down and their own obligation not to cooperate in any way. There was little bitterness and no anger, except on the part of the boy named Ralphie, who felt that he had been hit unnecessarily hard.

Riccio suggested that they all go into the school, where they could talk more comfortably, and led the way inside. Walking down a corridor, he asked the Stompers about Jerry, the boy who had been beaten up. They said he would be out of the hospital in a couple of days. "They thought he had a fractured skull," Ralphie said, "but all he had was noises in the head."

"I was with him when it happened," one of the other boys said. "There were four of them Cherubs in a car—Benny and that Bruno and two other guys."

"That Bruno ain't right in the head," another boy said.

"I got away because I was wearing sneakers," the first boy

said. "That Bruno came after me with that chain, I went right through the sound barrier."

Riccio pushed open a pair of swinging doors that led into the school gymnasium, and as I followed him in the dank, sweaty smell hit me like an old enemy; I had gone to a school like this and hated every minute of it. The windows were the same kind I remembered—screened with wire netting, ostensibly as protection against flying Indian clubs but actually, I still believe, to keep the pupils from escaping. Out on the floor, several boys were being taught basketball by a tall young man in a sweatsuit. Riccio went over to talk with him, and, returning, indicated some benches in a corner. "He says we can sit over there," he said. We moved over to the corner, where Riccio sat down on a bench while the boys grouped themselves around him, some on benches and others squatting on the floor and gazing up at him.

"All right," Riccio said. "What are you guys going to do? Is it on or off?"

The boys looked at Ralphie, who seemed to be the leader. "We ain't going to call it off," he said.

"They started it," one of the others said.

"They japped us," a third boy said, meaning that the Cherubs had taken them by surprise. "You want we should let them get away with that?"

"All right," Riccio said. "So they jap you, they put Jerry in the hospital. Now you jap them, maybe you put Bruno in the hospital."

"I catch that Bruno, I put him in the cemetery," Ralphie said.

"So then the cops come down on you," Riccio went on. "They bust the hell out of you. How many of you are on probation?" Two of the boys raised their hands. "This time they'll send you away. You won't get off so easy this time. Is that what you want?" The boys were silent. "O.K.," Riccio said. "You're for keeping it on. That's your decision, that's what you want. O.K. Just remember what it means. You can't relax for a minute. The cops are looking to bust you. The neighborhood thinks you're no good, because you're making trouble for everybody. You can't step out of the neighborhood, because you'll get jumped. You got to walk around with eyes in the back of your head. If that's what you want, O.K. That's your decision. That's how you want things to be for yourself. Only, just remember how it's going to be."

Riccio paused and looked around him. No one said anything. Then he started on a new tack. "Suppose the Cherubs call it off," he said. "Would you call it off if they do?"

"They want to call it off?" a boy asked.

"Suppose they do," Riccio said.

There was another silence. The basketball instructor took a hook shot, and I watched the ball arc in the air and swish through the net without touching the rim. The room echoed with the quickening bounce of the ball as one of the players dribbled it away.

"We ain't going to call it off," Ralphie said. "They started it. We went to their lousy dance and we didn't make no trouble, and they said we stole their lousy coat. Then they jumped Jerry, and that Bruno gave him that chain job."

"They say you guys jumped Benny after the dance," Riccio told them.

"He started it," one of the boys said.

"Don't you see?" Riccio said. "No matter who started what, you keep it up, all it means is trouble. It means some of you guys are going to get sent away. You think I want to see that happen? Man, it hurts me when one of you guys get sent away."

"We ain't calling it off," Ralphie said.

"Suppose they want to call it off," Riccio said.

"They're punks," Ralphie said. He stood up, and then others stood up and ranged themselves behind him. They looked like a gang now, with their captain out in front to lead them. Riccio sat where he was, looking up at one face after another.

"Just because they had a dance," Ralphie said. "You know what? We were going to have a dance, too. And not in the lousy Y.M.C.A. In the American Legion."

"Why didn't you?" Riccio asked.

"They took away our worker," one of the other boys said. "They wouldn't give us the American Legion hall unless we had a worker."

"You'll get the worker back," Riccio told them. "He'll come back in a week or two, and then you can have your dance."

"He said he was coming back last week," Ralphie said bitterly.

"I'll tell you what," Riccio said. "I'll talk to the people down at the Legion. Maybe if they know I'm working with you, they'll give you the hall."

"We were going to have an eight-piece band," one of the boys said.

"I'll see what I can do," Riccio said. "But you know how it is when it gets around that you're swinging with another crew. You'll have trouble getting the hall. And even if you do, who wants to come to a dance when there might be trouble? The girls won't want to come—they'll be too scared."

"You sure the Cherubs said they want to call it off?" a boy asked.

"I'm going over there right now," Riccio said.

"They want to call it off, let them call it off," Ralphie said. He stood there for a moment, a young Napoleon, and then turned and started for the door. The others followed him, some of them waving to Riccio and calling goodbye. Then they were gone, leaving only Riccio and me and the basketball players. The ball bounced off the backboard and over to the benches, and Riccio caught it and, still seated, took a one-handed shot at the basket. He missed, shook his head ruefully, and stood up.

We walked out to his car, and when we were driving through the streets again, he said, "I'm glad they told me about the dance. It gives them a reason for calling it off." I remarked that the boys hadn't sounded to me as if they wanted to call it off. "If they didn't want to call it off, they wouldn't have listened to me," he said. "They wouldn't have hung around that long. They want to call it off, all right—they're scared about what happened to Jerry. Only, they don't know how. They don't want to be accused of punking out."

We drove past the housing project where Benny lived. "The Cherubs hang out in that candy store down the block," Riccio said. He pulled up in front of the shop, which I could see was crowded with youngsters, and said, "Wait here while I take a look." He went inside, came out again, and got back in the car, saying, "The Cherubs aren't here yet, so we'll wait." We both settled back and made ourselves comfortable. It was only nine-thirty, but the neighborhood was deserted. The candy store was the only shop in sight that was open, and ours was the only car parked on the dark street. Above and behind the tops of the brownstones rose the great bulk of the housing project, like some kind of municipal mausoleum, but dotted here and there with lights as evidence that life persisted inside. Two boys came down the street and were about to enter the candy store when Riccio called out, "Hey, Benny!" They turned and walked over to the car, and Riccio said. "Get in. It's too jammed in there." They slid into the back seat, and Riccio, turning to face them, said to me "You know Ben, don't you?" and introduced me to the other boy—Bruno, the one who had used the tire chain on Jerry. He was very thin, and had enormous eyes. "I've just been over with the Stompers," Riccio said, without preamble. "I think they'll call it off if you'll call it off."

"We won't call it off," Bruno said.

"Not even if they do?" Riccio asked.

"Man, they *ruined* our dance," Benny said.

"Nobody ruined your dance," Riccio said. "Your dance was a big success. You had one of the best dances around here." He went on to give them the same arguments he had given the Stompers. They listened restlessly, shifting in their seats and looking everywhere but at him. "Well, how about it?" Riccio said, finally.

"We call it off, what else are we going to do?" Bruno asked.

"There's other things to do besides breaking heads," Riccio said, and then I jumped as the car shook from a violent bang against its left side and the head of a policeman suddenly appeared in the window next to the driver's seat.

"Out of the car!" the policeman said. "All of you! Out!"

"Boy, you scared me, Officer," Riccio said.

"Get out of the car!" the policeman repeated. "*Now!*"

"We're not doing anything wrong," Riccio said. "We're just sitting here talking."

"Get out of that car!" the policeman said, and with that we

found ourselves staring at a gun, which he was pointing straight at Riccio's head. It looked as big as a cannon.

"Jesus, Rick, get out of the car!" Bruno whispered from the back seat. "I'm on probation. I don't want to fight with the law."

"I'm getting out," Riccio said. He opened the door on his side and the policeman stepped back, but not quickly enough. The door hit his hand and knocked the gun to the pavement.

"Oh, Christ!" Benny said. "Now he'll kill us all!"

I shut my eyes, then opened them. The policeman had dived to the ground and recovered his gun. "O.K.—all of you," he said tightly. He motioned with his gun, and we all got out of the car and stood beside Riccio. "Face the car and lean against it with your hands on the top," the policeman said. We did, and he ran his free hand down the sides of our clothes, searching for weapons. Finding none, he said, "O.K., turn around." We turned around, and he said to Riccio, "This your car?" Riccio nodded, and the policeman asked for his license and registration. Riccio handed them over, and the policeman peered at them and then went around to compare the number on the car's license plates with the one on the registration. When he saw that the numbers matched, he said to Riccio, "Open the trunk." Riccio opened the trunk, and the policeman looked inside. Then he closed the trunk.

"Satisfied?" Riccio asked.

"Shut up," said the policeman.

"We didn't do anything," Riccio said. "What right have you got subjecting us to all this humiliation?"

"I'll crack this thing over your head," the policeman said, but his voice now betrayed a lack of conviction. "You're pretty old to be hanging around with kids. What the hell do you do?"

"I'm a teacher at Manual Training High School," Riccio told him.

"Well, why didn't you say so?" the policeman said. He put the gun back in his holster, and Benny exhaled slowly. "How the hell am I supposed to know who you are?" the policeman went on. "It's a suspicious neighborhood."

"That's no reason to treat everybody in it like criminals," Riccio said.

"Here," the policeman said, handing Riccio his license and registration. He seemed glad to get rid of them. Riccio and the rest of us climbed back into the car. "You see some guys in a car with some kids, how the hell are you supposed to know?" the policeman asked.

Riccio started to answer, but Benny, from the back seat, broke in, "Hey, Rick, let's cut out of here, man. I got to get home."

"Sure, Ben," Riccio said over his shoulder, and then drove off, leaving the policeman standing in the street. As soon as we were well away, the boys started talking excitedly.

"Man!" Benny said. "You could of got your head kicked in!"

"Did you see that gun?" Bruno said. "A thirty-eight. He could of blowed you right apart with that gun!"

"Man, I thought we were *gone!*" Benny said. "And we weren't even doing anything!"

The idea of their innocence at the time appealed to the boys, and they discussed it at some length. They both got out at the housing project, still talking. "I'm setting something up with you and the Stompers," Riccio said. "Just two or three guys from each side to straighten this thing out. All right?"

"Did you think that cop was going to shoot you, Rick?" Bruno asked.

"He was just jumpy," Riccio said. "Now, look. I'll get a place for us to meet, and we'll sit down and talk this thing out. O.K.?"

"Man, I thought we were *all* going to be busted," Benny said. "And for *nothing!*"

They drifted away from the car, laughing, and Riccio let them go. "I'll be in touch with you, Ben," he called. Benny waved back at us, and we watched them as they disappeared into the depths of the project.

I asked Riccio if he was always that tough with policeman, and he looked surprised. "I wasn't trying to be tough," he said. "That guy's job is hard enough—why should I make it any harder? I was making a point for the kids. I always tell them, when you're right, fight it to the hilt. I thought we were right, so I had to practice what I preach. Otherwise, how will they believe me on anything?"

Riccio invited me to go home with him for coffee, but I said I'd better be getting along, so he drove me to the subway. As I got out, he said, "I'm going to try to get them together this week. If I do, I'll let you know." We said good night, and I went down the subway stairs. On the way home, I bought a newspaper and read about a boy in the Bronx who had been stabbed to death in a gang fight.

I did not hear from Riccio again that week. The following week, I called him one night at about ten o'clock. His wife answered the phone, and said to me he was out somewhere in the neighborhood. She sounded upset. "It used to be like this when he was working for the Youth Board," she said. "He'd go out, and I'd never know when he was coming back. Three in the morning, maybe, he'd come back, and then the phone would ring and he'd go right out again. I told him he'd get so he wouldn't recognize his own children."

The next day, Riccio called me. He sounded discouraged. "They had another rumble," he said. "The Stompers came down to the housing project and broke a few heads. I got there too late." Fortunately, he added, it hadn't been too bad. A few shots had been fired, but without hitting anyone, and although a Cherub had been slashed down one arm with a knife, the wound wasn't serious, and nobody else had been even that badly hurt. Riccio told me he was going out again that night, and I could hear his wife say something in the background. He muffled the phone and spoke to her, and then he said to me, almost apologetically, "I've got to go out. They don't have a worker, or anything. The newspapers have raised such a fuss that the Youth Board's got its workers running around in circles, and it hasn't enough of them to do the job anyway, even when things are quiet. If somebody doesn't work with these kids, they'll end up killing each other." Then he told me he still had hopes of a mediation meeting, and would let me know what developed. Ten days later, my telephone rang shortly before dinner, and it was Riccio again, his voice now full of hope. He said that he knew it was very short notice, but if I still wanted to be in on the mediation session, I should meet him at eight o'clock in a building at an address he gave me. "I got it all set up at last," he concluded.

By the time I reached the building—a one-room wooden structure in an alley—it was five minutes after eight. Riccio was already there, together with three Cherubs—Benny and Bruno and a boy he introduced to me as Johnny Meatball.

"I was just waiting until you got here," Riccio said. "Now I'll go get the Stompers." He went out, leaving me with the three boys. The room had a fireplace at one end, and was furnished with a wooden table and several long wooden benches. It was hard for me to believe that I was in the heart of Brooklyn, until I read some of the expressions scrawled on the walls. I asked Benny who ordinarily used the place, and he replied, "Man, you know. Them Boy Scouts."

Bruno said he had gone to a Boy Scout meeting once, because he liked the uniforms, but had never gone back, because the Scoutmaster was a creep. "He wanted we should all sleep outside on the ground," Bruno said. "You know—in the woods, with the bears. Who needs that?" This led to a discussion of the perils of outdoor life, based mostly on information derived from jungle movies.

It was a desultory discussion, however. The boys were restless, and every few minutes Benny would open the door and look out into the alley. Finally, Bruno said, "The hell with them. Let's cut out."

"I'm down for that," Johnny Meatball said.

"They ain't coming," Bruno said. "They're too chicken."

"I give them fifteen minutes," Benny said.

All three became quiet then. I tried to get them to talk, as a way of keeping them there, but they weren't interested. Just before the fifteen minutes was up, the door opened and Riccio walked in, followed by two Stompers—Ralphie and Eddie, the boy we had met going home to hide his gun. They held back when they saw the Cherubs, but Riccio urged them in and closed the door behind them. Though the Cherubs had bunched together, looking tense and ready to fight, Riccio appeared to pay no attention, and said cheerfully, "I went to the wrong corner. Ralphie and Eddie, here, were waiting on the next one down the street. He pulled the table to the center of the room. "You guys know each other," he said to the five boys. Then he pulled a bench up to each side of the table and a third bench across one end. He sat down on this one, and motioned to me to sit beside him. The boys sat down slowly, one by one—the Cherubs on one side and the Stompers on the other.

"There you are," Riccio said when everybody was seated. "Just like the U.N. First, I want to thank you guys for coming here. I think you're doing a great thing. It takes a lot of guts to do what you guys are doing. I want you to know that I'm proud of you." He smiled at them. "Everybody thinks all you're good for is breaking heads. I know different—although I know you're pretty good at breaking heads, too." A couple of the boys smiled back at this, and all of them seemed to relax a little. "All right," Riccio went on. "What are we going to do about this war? You each got a beef against the other. Well, what's the beef? Let's talk about it."

There was a long silence. The boys sat motionless, staring at the table or at the walls beyond. Riccio sat as still as any of them. They sat that way for at least three minutes, and then Bruno stood up and said, "Ah, let's cut out of here."

"Man, sit down," Benny said. He spoke calmly, but his voice carried authority. Bruno looked down at him and he looked up at Bruno, and Bruno sat down. Benny then turned to the two Stompers across the table. "You tried to ruin our dance," he said.

"Your guy said we stole his lousy coat," Ralphie said.

"You jumped Benny on the street," Johnny Meatball said. "Three of you guys."

"He started a fight," Ralphie said.

"Man, that was a *fair* one!" Benny said.

"You started it," Ralphie said.

"There was just the two of us," Benny said.

"You were beating the hell out of him," Ralphie said. "What did you want us to do—let you get away with it?"

The logic of this seemed to strike the Cherubs as irrefutable, and there was another silence. Then Eddie said, "You beat up two of our little kids."

"Not *us*," Benny said. "We never beat up no little kids."

"The kids told us some Cherubs caught them coming home from the store and beat them up," Eddie said.

"Man, we wouldn't beat up *kids*," Benny said.

"You got that wrong," Johnny Meatball said, backing Benny up.

"Those kids were just trying to be wheels," Bruno said.

The Cherubs were so positive in their denial of this accusation that the Stompers appeared willing to take their word for it.

There was another pause. Riccio sat back, watching the boys. They were now leaning across the table, the two sides confronting each other at close quarters.

"Remember that time at the Paramount?" Ralphie asked. "When me and Eddie was there with two girls?"

"Those were *girls*?" Bruno asked.

"Shut up," Benny said.

Ralphie then said to Benny, "Remember we ran into eight of your crew? You ranked us in front of the girls. We had to punk out because there was so many of you."

"You want we should stay out of the *Paramount*?" Benny asked incredulously.

"It wasn't right," Ralphie said. "Not in front of the girls. Not when you knew we'd have to punk out."

After thinking this over, Benny nodded slowly, acknowledging the justice of the argument.

Ralphie pressed his advantage. "And you been hanging out in our territory," he said, naming a street corner.

"Man, that ain't your territory," Benny said. "That's *our* territory."

"That ain't your territory," Ralphie said. "We got that territory from the Dragons, and that's our territory."

The argument over the street corner grew hotter, and after a while Riccio broke it up by rapping on the table with his knuckles and saying, "I got a suggestion—why don't both sides give up the territory?" He pointed out that the corner had nothing to recommend it, being undesirable for recreation and difficult to defend. After debating about that for a minute or two, both sides agreed to relinquish their claim to the corner. Riccio had what he wanted now; I could feel it. The boys had lost the sharp edge of their hostility. Their vehemence became largely rhetorical; they were even beginning to laugh about assaults each side had made on the other.

"Hey, Ralphie," Bruno said. "You're a lucky guy, you know that? I took a shot at you the other night and missed you clean."

"You took a *shot* at me?" Ralphie asked.

Bruno nodded. "The night you came down to the project. I was waiting with a thirty-two, and you came down the street and I took a shot at you."

"I didn't even hear it," Ralphie said.

"There was a lot of noise," Bruno said. "I was right across the street from you."

"You must be a lousy shot," Eddie said.

"It was dark out," Bruno said.

"You know, you could have killed him," Riccio told Bruno.

"I wasn't looking to kill him," Bruno said.

The other boys proceeded to kid Bruno about his marksmanship—all except Ralphie, who had become subdued. After a few minutes, Riccio looked at his watch and said, "Hey, it's ten o'clock. We got to get out of here before they close the place." He stood up, stretched, and said casually, "I'm glad you guys are calling it off. You're doing the smart thing. You get a lot of credit for what you're doing."

"You took a shot at me?" Ralphie said again to Bruno.

"What's past is past," Riccio said. "There's no reason you can't get along from now on without breaking heads. If something comes up, you do what you've been doing tonight. Mediate. Get together and talk it over. Believe me, it's a lot easier than breaking heads."

"What if we can't together?" Bruno asked. "Suppose they do something, and they say they didn't do it and we say they did it?"

"Then you have a fair one," Eddie told him. "We put out our guy and you put out your guy. We settle it that way. That's O.K., ain't it, Rick?"

"It's better not to do any bopping at all," Riccio said.

"I mean, it ain't wrong," Eddie said. "It ain't making any trouble."

"Suppose we have a fair one and our guy gets beat?" Bruno asked.

"Man, you don't put out a guy who's *going* to get beat," Benny said.

The boys were on their feet now, all mixed together. A stranger might have taken them for a single group of boys engaged in rough but friendly conversation. "Listen, we got to break this up," Riccio said. He told them again how proud he was of them, and then he advised the Cherubs and the Stompers to leave separately. "Some cop sees the five of you walking down the street, he'll pull you all in," he said. So the three Cherubs left first, with Benny in the lead. They said goodbye very formally, shaking hands first with Riccio, then with me, and then, after a little hesitation, with the two Stompers. When they had gone, Ralphie sat down again on his bench. "That crazy Bruno," he said. "He took a shot at me."

A few minutes later, the Stompers stood up to go. Riccio said he would be around to see them and help them plan their dance. They thanked him and left. Riccio looked around the room. "I used to come here when I was a kid," he told me. "I got my name carved on the wall somewhere." He looked for it for a moment, without success, and then said, "Well, we might as well run along."

We went outside and got into Riccio's car. "Evelyn said if it wasn't too late, she'd have coffee and cake for us," Riccio told me, and I said that would be fine. He drove to his house and, after parking, leaned back in the seat and lit a cigarette. "I want to slow down a little before I go upstairs," he said. We sat there quietly for a few minutes. I could hear the whistles of ships down in the harbor. "Benny and Ralphie," Riccio said finally. "Those are the two to concentrate on. Maybe Eddie, too. But that Bruno—I don't know how far you could get with him. He's a disturbed kid. But you have to try. You have to try to reach him, That's the whole trick—reaching them. If I could have reached Tommy Hanlon, he wouldn't be dead now. I was just starting to reach him when he died. The last real talk we had, he told me he was scared to get a job. He'd quit school very early, and he couldn't read or write very well. He was scared if he got a job they'd make him do arithmetic and he'd look stupid. He was scared that they might send him over to Manhattan on the subway and he wouldn't be able to read the station signs. He'd never been out of Brooklyn. This was a kid there wasn't anything anti-social he hadn't done. Short of murder, there wasn't a thing. He broke into stores, he broke into cars, he molested girls. And, of course, he was on narcotics. I tell you, I used to look at this kid and think, How the hell can you defend a kid like this to society? And I'd think, How the hell can I help him? What can I do? This is too much. At the same time, he was such a nice-looking kid, I mean, he had a very nice face. Never mind what came out of his mouth—he had the dirtiest tongue I ever heard on a kid. But I worked with him, and he was starting to come around. He was starting to trust me. I don't think he'd ever trusted anybody in his whole life. I was his father. I was his mother. I was his best friend, his father confessor. I was all the things this kid had never had. And he was starting to move a little. The gang ran a dance, and he volunteered for the sandwich committee. You know what that meant? The kid was participating socially for the first time in his whole life. And he worked twice as hard at it as anybody else. I was starting to reach him. And then I quit the Youth Board."

Riccio fell silent again. "I had to quit the Youth Board," he said presently. "I had a wife and two kids, and I wasn't making enough to support them. I was spending more time with these kids than with my own. So I quit. The day I quit, I went down the street to tell the kids. They were in the candy store and Tommy Hanlon was with them, and he looked at me and said, 'What did you quit for?' I told him I had to, and tried to explain why. 'You know, I'm on the stuff again,' he said. And I said, 'Yes, Tommy, I heard you are, and I'm very sorry.' And he said, 'What do I do now?' And I said, 'Tommy, I'll always be around. We can still talk. You can still come and see me.' Then some other kid called me over to talk to him, and when

I looked around Tommy was gone. Two weeks later, he was dead."

Riccio paused, this time for a long while. His cigarette had gone out, and he looked at it blankly and threw it out the window. "I know," he said. "The kid destroyed himself. He was a disturbed kid. If he wasn't disturbed, he wouldn't have been on narcotics in the first place. I went to the funeral and I looked in the casket and saw him laying there in a suit, with a decent haircut and his face all washed—and looking like a little old man. And I watched that kid's father getting drunk with that kid laying there in the casket. And I wanted to get up there at the funeral and, everybody who was there, I wanted to shout at them, 'You're the people who caused it! All you big adults! All you wise guys on street corners that feel sorry for the kid! Now you throw away your money on flowers!' I wanted to grab them by the throat."

He paused again, and then said, his voice low, "We hear about the soldier, a normal guy, who goes through all the tortures of war and all this brainwashing—takes everything they throw at him—and comes home a hero. Well, here was a kid that had everything thrown at him, too. Only, he was all mixed up, and still he took everything anybody could throw at him for seventeen years, and that was all he could take, so he collapsed and died."

Riccio abruptly pushed the car door open and got out. I got out on my side, and we went into the house together. Mrs. Riccio was both surprised and relieved to have her husband back so early. She asked if things had gone well, and Riccio assured her that things had gone very well. She went into the kitchen to make the coffee, and Riccio and I watched a quiz program on television until she came back. The three of us chatted awhile over our coffee and cake, and then, just before saying good night, I asked Riccio if Mickey had ever found the coat he lost at the dance. Riccio said that he hadn't but that the Cherubs had given him the eighteen dollars and he had bought a new one.

Riccio called me a few days later to tell me that the Cherubs and the Stompers were observing their armistice but that the enmity between Ralphie and Bruno had become so pronounced that they had decided to settle it with a fair one. Both gangs had gone to Prospect Park one night to watch the two of them have it out. A squad car had happened along, and the policemen had run the whole bunch of them in. Riccio was on his way to court to see what he could do for the boys.

AGGRESSION IN A BOYS' STREET-CORNER GROUP

Walter B. Miller, Hildred Geertz, and Henry S. G. Cutter

THE ADOLESCENT street-corner group or juvenile gang is commonly conceived of in sociological and psychological literature both as a major breeding ground for delinquent activity and as a structural form for implementing its execution. Almost without exception the gang is described as aggressive, hostile, and rebellious.[1] Aggression is seen as an important component in delinquent behavior; indeed, "aggressive acting out" and "delinquency" are virtually equated by some authors. How accurate is this picture? How aggressive or rebellious is the average corner gang? What are actual forms of aggressive action and sentiment, how prevalent are they, at whom or what are they directed, and what functions do they serve? The present study attempts to answer these questions through systematic examination of the day-to-day behavior of one corner group, the Junior Outlaws, during a one-year period.

One popular misconception perceives the corner group as one whose members engage *primarily* in delinquent activity.[2] This fallacy has several sources. First, corner-group behavior

Reprinted by special permission of The William Alanson White Psychiatric Foundation, Inc. Originally published in *Psychiatry*, 24 (November, 1961), pp. 283–398. Copyright 1961 by The William Alanson White Psychiatric Foundation Inc.

reported in newspapers is not only "delinquent" but also spectacular and newsworthy; the bulk of customary, recurrent, and nonspectacular daily behavior is generally ignored. Second, scientific investigations which examine the *entire range* of corner-group activity are rare. Third, investigators tend to assume that the most delinquent groups are the best sources of information on delinquency; consequently, extreme and nonrepresentative forms of behavior and types of individuals emerge as "typical" of all behavior of all members of all street-corner groups.

The present study concerns a group which falls near the center of a range of behavior from highly delinquent to negligibly delinquent, and is therefore fairly representative rather than an extreme example. Attention is focused *not* on specifically delinquent behavior, but on a broader area—that of aggression. Data on the "normal" day-to-day manifestations of aggressive behavior in a fairly typical, lower-class, adolescent corner group, observed in its natural milieu, should provide a useful base line against which to gauge the forms and nature of aggressive behavior manifested by such youngsters in other settings such as the school, correctional institution, treatment center, and social agency.

THE JUNIOR OUTLAWS

The Junior Outlaws was one of a set of age-graded subdivisions of a larger street-corner aggregate known as the Outlaws. During the study period, four such subdivisions, each including about twenty boys, were active in the Outlaw area. They were referred to by study personnel as the Midget Outlaws (11-13), the Juniors (13-15), the Intermediates (15-17), and the Seniors (18 and over). These labels, however, were not systematically used by the Outlaws, who called the Juniors the "little kids," the Intermediates the "big kids," the Seniors the "BIG kids," and the Midgets the "LITTLE kids." Smaller groups of slightly younger girls were associated with each subdivision, comprising a more loosely organized series of female age-grades paralleling the structure of the boys' groups. The Outlaws, including all divisions, numbered about 100 persons.

The core group of Junior Outlaws consisted of 18 white Catholic boys between the ages of 14 and 16. During the study year, seven boys became involved with official agencies as a result of delinquent acts. Of these, one boy, who was already on probation, became involved with the courts twice during the study year—once on a charge of auto theft and once on a lewdness charge. Three of the other boys were put on probation during the year—one for auto theft, one for auto theft and habitual truancy, and the third for auto theft and creating a public disturbance. The three others were arrested on suspicion, but released without sentence.

In addition to these official delinquencies, group members were observed committing or reliably reported to have committed thirty arrestable acts for which no official action was taken. These included five instances of car theft, six of petty theft, nine cases of assault, seven alcohol violations, one instance of trespassing, and two cases of creating a public disturbance.

The most important persons in the street-corner world of the Junior Outlaws, outside of their own group, were members of other Outlaw age subdivisions, neighboring corner groups, and several community adults who maintained continued contact with the boys—particularly a variety store proprietor, a drugstore owner, and a poolroom manager. Another group of adults played significant roles in the boys' lives by virtue of the fact that their occupational duties entailed recurrent contact with the group. These included employees of the metropolitan recreation department (playground directors and umpires) and staff members of settlement houses and gyms where the group engaged in athletic activities. Other adults present in the neighborhood but playing very small parts in the lives of the boys were policemen, priests, and other shopkeepers.[3]

DATA COLLECTION AND ANALYSIS

Base data were collected by a trained social worker who maintained intensive and continued contact with the Junior Outlaws in their indigenous cultural milieu for a period of two and one-half years. The worker engaged with the group in a set of customary activities ranging from "hanging out" to organized athletics, and thus became involved with group members on a very intimate level, participating with them in many aspects of their "natural" life in their "natural" theater of operations—the local community. During this period, the worker kept records which provide a richly detailed running account of events as they occurred. While the worker was aware that these records would be subjected to scientific analysis, he was not aware what specific research interests would be developed through them.

The method of analysis employed was designed to take advantage not only of the qualitative richness of the worker's records, but also of the consistency in level of reporting, which made them amenable to quantitative study. For purposes of quantitative study, every instance of an overtly aggressive act or sequence of acts recorded by the worker during the study year was extracted from the records. An aggressive act—the basic unit for quantitative analysis—was defined as any overt, observable action performed by a specific individual or group and directed at an identifiable object or target which could be reliably characterized as "aggressive" in form or intent. Each act extracted from the records was typed on a McBee Keysort card, and coded according to a complex set of categories for actor, form, intensity, object or target, and social context and other descriptive details.[4]

PATTERNS OF AGGRESSIVE BEHAVIOR

Using these coded data to supplement qualitative analyses, it was possible to seek quantitative answers to the following four questions: (1) What were the primary objects or targets of aggressive behavior by the Junior Outlaws, and what was the relative importance and frequency of these targets? (2) In what form was aggression customarily expressed, and what was its range of intensity? (3) What was the relationship between the form of aggressive behavior and its social and interactional context? (4) What was the content of aggressive statements, what personal qualities came under attack, and what was the evaluative content of derogation. The social context of aggression among the Junior Outlaws is treated at length elsewhere,[5] but findings with respect to the other questions are presented below.

Targets of Aggression

One of the most striking and clear-cut findings of the study was that most of the aggressive actions performed by members of the Junior Outlaws were directed at one another. Seventy percent of the aggressive actions of all types, from good-natured ribbing to outright physical attack, were directed at fellow group members. Table 1 shows the distribution of aggressive actions performed by the Junior Outlaws according to category of target.

The remarkably high proportion of acts directed at group members is, to some degree, a function of interaction—that is, the more frequent the contact, the greater the opportunity for aggressive expression. In fact, all but a few aggression targets were specific individuals within the immediate interactive environment of the group rather than abstract institutions or persons out of hearing. Aggression, as reported in these records, is an interactive phenomenon, not a one-sided attack on impersonal objects or persons or institutions outside the boys' actual social world. However, it is also evident that distribution of target choice was not simply a function of interaction frequency; examination of the 30 percent of the acts directed to nongroup targets shows that some targets with relatively high interaction frequency received relatively low proportions of aggression. For example, although the Junior Outlaws interacted with neighborhood adults—especially the owners of stores where they hung out daily—even more frequently than with local adolescents, the adults were subject to a far smaller proportion of aggression. Adults as a whole, in fact, were objects of very little expressed aggression —direct or indirect—contrary to a highly prevalent conception of such gangs as seething with hostility against the adult world. Surprisingly, even adults such as policemen and schoolteachers, whose roles entailed the exercise of disciplinary or restrictive functions and thus might have been ex-

TABLE I. *Proportion of Aggressive Acts by Junior Outlaws Directed Toward Different Targets* (N = 1,490)

Targets of Aggression	Percentage of Acts By Sub-Groups	Total
Junior Outlaws		70.4
Other local adolescents		
Male peers, not Outlaws.	5.8	—
Intermediate Outlaws	2.7	—
Senior Outlaws	2.1	—
Girls	1.2	—
Total	—	11.8
Neighborhood adults in frequent contact with Junior Outlaws		
Recreation workers	5.0	—
Storekeepers	1.9	—
Total	—	6.9
Corner-group social worker	—	5.0
Other adults in regular contact with Junior Outlaws		
Teachers	1.8	—
Clergy	0.4	—
Police	0.2	—
Total	—	2.4
Family members		
Father	0.8	—
Brother	0.7	—
Mother	0.3	—
Sister	0.1	—
Total	—	1.9
All other targets		
Other adults	1.0	—
Property	0.3	—
Jews and Negroes*	0.2	—
Generalized "they"	0.1	—
Total	—	1.6
		100.0

*Acts directed at persons solely in terms of their ethnic status were separated from other targets as a crude measure of the degree of ethnic out-group aggression. The proportion of such acts was strikingly low.

pected to draw considerable face-to-face or behind-the-back aggression, were objects of only a minute proportion of all recorded aggressive behavior.[6]

Form and Intensity of Aggressive Behavior

Simple physical attack against persons or property was rare, comprising less than 7 percent of the 1,395 aggressive acts—a fact which contradicts another common misconception of gang boys as brawling and destructive. A picture begins to emerge of a type of group in which aggression as-asumed a very narrow range of expression: narrow in choice of targets, narrow in form, and also limited in intensity.[7] In none of the 95 physically aggressive acts performed by members of the group, including acts reported to the field worker and those observed by him, was a weapon of any description employed. In all but 7 of these 95 acts, the emotional state or "charge" accompanying the act was adjudged to range from "no evident charge" to "mild anger or irritation." All 7 acts of physical aggression involving "genuine anger" were directed at fellow group members.

For the 94 percent of the aggressive acts that were not physical (mostly verbal, a few gestures and grimaces), a similar situation obtained: only 2 percent were rated as involving "genuine anger," none as involving "uncontrollable fury."

This general pattern of aggressive behavior—sharply limited to nonphysical forms, and of low intensity—prevailed in widely varying contextual circumstances. There were two major exceptions: toward *adults* physical aggression was almost entirely absent, and toward *girls* of their own age aggression was predominantly physical. The patterning of aggression to female peers reflected distinctive aspects of lower-class adolescent male-female interaction and could be characterized as "aggressive in form only."[8]

Verbal aggression was expressed in a number of forms ranging from direct derogation to sarcasm. Eight such forms were distinguished: (1) direct derogation and devaluation (He's just a punk!); (2) direct expression of hostility and antagonism (You stink!); (3) hostile commands (O.K., clear out!); (4) joking, kidding, and teasing (You're acting like a buncha juvenile delinquents); (5) threat of physical aggression (I'm gonna *cream* you!); (6) hostile interrogation (Who asked *you*?); (7) defensive reactions (Whata ya mean, *I'm* stupid?); (8) irony and sarcasm (Here comes the big *lover*). The proportion of verbal acts assignable to each of these categories is shown in Table 2.

TABLE 2. *Form of Verbal Aggression* $(N = 1,294)$

Category	Percentage of Acts
Derogation, devaluation	42.2
Direct hostile statement	23.2
Hostile command	8.5
Joking, kidding, teasing	8.3
Threat of physical aggression	6.0
Hostile interrogation	5.7
Defensive reaction	5.3
Irony, sarcasm	.8
Total	100.0

The bulk of verbal aggression (65.4 percent) took the form of direct hostile statements and derogation. Subtlety was not a characteristic of verbal aggressive expression—very few remarks were ironic or sarcastic. Most verbal attacks were aimed bluntly and directly at the specific object of aggression rather than derogating by implication or through a third party, except for infrequent statements such as "Your whole *family* is soft in the head."[9] Even joking aggression was of low frequency (8.3 percent). Both the low intensity of verbal aggression and relative rarity of physical aggression support a general characterization of Junior Outlaw aggression as a continual flow of direct, overt, low-intensity action directed predominantly to fellow in-group members.

The Content of Verbal Aggression

Study findings have indicated clearly the inadequacy of explaining the aggressive behavior of the Junior Outlaws as a simple venting of subjective feelings of anger generated by intrapsychic impulses; virtually every aggressive action of group members was deeply embedded in a social matrix; acts were directed at specific social targets and involved specific issues, qualities, and areas of group concern. What were these issues and concerns? What personal qualities or behaviors evoked aggressive responses? And, finally, what purpose was served by the constant flow of aggressive activity?

Many of the acts of verbal aggression directed by the Junior Outlaws at one another and nongroup members contained an explicit evaluative component—that is, persons were derogated or ridiculed because they acted in certain ways or manifested certain qualities; irritation or anger was manifested because of failure of the target to conform to certain standards of expected behavior. The personal qualities, ways of behaving, practices, or issues which became implicated in aggressive expression were designated the "content" of aggressive statements.[10]

Content of intragroup aggression.

In the continuing flow of intragroup aggressive exchange, certain areas were subject to consistent concern. Table 3 lists in rank order qualities and issues which figured in aggressive expression. Although the boys' actual speech lent itself to content categories that could be labeled in either valued (Why don't you get wise?) or devalued (What a dumb jerk!) form, Table 3 uses the pejorative phrasing throughout to faciliate comparability.

The listing is significant for what it includes and what it omits, as well as for denoting the different weighting of various objects of concern. By indicating what one is railed at or scoffed at for *not* being or doing, the listing furnishes clues to the Junior Outlaws' conception of the "ideal" corner boy. He is, first and foremost, skilled and competent in a range of physical and athletic accomplishments; he does not disrupt group enterprises by disorderly behavior; he is a faithful participant in group activities, and dependable in fulfilling group obligations. Despite his skill and competence, he is properly modest, and, in particular, refrains from boasting, self-aggrandizement, and behaving as a star or prima donna

TABLE 3. *Identifiable Personal Qualities or Forms of Behavior Subject to Intragroup Verbal Aggression* (N = 454)

(1)	Incompetence, lack of skill (primarily athletic)	11.7
(2)	Disorderly or disruptive behavior	8.6
(3)	Insufficient participation in collective activities	7.9
(4)	Laxness in payment of club dues	7.4
(5)	Arrogance, conceit, self-aggrandizement, "bossiness"	5.7
(6)	Stupidity, ignorance, lack of knowledgeability or sophistication	5.7
(7)	Dishonesty, untrustworthiness	5.5
(8)	Softness, physical weakness	5.3
(9)	Violation of game rules	4.6
(10)	Excessive "roughness" in athletics	3.7
(11)	Sexual ineptitude, impotence	3.7
(12)	Abstaining from drinking, gambling, profanity	3.5
(13)	Laxness, default in debt repayment	2.6
(14)	Incompetence, ineptitude (nonathletic)	2.2
(15)	Insufficient effort in group enterprises	2.0
(16)	Uncooperative "team" behavior	2.0
(17)	Inconsiderateness	2.0
(18)	Cowardice	2.0
(19)	Insufficient self-esteem	1.8
(20)	Disrespect to adult women	1.8
(21)	Law-abiding behavior	1.7
(22)	Faithful school attendance	1.6
(23)	Insolvency	1.3
(24)	Inability to "hold" liquor	.9
(25)	Excessive cleanliness, industriousness	.9
(26)	Insubordination to group leaders	.7
(27)	Overdependency, insufficient autonomy	.7
(28)	Evasiveness, underhandedness	.7
(29)	Effeminacy	.6
(30)	Insufficient control of anger	.4
(31)	Stinginess	.2
(32)	Quarrelsomeness in group	.2
(33)	Disloyalty to group	.2
(34)	Inadequate support for the "team"	.2
	Total	100.0

in collective events. He is smart in the sense of being knowledgeable as to what is current in the world of the corner and its concerns, informed as to game rules, and able to hold his own in rapid-fire repartee. He is scrupulously honest in his dealings with fellow group members, especially in money matters, and is sensitive to and adheres to conceptions of fair play in contests of various sorts. He is physically strong, but careful not to take unfair advantage of this strength in dealings with fellow group members. He is "smooth" with the girls, and sexually potent. He drinks, swears, and gambles but recognizes that there are both appropriate and inappropriate circumstances for these activities.

A rough conceptual distinction may be made between those items which denote personal attributes or qualities of the individual (strength, skill, honesty) and those which refer more directly to the requirements of group solidarity or harmonius group relations (orderliness, fair play). Comparing the ten highest ranked items (66 percent of all orientations) to the ten lowest ranked (5 percent) shows that in the top ten, eight items are referrable to the maintenance of group solidarity and reciprocity (orderliness, participation in group activities, fulfillment of group obligations, payment of club dues, nonself-aggrandizement, trustworthiness, fairness, physical aggression control), while for the bottom group, six out of ten refer more directly to personal characteristics (cleanliness and industriousness, personal autonomy, straight-forwardness, masculinity, anger control, generosity). Of course, these two types of item are not unrelated. If achievement of effective group interaction and achievement of competitive success by the group are seen as mutually dependent, then such personal qualities as skill, smartness, and strength can be seen as essential components both of individual prestige and group prestige, so that successful individual achievement at the same time serves fundamental collective ends.

A further instructive comparison may be made between the top twelve "ideal" qualities of the Junior Outlaws and the twelve qualities specified in the Boy Scout oath, assuming the latter to represent an adult middle-class image of the "ideal" middle-class boy.[11] The two lists have one direct correspondence (Scout: trustworthy; corner boy: honest); three partial correspondences (Scout: loyal, helpful, friendly; corner boy: dependable group participant, fills group obligations, orderly in group situation), and eight noncorrespondences. Reference to obedience and bravery is absent from the Junior Outlaws' top twelve, although occurring later in the list. The items of courtesy, kindness, cheerfulness, thrift, and reverence, notably absent from the total listing, might be seen as "core" concerns of middle-class adults regarding male adolescents which command little attention from lower-class corner-group members. On the other hand, the Boy Scout listing does not include the items of smartness (worldly sophistication and nongullibility), physical strength (although that is cited in the Scout Oath), sexual skill and potency, and adeptness in drinking, gambling, and profanity. These items might be seen as special concerns of street-corner boys which are not verbalized as desirable by middle-class adults.

The partial correspondences (loyalty, helpfulness, friendliness) are significant in that the Boy Scout code enjoins application of these qualities to everyone, including—or, perhaps, especially—adults, while the Junior Outlaws saw loyalty, helpfulness, and friendliness primarily as requirements of the in-group situation. In the out-group situation they were either negligibly applicable or, in many instances, directly proscribed.

Another useful comparison can be made by pairing listed items which imply apparently contradictory or opposing injunctions. Some of these are: *orderly behavior* (8.6) and *unlawful behavior* (1.7); *modesty* (5.7) and *evident self-esteem* (1.8); *straightforwardness, candor* (.7) and *smartness, wariness* (5.7); *toughness, strength* (5.3) and *control of physical aggression* (3.7); *obedience, tractability* (.7) and *independence, autonomy* (.7).

These apparent contradictions may be explained by considering two factors—first, certain standards were differentially or oppositely applied in the in-group and out-group situations, and second, the group code not only defined valued qualities, but also made fairly nice distinctions as to the *limits* of acceptable behavior. One should not be too boastful or self-aggrandizing, but neither at the same time should he be too modest or self-effacing; a "healthy" degree of self-respect would appear to be the group norm. One should be physically vigorous, tough, and strong, but should also confine the exercise of his strength and fighting skill to those areas where such behavior is appropriate or demanded, and exercise due restraint in other areas. One should be honest, aboveboard, and "on the level" with his colleagues, but at the same time he should not be overly trusting, gullible, or insufficiently wary of being "conned." He should accept legitimate authority with good grace and subordinate his individual desires to group requirements, but at the same time he should have the capacity for reaching decisions on his own, and exercising autonomy in directing his affairs. He should be fluent—even creative—in profanity, but should totally mute profane expression in the presence of adult women, especially mothers and nuns. He should drink readily and frequently but not to the point of losing control over his actions.

The explicitness of the behavioral code of the Junior Outlaws—the niceness of the distinctions it afforded, and the pervasiveness and effectiveness of sanctions against violation—reflects anything but the condition of "normlessness," "identity diffusion," or "anomie" sometimes attributed to delinquent gang or slum youngsters. The Junior Outlaws' code of behavioral standards is comparable in specificity to that of the Arthurian knights or Samurai warriors, and, in fact, stresses many of the same qualities. Aggression is expressed in this group not because members feel frustrated at the absence of any firm and guiding set of behavioral controls and thus lash out in diffuse and restless anger, but rather as the result of violations of a specific and precisely defined set of standards which delineate an explicit and consistent model of estimable behavior.

In order to explore the functions of the aggressive enforcement of these behavioral standards, the qualities and issues of Table 3 were grouped, in their positive forms, with some items merged, into the following four clusters:

(1) *Qualities and behaviors which serve to maintain group solidarity, reinforce group cohesion, or facilitate the coordination of collective action.* These would include the items orderly behavior (8.6 percent of acts); dependable participation (7.9 percent); fulfillment of financial obligations (7.4 percent); adherence to operating rules (4.6 percent); loyalty, energetic support (4.4 percent); control of physical aggression (3.7 percent); obedience to authority (.7 percent); and control of verbal aggression (.6 percent). These total 37.9 percent of the acts.

(2) *Qualities and behaviors which serve to secure and maintain relations of mutual equality among group members or to insure reciprocity in intragroup relations.* These include modesty (5.7 percent); trustworthiness (5.5. percent); debt repayment reliability (2.6 percent); considerateness (2.0 percent); openness, candor (.7 percent); generosity, willingness to share (.2 percent). These total 16.7 percent.

(3) *Personal attributes or qualities which serve as criteria of group acceptance and form the basis of prestige conferral.* These include skill, competence (13.9 percent); physical strength, masculinity, toughness (5.9 percent) sophistication, knowledgeability, smartness (5.7 percent); adeptness in drinking, gambling, profanity (4.4 percent) sexual potency, adeptness (3.7 percent); bravery (2.0 percent); adequate self-esteem (1.8 percent); solvency (1.3 percent); self-reliance (.7 percent). These total 39.4 percent.

(4) *Qualities and behaviors which are recognized as prestige-conferring for adult reference groups.* These include, in addition to respect to adult women (1.8 percent), qualities such as lawfulness (1.7 percent), regularity in school attendance (1.6 percent), and cleanliness and industriousness (.9 percent, which they ostensibly derided, but whose importance they recognized, as will be discussed below. The total is 6.0 percent.

These four groupings, as already mentioned, are not mutually independent; for example, modesty, candor (cluster 2), and industriousness (cluster 4) could also be considered as personal qualities, or trustworthiness (cluster 2) and competence (cluster 3) could be seen as related to effective collective action. However, assigning items to these particular groupings furnishes a key to four interrelated functions of intragroup verbal aggression represented by the four clusters, namely, the maintenance of group cohesion and effectively coordinated action, the maintenance of relationships of equality and reciprocity among a group of peers, the delineation and enforcement of a specific set of standards of personal worth and group acceptance, and the communication of group definitions regarding certain standards and behaviors known to be of concern to outside groups.

The relative weightings of the four clusters are of interest. Group cohesion maintenance and personal attributes are accorded almost exactly equal attention, and figure in three-fourths of all aggressive expression. Reciprocity maintenance receives less than half the attention granted group cohesion and personal qualities, while concern with extragroup standards constitutes only 6 percent of the total.

The prominence and character of cluster 1 items evidently reflect basic operational requirements of collective action in whatever context it occurs.[12] In this area, the issues which become involved in aggressive action derive to a large extent from conditions inherent in the operation of a face-to-face collectivity, relatively independent of the age or social class status of group members. Items refer to three basic requirements of effectively coordinated action—the maintenance of harmonious interpersonal relations, the fulfillment of group obligations, and adherence to a legitimatized order. These conditions must obtain regardless of the character of the group.

On the other hand, the weightings of items within these clusters do reflect several particular conditions of group members, such as their age status, and the fact that the group was essentially autonomous and unaffiliated, with voluntary membership and authority originating within rather than without. The high amount of attention devoted to keeping order, so that group business could proceed, reflects the fact that the Junior Outlaws were fifteen-year-old boys. At this age adolescents tend to be highly active and motile. As shown in the discussion of form of aggression, a persisting pattern of mutual teasing, insult interchange, chasing, and roughhousing was a constant concomitant of this group's usual interaction.[13] Under these circumstances, group members were frequently constrained to admonish one another—"O.K., you jerks, cut out the rough stuff. Let's get down to business," or "C'mon, quit raising hell so we can get something done." The degree of attention to the control of physical aggression also reflects the age and class status of the group; among older or higher-class males there would probably be far less necessity to curb actual physical aggression as a condition of collective effectiveness. It is also significant here to note the low degree of expressed concern with control of verbal aggression. It is evident that mutual invective, quarreling, derogations, and aggressive commands were accepted by the group as an expected if not necessary condition of group interaction; opposition to this pattern took the somewhat anomalous form of verbal aggression to curb verbal aggression, and this was done to keep such aggression within reasonable limits rather than to extinguish it. This might indicate an implicit recognition by the group of the indispensable role played by verbal aggression in facilitating higher-order objectives of the group.

The stress on fulfillment of collective obligations reflected to some degree the voluntary nature of group membership. The group controlled no official sanctions such as witholding of salary or dismissal, so that the extent to which an individual would pitch in and help or show up for scheduled events depended on his personal incentives. Important competing interests which inhibited dependable participation were a good show at the local movie theater, or a professional athletic event; school work or activities had slight force as competing demands; interest in girls and dating sometimes took precedence for a few of the boys. Very occasionally a boy would cite home obligations as a reason for lax participation. Stress on payment of dues reflected not only the fact that the boys had limited spending money, but, more importantly, a shared pattern of immediate gratification; what money came in was generally spent shortly afterwards on food, liquor, and cigarettes, or in gambling, so that by club meeting time, cash was depleted or nonexistent.

It is also of interest to note that violation of procedural rules received far more attention than disobedience to individual authority. This is in line with the essentially egalitarian nature of the Junior Outlaws, wherein collective activity was ordered primarily through mutual adherence to a known set of operating rules rather than by commands of leaders.

The lower-class adolescent corner group is sometimes pictured as an autocratic despotism, with one able and forceful leader making the primary decisions for the group and enforcing them by a rigorous exercise of personal authority. This situation did not obtain among the Junior Outlaws. The items in cluster 2 indicate a stress on the mutuality of intragroup interaction, with the expression of aggression serving as a device for inhibiting individual attempts to assume authority prerogatives or claim personal prestige beyond limits acceptable to the group. The sanctions against undue self-aggrandizement served as a significant counterpressure to the high stress on individual achievement noted under cluster 3. Any claims of superior personal eminence, ability, or prominence by a group member produced an almost automatic outpouring of mockery, scorn, and belittlement by those within hearing. An assertion such as, "Man, I can *smother* any of you cats in pool," would evoke an instant barrage of hoots, guffaws, and counterclaims—"Man, you couldn't beat them little *girls* over there in a marble game," and the like. The group ethic demanded a high degree of status equality, and aggression was directed at attempts by individuals to elevate themselves above the common level. Sanctions were also leveled at attempts by individuals to assume undue authority or order others around. Such attempts would elicit this kind of response, "Whataya tryin' to do— be the big boss?"

Coupled with pressures permitting only a limited degree of status differentiation within the group was a stress on the reciprocity of relations, the fulfillment of mutual obligations, and sharing of limited resources. Money and cigarettes were the primary objects of exchange. Group members who had were expected to share with those who had not by lending small sums of money, or furnishing cigarettes to the cigaretteless. However, there was high sensitivity to the accumulated obligations of fellow members, and one could legitimately refuse further giving or lending until prior obligations were fulfilled. The cigarette "moocher" in particular received strong sanctions; at some point in a one-way process of furnishing cigarettes to another, the donor would complain, "Ah, you're always broke and bumming cigarettes. No more until you even up."

Group members were also expected to be honest and aboveboard in intragroup dealings; a prime epithet was that a group member was "sneaky," or trying to "pull something" on his mates. It was also expected that group members would not conceal their personal affairs from other group members; keeping secrets or acting "on the sly" was condemned.

On the other hand, skill in duplicity, evasion, and concealment when directed at groups such as the police or schoolteachers was lauded; here as elsewhere differential standards of proper behavior were applied to those within the group and those outside.

The nature of the items in cluster 3, personal qualities held in esteem by the Junior Outlaws, was indicated by members' attributing the negative aspect to the aggression target; group members would be teased, ridiculed, or castigated as inept, sissified, "square," stupid, and the like. The attribute most frequently referred to was skill or competence. Reflecting a prevalent American stress on achievement, Junior Outlaws measured one another in terms of what they could do. But the nature of this achievement reflected the special concerns of the group. Virtually all reference to individual competence involved skill in athletics, sports, or games. Prestige was accorded the skillful ballplayer, the able cardplayer, the accomplished pool shark. Group concepts of competence virtually never involved academic, technical, or occupational skills. Artistic, musical, or literary capability received no attention. The personal skills most deeply esteemed by the Junior Outlaws related directly to those acts of physical strength and dexterity which conferred competitive advantage in direct contests with male peers.

The qualities of smartness and toughness were accorded about equal concern. With a single exception, none of the acts oriented to smartness involved academic or scholastic ability. Peers were adjudged as stupid or "square" when they appeared to be inadequately informed concerning game rules, parties, cards, hit songs, or techniques of rule violation. Also devalued was general mental slowness or the inability to grasp rapidly what was going on. The concept of toughness involved a combination of physical strength and endurance, fighting prowess, avoidance of softness or sentimentality, and properly "masculine" behavior. Although infrequently used as an epithet, the accusation of effeminacy was one of the group's most potent insults. Also involved in the possession of manly qualities were skill in gambling, fluency in profanity, and readiness to engage in drinking. The ability to "score" with women and skill in "making out" were also closely allied with the general concept of masculinity.

In addition to forming a conception of what was most admirably male, several of the same qualities were also seen as the particular attributes of *adultness*, insofar as they were recognized prerogatives of the adult male. Lacking these qualities was a sign not only of questionable masculinity, but of a despised "babyishness" as well. The last three items in the individual attributes cluster also involve the concept of adultness. As mentioned above, the Junior Outlaws were subject to somewhat conflicting pressures in regard to personal autonomy; on the one hand, collective welfare involved the subordination of self to collective ends; on the other, the much sought-after adult status required evidence of a certain degree of autonomy, and the capacity to stand on one's own two feet. Although there was very little emphasis on the possession of money as a criterion of status, there was some feeling that constant and complete insolvency was degrading, so that a group member who was always cadging cigarettes and borrowing money would be accused of being a "bum."

The comparison of qualities valued by Boy Souts and Junior Outlaws indicated several items, such as thrift and courtesy, which were not involved in Junior Outlaw aggression. These omissions support the frequent assertion that good manners, correct etiquette, and saving for the future are of greater concern to middle-class than lower-class youngsters. Several other qualities which are absent from the Junior Outlaws' personal-worth list are of significance. The financial or social-class level of the boys' families was never utilized to indicate prestige or its lack. Religiosity or church attendance did not figure in aggressive behavior. The boys' occupational status or job-holding experience was at no time referred to in aggressive expression.

Most of the items in cluster 4, which includes several qualities defined by the boys as concerns of groups outside their immediate cultural milieu, were always referred to in a mocking, derisive manner; concern over cleanliness, industriousness, lawfulness, or school regularity was seen as a sign of "squareness" or lack of sophistication. However, little real malice or animus characterized such expression. These values of adult groups were seen as rather laughable and "square," but of relatively insignificant import. This mode of reference indicated that the Junior Outlaws were well aware that these characteristics were seen as important by outside groups, at the same time affirming the fact that they themselves were using quite different criteria of estimability. Item 1, respect to adult women, however, was taken very seriously and violation commanded real indignation. Disrespectful behavior to nuns and mothers was tabooed. This may reflect the Irish Catholic background of the majority of group members.

Aggression toward nongroup members.

Acts of verbal aggression directed against persons outside the corner group were not sufficiently numerous to permit meaningful quantitative analysis. However, some qualitative generalizations may be made.

Verbal aggression toward members of older Outlaw segments concerned two general areas. The first related to the paternalistic or older-brother role assumed by the older boys—the amount of help they gave or offered, the dependability of that help, their domineering tendencies, their fairness as umpires; the second involved the same set of personal-worth standards the boys applied to themselves—adultness, capacity for alcohol, athletic competence, self-control, and so forth. Aggression toward non-Outlaw peers concerned primarily the same personal characteristics, which served as criteria for judging the worth or acceptability of nongroup peers.

Aggression toward adults assumed a different form. Remarks addressed to or concerning recreation department officials referred to their fairness or unfairness as umpires, their lack of kindness, and their domineering manner of exercising authority. There were no remarks about specific personality characteristics. Parents were criticized for being domineering, too talkative, clever at outwitting the boys' attempts at deception, and drinking too much. Teachers were accused either of incompetence or unwillingness to help. Priests were seen as negativistic and moralistic, shopkeepers as stingy or inconsiderate.

There were thus two major patterns of verbal aggression toward nongroup members. To boys of their own age or slightly older, the Junior Outlaws applied standards of evaluation similar to those used in their own group—measuring their peers in terms of competence, sophistication, toughness, masculinity, and so forth—except that the set of standards relating to group cohesion and collective action, which figured so prominently in intragroup aggression, was never applied to nongroup members.

In the case of adults, aggressive comments reflected a consistent resentment of impersonal treatment—unkind or inconsiderate actions which appeared to the boys to deny them the status of individual human beings worthy of personal consideration. Related to this was a theme of resentment of authority, directed not so much at the exercise of authority itself, but against what was seen as injustice or unfair exploitation of positions of authority. In the case of older persons, then, the content of aggressive expression involved three primary areas: the adequacy of nurturance, the impersonality of treatment, and the unjust exercise of authority.

Analysis of the content of Junior Outlaw verbal aggression has indicated that whatever the intrapsychic forces generating aggressive behavior, and whatever the emotional functions it served, such aggression served important positive functions for Junior Outlaws qua group members. It was an essential element of behavioral mechanisms which operated to delineate standards of personal worth, to facilitate effective collective functioning, to maintain relations of reciprocity and equality, to define attitudes toward those outside the group and their values, to indicate the *limits* of acceptable behavior, and to provide effective sanctions against deviation from group-supported standards.

The ultimate sanction for not conforming to these standards was exclusion from the corner group. In fact, punishment by expulsion was a constant theme in Junior Outlaw conversations, and actually occurred several times during the study year—for example, one boy was ostracized twice for "childish" behavior. The reward for conformity and achievement within this framework was high prestige. In addition, there was a further source of legitimacy for these aggression-supported norms—the reputation of the entire group vis-à-vis other corner groups in the vicinity. Athletic merit, fighting prowess, and sophistication were not only standards which governed acceptance or rejection by the group, but also the standards by which the reputation of each corner group as a unit was measured. Aggression in the service of group-condoned norms thus had a community-based source of legitimacy.

THE NATURE AND FUNCTION OF CORNER-GROUP AGGRESSION

Aggression may be analyzed from many points of view and within many different frames of reference. Psychodynamic approaches stress intrapsychic forces which generate aggressive impulses, and mechanisms such as displacement, sublimation, and catharsis which are utilized by the personality to cope with such impulses. Social-psychological theory explores the frustration-aggression hypothesis, whereby socially or intrapsychically generated strains are seen as contributing to such aggressive behavior as prejudice and warfare. Some psychiatrically oriented approaches conceive of the hostile acting out of aggressive impulses as a major force in the disruption of group solidarity or in the genesis of criminal behavior.

The present study has produced a picture of aggression as an integral component of the customary day-to-day behavior

of a group of adolescent street-corner boys. The study has
developed a fairly consistent set of findings. The Junior Outlaws manifested an extremely narrow range of aggressive
expression, sharply limited in choice of target, and, even
more remarkable, in form and emotional intensity. Acts of
physical aggression were rare. The social world of group
members was narrowly circumscribed: their activities were
usually restricted to the safe confines of a known and predictable neighborhood, and forays beyond its limits were felt
to be dangerous. They were cautious in their dealings with
persons outside their own corner group, particularly with
adults. There was a striking absence of expressed aggression
toward generalized entities such as Jews, Negroes, Com-
munists, or "rich people," or toward larger institutions such
as "school" or "the police."

Aggression was predominantly a characteristic of interaction *within the corner group*, and only rarely an aspect of
relations with outside groups. Aggressive actions toward the
adult world were not markedly antagonistic or rebellious, but
rather entailed resentment of perceived injustices and impersonal treatment. Ostensibly aggressive behavior toward
girls of the same age actually involved negligible hostile intent, but rather served as a somewhat awkward and indirect
method of expressing affection. Most aggression toward members of other corner groups was essentially "testing" behavior,
a means of estimating relative status and threat potential.

Aggressive expression within the corner group itself, rather
than appearing as disruptive or disintegrative, served as an
effective device for producing and maintaining group cohesion. Actions or personal characteristics which evoked aggressive reactions involved, for the most part, failure to contribute toward group ends, disruption of concerted activities,
or failure to maintain expected relationships of reciprocity
and equality. Other aggressive comments concerning personal
characteristics served to define and affirm standards of eligi-
bility and group acceptance.

The consistently low level of emotional "charge" suggests
that for most group members aggression was much more
directly related to their roles as corner-group members, re-

flecting pressures to conform to group norms, than to inner wellsprings of malice and rebellion. These conclusions further suggest that the corner group—rather than generating resentment and consequent criminal acts against the outside world, or transforming personality conflicts into delinquent behavior—in actuality served to absorb the great bulk of its members' personal hostility.

This absorptive capacity of the corner group would appear to obtain regardless of the ultimate source of aggressive drives in boys of this age and sociocultural group. Some authors have suggested that child-rearing practices of urban lower-class families produce a character structure which, particularly in adolescence, involves an unusually high aggressive potential; others maintain that the life situation of lower-class boys entails a set of insoluble dilemmas which make the transition to adulthood extremely difficult, with a consequent generation of hostility and criminal behavior.[14] Others, including the present writers, suggest that the lower-class cultural milieu itself generates and transmits emphases on strength, fighting prowess, toughness, and the quest of risk, all of which may achieve fulfillment in certain forms of crime, and that the cultivation of competence in individual and collective aggressive action is a highly functional component of the role of the lower-class male—especially in the light of the persisting social indispensability of the combat soldier.[15] But whatever factors are postulated as productive of aggressive behavior, the lower-class street-corner group serves for its members as a major device for handling aggressive expression. However, this study fails to support a widely held conception that such groups operate as a funnel through which aggressive tensions and destructive impulses are vented on outside groups, but indicates instead that they provide an arena in which aggression is played out, its force dissipated in a continuing, persistent, low-level flow, directed at members of the group itself.

What light is thrown on the causes of delinquent behavior by these generalizations as to the form and functions of corner-group aggression? The Junior Outlaws cannot be considered a severely delinquent group, but it also cannot be considered nondelinquent. Study findings suggest three primary conclusions as to the relationship between aggression and delinquency: (1) Active malice toward adult groups was a negligible factor in the motivation of delinquent acts. (2) The desire to demonstrate possession of personal qualities which served as criteria of group acceptance and prestige— for example, toughness and smartness—and thus avoid group censure, was a highly significant component in the motivation of delinquent acts. (3) Engaging in extragroup aggression as a device for reducing intragroup aggression entailed, primarily, collective aggressive contests against similarly circumstanced groups of peers, thus providing one component of the motivation for gang fights.

The picture of corner-gang members as angry, frustrated boys lashing out in rebellious fury against the adult world is not substantiated. Table 1 shows that adults or symbols of the adult world were the object of only about 10 percent of total group aggression, with such aggression of consistently low intensity. Physical attack on adults was virtually nonexistent. Virtually no vandalism or other property damage was noted, and auto theft, which might be seen as a way of expressing aggression toward adults, appeared primarily as a means of demonstrating group-valued qualities of daring and resourcefulness. The Junior Outlaws, in common with all adolescent groups, did evince hostility to adults and used this shared hostility as a device for affirming group solidarity, but such hostility had little evident relation to specifically delinquent activity.

The behavioral context of Junior Outlaw delinquencies (primarily theft, assault, and alcohol violations) indicates that the desire to gain prestige and achieve personal stature in the eyes of one's peers was far more important than the impulsive or uncontrolled venting of anger. Most delinquent acts were collectively performed, thus inevitably involving collective validation and a degree of controlled planning. Individual delinquencies were seldom concealed from the group, but rather were publicly reported in a manner designed to elicit approbation and admiration. In some instances, group members engaged in delinquent actions such as alcohol violations following assertions that they lacked manliness, daring, or sophistication.

Under usual conditions, aggression manifested by the Junior Outlaws was adequately accommodated by mechanisms thus far described. A group of this type, because it is a cohesive organization of peers with limited intragroup power or status distinctions, can tolerate a fairly high level of intragroup aggression. In addition, overtly hostile action toward those outside its circle is dangerous, possibly provoking harmful retaliation. The front of bravery and toughness assumed by the corner boy conceals considerable fear and caution, and 'safe' targets for aggression are welcome. Further, as stated above, a certain level of intragroup aggressive behavior is functional for maintaining the stability and cohesiveness of the group. Periodically these established devices appeared inadequate to handle rising levels of aggressive potential, and the group's response sometimes involved a collective attack on out-group peers. A major consequence of these engagements appeared to be the enhancement of group solidarity— both in that the catharsis resulting from collective assault provided a safety valve for accumulated aggressive tensions, and in that shared effort against a common enemy served to mitigate intragroup differences.

A final conclusion relates to the extent to which the patterning of aggressive behavior by the Junior Outlaws can be considered abnormal or pathological. Psychiatric literature frequently characterizes gang members as "disturbed," and sees their patterns of collective behavior as manifestations of individual or social pathology. The handling of aggressive tendencies inevitably generated by day-to-day human interaction represents a universal problem for which different societies have developed different adaptations. Although it is difficult to establish standards by which to rate as more or less normal the various methods used by different cultural systems, psychiatric experience does furnish guides as to what ways of handling aggression appear to be abnormal ways in contemporary urban American society. These include such devices as isolation or withdrawal from social interaction (thus avoiding both targets and instigators of aggression), depressive states resulting from turning hostility in on oneself, with suicide an extreme manifestation, excessive use of alcohol, resort to drugs or narcotics, patterns of irrational hatred for selected social targets, and projection of subjective feelings of hostility on to external agencies.

Gauged against such methods of dealing with aggression, the mechanisms utilized by the Junior Outlaws could scarcely be characterized as abnormal. On the contrary, they appear as an organized, efficient, and dynamically balanced system, performing stabilizing and integrative functions for both the group and its members. From this perspective, this type of adolescent group appears not as a defective or pathological organism, but as a highly effective device for accommodating a universal human problem in a manner particularly well geared to the conditions of its cultural milieu.

On Property Crimes
and Delinquent Subcultures

As NOTED in the introductory chapter, stealing, particularly among males, tends to take place in groups. Cloward and Ohlin have hypothesized that "criminal subcultures" among young people emerge in communities in which adults who are engaged in systematic criminal behavior are integrated into community life.[1] Cohen and Short have argued that "semiprofessional theft" occurs most often as an emphasis of individuals and cliques within the gang rather than in the form of a fully developed criminal subculture, though the latter clearly occurs in adulthood for those who become committed to crime as a means of livelihood.[2] The issue is thus whether—or to what extent—criminal activities become a distinct subculture among juvenile gangs or a subcultural emphasis within gangs. We have adopted the latter view on the basis of limited evidence from Chicago and other cities.

In the Chicago study systematic analysis of detached-worker reports on the behavior of gang boys revealed no criminal factor or configuration of offenses. The following discussion is relevant:

> Conflict and retreatism emerge as fairly distinct emphases in terms of factor structure, but criminal behavior does not. Observational data clarify the relation between various types of "criminal" behavior and other types of delinquency . . . . We know, for example, that tough, conflict-oriented boys sometimes display and utilize their neighborhood "rep" by charging small amounts from younger boys for "protection" or by "shaking down" paper boys. Members of such gangs are known to purse-snatch, shoplift, and burglarize. The norms of the gang regard these as acceptable ways of

acquiring a little "bread" to buy a bottle of wine, a bite to eat, one's share of the cost of a game of pool, and the like.

By contrast, these criminal activities are directed toward the acquisition of larger sums of money when related to drug use. Even a "nickel bag" of marihuana costs five dollars. Pills are less expensive but the habit requires a continuous supply, and heroin is very expensive. In addition to robbery and theft, pimping emerges as a retreatist-related activity consistent with the joint emphasis on "kicks" and "hustles."

Auto theft often is part of a complex which involves dressing up one's own auto, "souping up" the motor, etc. These things require money or appropriate auto parts. Groups highest on this factor are known also to sell parts of stripped autos. Forgery and bribery are also related to . . . [authority protest]. Observational data suggest that both are relatively petty among our boys, involving attempts to cash forged checks in small denominations and bribing policemen who apprehend them in various delinquencies. Gambling and theft, which are the only criminal items with moderate loadings on . . . [the stable corner boy pattern], are part of a recreational rather than a criminal pattern. No criminal item has even a moderate loading on . . . [the stable sex-maturity pattern].[3]

The Chicago researchers did locate a criminal clique of eight boys within a large aggregation of "hanging groups" which coalesced sporadically and in widely varying numbers for activities such as drinking, athletic contests, occasional drug use, driving around in cars, and general hell-raising. The criminal clique did not form a hanging group themselves—indeed they avoided visibly cliquing-up on the street. They became a clique only when they were not with the other groups, gathering in each other's homes or elsewhere quite secretively to discuss and plan theft activities. Their leader told the detached worker—and this was confirmed by the other boys—that they had joined together specifically and exclusively for the purpose of promoting thieving operations.

They engaged extensively, and successfully for approximately two years, in auto stripping, burglary, and shoplifting, eschewing such "heavy stuff" as robbery and "shakedown." The detached worker assigned to these boys indicated that "Bobby and his guys talk about what they are doing in one room, while Bobby's old man, who used to be some sort of wheel in the syndicate, talks to his friends about the 'old days' in the next room."[4] There is evidence, also, that Bobby enjoyed a considerable degree of police immunity for several months.

From observations and interviews in New York City, Spergel also finds that behavior adaptations of delinquents vary systematically, but with much "overlapping" in the degree of involvement of youngsters in racket and theft behavior, in conflict, and in drug use.[5] The distinction between rackets and theft was not made by Cloward and Ohlin, but it is not inconsistent with their rationale, and Spergel's empirical observations are supportive. Briefly, "rackets" are *organized* forms of criminal endeavor, such as policy or numbers and loan shark activities engaged in for profit and with provision for legal protection, if not for juvenile enterprises of this sort, at least for their adult counterparts. "Theft" refers to pervasive activities which are less well planned, organized, and executed, at times for profit, but often chiefly for "kicks" and the establishment of "rep." Examples are joy riding, stripping of auto parts, apartment burglary, and robbery.

Further commentary on theft activities within gangs will be found in the selections which follow, particularly in this section, but also in later sections.

The following selections are separated in time by nearly 30 years. The first, again from Chicago, is a classic discussion of play and comradeship as the major motivational themes of gang delinquency. The second, from New York City, describes a gang of boys who are somewhat older and more sophisticated in their activities, including theft. Differences between these accounts, it may be suggested, reflect the increased sophistication which comes with age and with exposure to organized and professional criminal activities at the adult level.

JUVENILE DELINQUENCY:
A GROUP TRADITION

Clifford Shaw

IT IS frequently assumed that the motivating tendencies involved in the development of the attitudes and behavior patterns of the delinquent are of a very different character from those imputed to individuals whose conduct is in accordance with the laws of conventional society. Delinquency is very often regarded by the general public as an expression of "innate perversity," "inherent viciousness," or "willful disobedience." Despite the rather widespread acceptance of this belief, there is considerable evidence to substantiate the assumption that the wishes and desires underlying the delinquent boy's participation in the unlawful practices of his group are essentially not unlike those of members of groups whose activities meet with conventional social approval. Presumably the fundamental social wishes or desires of the members of delinquent and nondelinquent groups are of the same character, although their overt form of expression may vary widely according to the cultural standards of the respective groups.

. . .

The member of a delinquent group may achieve recogni-

Reprinted from *Child Welfare Pamphlets, No. 24*, Bulletin of the State University of Iowa, Iowa City, 1933.

EDITOR'S NOTE: Though his intention was to illustrate the manner in which the delinquent group came to satisfy the "four wishes" hypothesized by W. I. Thomas as motivating behavior, Clifford Shaw here presents cases which have been utilized to establish the presence of a group tradition of stealing, and of the development of criminal subcultures. Earlier research by Shaw and McKay[1] had established that more than 90 per cent of the boys brought before the Juvenile Court of Cook County (Chicago) for *stealing* were implicated with companions, a higher percentage than for other offenses.

tion and derive a feeling of superiority by displaying courage in committing a daring crime, by refusing to divulge to the police the identity of his confederates in delinquency, or by virtue of the fact that he has a long record of delinquency or has served a period of incarceration in a correctional institution. The boy in a conventional group may achieve similar satisfaction by receiving honors for scholastic achievement, by excelling in sports, or by virtue of the fact that his family has prestige and prominence in the community. In like manner, the form of behavior involved in the satisfaction of the desires for security, response, or new experience may vary widely as between members of delinquent and nondelinquent groups.

In many cases, especially in the deteriorated areas where there is a paucity of facilities for socially acceptable forms of supervised play, participation in delinquent activities may constitute the only available means for the satisfactory expression of the boy's social wishes. The cultural standards of his group may be such as not to tolerate socially approved forms of expression; they may represent a complete reversal of the standards and norms of conventional society. As stated previously, forms of behavior which result in personal degradation and dishonor in a conventional group serve to enhance and elevate the personal prestige and status of a member of the delinquent group.

The delinquent group, like all social groups, tends to develop its own rules of conduct by which it seeks to regulate and control the behavior of its members. It looks with disapproval upon those who violate its rules and views with approval those who conform and are loyal. In the older delinquent and criminal groups there tends to be a definite hierarchy of social groupings, which range all the way from the petty thief to the gangster.

Numerous case studies of delinquent careers and observations of persons who have had intimate contacts with delinquents and criminals suggest that the delinquent belongs to a social group whose cultural values and moral standards vary widely from those of the larger conventional society. The wishes or desires of the boy who grows up as a member of such a group find their natural expression in various forms of delinquent activities, which are in accordance with the behavior patterns, values, and expectations of the group. From this point of view, delinquency may be regarded as a natural adjustment of the boy to the expectations of the group of which he is a part. In other words, various forms of delinquent behavior become the objects toward which the wishes of the boy are necessarily directed in the course of his participation in the activities of the group.

One of the most obvious elements in the experiences of young delinquents is the thrill, stimulation, and excitement which they derive from their delinquent activities. This element is especially noticeable during the initial stages of delinquent careers. As is indicated in the following case, initial stealing episodes may take the form of fascinating and enticing games, with the usual rivalry and competition characteristic of such group activities among boys.

CASE NO. 2

When we were shoplifting we always made a game of it. For example, we might gamble on who could steal the most caps in a day, or who could steal caps from the largest number of stores in a day, or who could steal in the presence of a detective and then get away. We were always daring each other that way and thinking up new schemes. This was the best part of the game. I would go into a store to steal a cap, by trying on one and when the clerk was not watching walk out of the store, leaving the old cap. With the new cap on my head I would go into another store, do the same thing as in the other store, getting a new hat and leave the one I had taken from the other place. I might do this all day and have one hat at night. It was the fun I wanted, not the hat. I kept this up for months and then began to sell the things to a man on the west side. It was at this time that I began to steal for gain.

The formal routine of the school is often regarded by the delinquent boy as dull and monotonous compared to the activities of his group. All of the agencies dealing with problem boys find it difficult to compete with the thrill of adventure which the group is able to secure for itself through its delinquent practices.

CASE NO. 3

For awhile my life was made up of constant efforts to avoid the truant officer, the house detectives of the department stores, and my mother and brother when I should have been in school. The only time that I spent at home was at night and I never got home until ten or eleven o'clock. . . .

It wasn't long before my mother received a summons to appear with me in the juvenile court. When faced with this possibility of having to leave my mother and leave the gang, I felt miserable and cried. I couldn't understand how the judge could contemplate such cruelty. I, of course, promised to attend school regularly in the future and sincerely wished that I could. Yet I knew I would find it misery to attend school all day long every day. So dull an outlook did this present that school from that time onward was regarded by me as a punishment. And that was one punishment I tried hard to avoid. School, I thought, was a necessary evil that grown folks expected little children to endure. I didn't want to go and I couldn't see it in any other light but as a means to keep me from doing the things that I liked to do.

I, of course, attended school regularly for about two or three weeks, but it was no use. My heart wasn't in it. My mother would accompany me to see that I got as far as the school; but I never went inside if I could help it. Between going to school and stealing I chose stealing. I knew of nothing else to do, only these two things. . . .

It is a matter of general observation that individuals are most sensitive to the attitudes of approval and disapproval of those persons with whom they are most intimately associated or those who belong to their own club, sect, social class, or profession. The delinquent is no exception to the rule. He is much more responsive to the opinions and judgments of his companions in crime, or to the members of the criminal class in general, than he is to the larger society. He seeks to secure the esteem and approbation of his fellows by conducting himself in a manner acceptable to his group.

Who can tell the blackest tale, who can make crime most exciting and attractive, who can pour the wittiest amount of derision on rectitude, who can most cleverly "dodge" the jail officers, who can bear punishment in the most hardened manner—these are the heroes and objects of admiration to many of the inmates of a prison. If a man does not endure his punishment bravely, he's so teased and jeered by his fellow prisoners, that he not unfrequently commits, designedly, some flagrant breach of prison rule, in order that, by braving the punishment and enduring it without flinching, he may redeem his lost character of hardihood.

The manner in which the boy's participation in the delinquent practices of his group may contribute to his prestige and give him a feeling of pride and superiority is illustrated in the following case:

CASE NO. 7

When I was 8 years old I did my first job in the racket. This job was the biggest thrill I ever got in my life. It happened in April. That day I was hanging around with the oldest brother and his gang. They had been playing baseball all afternoon and I was watching them.

When it got too dark to play ball we all went into the alley to have a smoke and tell stories. The big guys got to talking about stealing, and my brother said he had a good place spotted where we would get some easy "dough" [money]. The place was a butcher shop in Thirty-first Street. The big guys planned everything, and I only listened. These guys were seven or eight years older than me and had pulled off a lot of big jobs before. They would never let me go with them on big jobs; but this night I went along and they didn't say a word. We all went to the butcher shop about 11:30 o'clock. It was very dark and everything was quiet, and I was nervous and stayed close to my brother. We all slipped around into the alley behind the butcher shop, and my brother and another big guy went up to the building to see if the doors were unlocked. My brother had been in the place a few days before to see how to get in and where the cash register was; and so he led the way. I and two other guys waited close to the alley between two buildings. We were going to give "jiggers."

In a little while my brother came back and said everything was locked tight. The owner lived over the butcher shop, so we couldn't make much noise by breaking the glass or jimmie the door. We all went up to the back door, and then my brother got a box and stood on it and tried the transom—and it opened. It was too little for my brother or the other guys to get through. Then I was thrilled when they said I'd have to crawl through the transom. That was the kick of my whole life.

I was only 8 and always was very little so I could get through the transom easy. I was scared but made up my mind to go through anyway. I was too thrilled to say no.

My brother lifted me up on his shoulders and I crawled through the transom. I hung down on the inside and stood on an ice box and then crawled down on the floor. The door was locked with a padlock and chain, but I was able to unlock the window and let the big guys in that way. The big guys looked for money first and found $22. Then we all got everything we wanted to eat and several cartons of cigarettes and ditched the placed.

When we got out, my brother divvied up everything and I got $4 and a lot of cigarettes. I felt like a "big-shot" after that night and the big guys said I could go with them every time they went robbin'. Almost every night we went robbin' and many times I had to crawl through transoms and one time through an ice-box hole. That's why the big guys called me the "baby bandit."

The criminal group has its heroes, its "big-shots," its prominent persons who have gained prestige and power in the delinquent world. Such persons are well-known in the delinquency areas of the city and are often emulated by the younger members of delinquent groups. To the young delinquent, the "big-shot" symbolizes success and power in the criminal world and represents an ideal to be achieved.

CASE NO. 8

Every boy has some ideal he looks up to and admires. His ideal may be Babe Ruth, Jack Dempsey, Al Capone, or some other crook. His ideal is what he wants to be like when he grows up and becomes a man. When I was twelve years old we moved into a neighborhood where there lived a mob of gangsters and big crooks. They were all swell dressers and had big cars and carried "gats." Us kids saw these swell guys and mingled with them in the cigar store on the corner. Jack Gurney was the one in the mob that I had a fancy to. He used to take my sis out and that way I saw him often. He was in the stick-up racket before he was in the beer racket and was a swell dresser and had lots of dough. He was a nervy guy and went in for big stuff. He was a mysterious fellow and would disappear sometimes for several days but always came back. He was looked up to as the leader of his mob and anybody would be glad to be in his place.

He never talked to me about crime, but I secretly looked up to him for his daring and courage. He was what a fellow would call a big shot to me. I liked to be near him and felt stuck up over the other guys because he came to my home to see sis.

CASE NO. 9

Naw, I don't wanna be a big lawyer or business man, I wanna amount to something. I wanna be a big shot, like "Polack Joe" (Joe Saltis, beer baron of the south side). Have all the guys look up to me. Have a couple of Lincolns, lots of molls, and all the coppers lickin' my shoes.

It is a matter of significance to note also that there is a general tendency among older delinquents and criminals to look with contempt upon the person who specializes in any form of petty stealing. Very frequently he is distrusted and regarded in much the same manner as the "rat" or "stool pigeon." "The common thief is not distinguished for manual dexterity and accomplishment, like the pick-pocket or mobsman, nor for courage, ingenuity, and skill, like the burglar, but is characterized by low cunning and stealth—hence he is termed the Sneak, and is despised by the higher classes of thieves . . . ."

It is possible that the stigma attached to petty stealing among members of older delinquent groups is one factor which gives impetus to the young delinquent's desire to abandon such forms of petty delinquency as stealing junk, vegetables, breaking into freight cars, stealing pennies from newsstands, and to become identified with older groups engaged in such crimes as larceny of automobiles and robbery with a gun, both of which are accredited "rackets" among older delinquent boys.

CASE NO. 10

In my racket, which was the auto racket, we wouldn't have a sneak thief of any kind. It takes guts to steal cars and we wouldn't trust our lives with a low piker like a petty thief. The way we looked at it was that if a fellow didn't have enough guts and ambition to do anything but jack-roll a poor old drunk man or snatch an old lady's purse [he] was a coward and no good in a hot racket. A sneak thief is looked down on by all real criminals and is not trusted. Stealing junk and vegetables is all right for a kid, but it's not a man's job. . . .

The delinquent's relationships with members of his gang often serve as the chief medium for the satisfaction of his desires for intimacy and companionship. These relationships usually are much more spontaneous and intimate than the formal contacts with teachers, probation officers, and even with members of the family group. In many cases the boy is much more confidential and has many more interests and sentiments in common with his companions than with his parents or other adults in the neighborhood. Consequently, the gang may exercise a control over the boy's conduct which is more effective than that of his parents and through its influence he may develop attitudes and forms of behavior which partially or completely isolate him from his family.

. . . a delinquent's relationship to his parents may assume the character of an emotional conflict, which not only complicates the problem of parental control but often leads to truancy from home and the development of attitudes of hostility and rebellion. In such cases, the family is usually rendered relatively ineffective as an agency for the training and control of the child. This conflict between the child and the parents and the consequent lowering of family restraint are particularly marked in the case of the children of foreign-born parents. They cleave to their Old World traditions and are largely unfamiliar with the standards of American life, while the children through their contacts with groups in the neighborhood develop attitudes and acquire forms of behavior which vary widely from those of the parents. The intimacy, sympathetic understanding, and companionship which the young delinquent secures through his contacts in these groups are indicated in such cases as the following:

CASE NO. 11

From the time I used to go to the markets and to West Madison Street with the old gang I had been attracted to throngs of people, not the Loop throngs, but the West Madison and South State Street throngs. I could not explain this irresistible interest, even if I wanted to. Perhaps it was the telepathy that is from one derelict to another. I do know full well that this human wreckage was always full of interest and mystery to my dreamy mind. Men of all nationalities and races, from the four corners of the earth, were there and brushed shoulders with the crooks and gunmen of the underworld. They were all attracted there, as I was, by the cheap movies, flophouses, cheap hashhouses, and most of all, by the human derelicts that make West Madison Street what it is. When blue and broken-up I would always find an old pal there to tell my troubles to and receive the sympathy that comes through mutual understanding. All the old bums and human wrecks were my family. We all ate at the same table and enjoyed ourselves at the same theaters. In fact, we consisted of a brotherhood whose object was mutual pity and sympathy. The brotherhood was made up of ordinary "'bos," pickpockets, panhandlers, petty thieves, "jack-rollers," and the other wrecks that compose the underworld. Here was my favorite haunt, because my friends made their rendezvous there. It seemed to me that here the lights gleamed brighter, the lures were stronger, and that there were more bums to hide me from the stares of snobbish people. . . .

In those sections of the city where a relatively large proportion of the boys are engaged in delinquent activities, it is often difficult for the delinquent to sever his relationships with his companions in delinquency and to establish satisfying contacts with nondelinquent boys. This problem is particularly difficult both because of the nature of the delinquent's attitude, which has been defined in terms of the activities, interests, and values of the delinquent group, and because of the attitudes of distrust with which the law-abiding elements of the neighborhood regard him. On the one hand, the delinquent often regards the boy who works or attends school regularly as a "chump," or as one delinquent put it, "only fools and horses work." On the other hand, the delinquent is distrusted by nondelinquents and is often excluded from contact with them. This difficulty which the habitual delinquent encounters in his attempt to develop relationships of intimacy and response with nondelinquent boys is suggested in cases like the following:

CASE NO. 12

When I got out of the reform school I went back home but I found out I didn't have any close friends I could go with, without getting pinched. I wanted to go straight and get a job but I couldn't very well, because when I was going straight I didn't have as many friends as if I was robbing. I didn't feel at home with these new fellows and I guess they didn't with me. I stayed away from my good pals for a little while but then I went back to them and got to robbing again and went to St. Charles School for Boys.

.   .   .

CONCLUSION

It is not possible from the foregoing data to determine the extent to which membership in delinquent groups produces delinquent behavior. One may ask whether the individual boy is delinquent because of the influence of his group or whether he selects delinquent companions because of a pre-established tendency toward delinquency. It is clear that many types of delinquencies are of such a character as to necessitate the participation of two or more persons in their execution. However, since it is found that delinquency in most cases is a form of group activity, that contact with delinquent groups often marks the beginning of the boy's career in delinquency, and that his initial delinquencies are often identical with the traditions and established practices of the group, it is probable that participation in the activities of such groups is one of the very significant contributing factors in cases of delinquency.

It is important to observe that the activities and social

values of play-groups and gangs among boys frequently reflect more general processes in the social life of the larger communities of which these groups are integral parts. This is characteristic of both delinquent and nondelinquent groups. In the delinquency areas, where there is very little conventional public opinion and homogeneity of cultural standards surrounding both the children and parents, many of the groups of delinquent boys are almost entirely isolated from conventional society. The neighborhood not only fails to surround the child with consistent cultural standards and to provide facilities for the satisfaction of wholesome play interests, but it subjects him to numerous influences which contribute directly to the development of tendencies toward delinquency. In this situation the moral standards and practices of many of the groups engaged in delinquency develop as a natural product of local neighborhood life and it is artifical to view them except as a part of these more general and inclusive situations.

The data presented in this paper afford a basis for assuming that various forms of delinquent conduct, especially stealing, are in large part a product of the social and cultural life of the groups in which the delinquent is a member. From this point of view, the differences in conduct between delinquent and nondelinquent boys reflect fundamental differences in group traditions, standards, and expectations. In a very real sense the behavior of many delinquent boys may be regarded as an adjustment to the cultural standards of the group and neighborhood in which they live. Viewed from the standpoint of the cultural patterns of his group, the delinquent's behavior in many cases is an approved form of conduct, although it is an offense against the laws of the larger social order. His reformation, on the other hand, is often regarded by his companions in delinquency as a violation of the standards of the group.

LEADERSHIP AND
THE POWER SITUATION

Herbert A. Bloch
and Arthur Niederhoffer

1. PAULIE

PAULIE had real prestige in the gang. His was the final say in all important decisions. Older than the other members, by seven or eight years, he maintained a certain air of mystery. The younger Pirates might indulge in wild adolescent antics. Paulie remained aloof. He hated the police, perhaps from experience with them. He rarely spoke to them at all as a Pirate. He organized and "cut" crap games for older men and frequently engaged in serious conversation with the hardened professionals on _____ Street, two blocks from the Pirates' headquarters.

From talks with more garrulous members, it was later on learned that Paulie was the mastermind behind some of the gang's most impressive coups. From his contacts, information was obtained as to the most inviting location to burglarize. It was he who developed the strategy and outlined the major stages of each campaign of burglary or robbery. At the same time, he never jeopardized himself by physically taking part in these dangerous forays. He relied on the loyalty to the gang code to protect him in case any Pirate was caught. And his confidence was justified since he was never implicated directly. There is no doubt that he made a considerable profit from the criminal activities of the gang. Another vital duty which he performed was to get rid of the considerable loot,

Originally published as Chapter 16 in Bloch and Niederhoffer, *The Gang, A Study in Adolescent Behavior*, New York: Philosophical Library, 1958, pp. 201–216. Reprinted by permission.

which might consist of jewelry, clothing, tools, or currency of large denominations. His contact with professional gangsters, fences, bookies, made him an ideal choice for this function.

2. LULU

Second in command was Lulu. (The feminine nickname is suggestive.) Lulu was about twenty years old. From all reports he was married and had one child, although no one had ever seen his family with him. His life was dedicated to the gang. He was the tactician of the group and had a tremendous talent for anything connected with tools or electricity. Combined with a devil-may-care attitude, his abilities made him an outstanding burglar. While ostensibly working in an auto repair shop, it was discovered later, Lulu was repainting stolen automobiles, changing engine numbers, and selling them as his own. In fact, he "proved" ownership of his two automobiles by presenting forged registration certificates to the police. His proudest possession was a Cord automobile which had become a real collector's item. It turned out that the Cord, too, had been stolen. He had done such a clever job of disguising its identifying characteristics that, in spite of its rarity, he was able to avoid detection.

Lulu took care of the details of all the burglaries. He "cased the jobs"; looked over the wiring layout; learned the habits of the patrolman on the post; secreted burglars' tools in the building to be burglarized. Specific instances of his methods in planning a crime prove that he justified the gang's confidence in him. In an unguarded moment, he revealed that he had raced his car from the nearest Holmes Protective Service office to a jewelry store in order to time the period between an alarm set off by a broken window and the arrival of the Holmes' men at the scene. Consequently, he knew that it would give a thief three minutes and twenty seconds to clean out the window and make a getaway. That jewelry store had been burglarized in just such a fashion several months before. But continued success made Lulu too self-confident and careless. This finally led to his downfall.

3. SOLLY, THE DIPLOMAT

In view of the gang's frequent contacts with the police, a member with a personality suited to this new role responded. This was Solly, the diplomat. If there had not been constant police interrogation, Solly probably would have remained an undistinguished lesser light among the Pirates. Compared to the others, he was quiet and unassuming. A peculiar, neutral quality to his speech and behavior, the ability to listen quietly to a long harangue from an irate patrolman, and then by some noncommittal answer to pacify the speaker, taught the gang that they were better off when they let Solly do most of the talking in police encounters. With experience, he grew very adept at handling these matters which meant so much to the existence of the gang. Solly played the part of the decent fellow commiserating with the police over the bad habits of the other Pirates. He gave the impression that he was on the side of the law and eager to contribute any information that would be of value to the police in their search for burglars and other criminals. But all that he actually volunteered was hearsay reports of past activities about which nothing could be done. Never was there a shred to enable the recipients of the information to take positive preventive action.

However, in Solly's revelations about certain crimes, he inadvertently exposed the Pirates' connection to the burglaries in the sector. He strengthened to a conviction what had been conjecture and eliminated conclusively the possibility of coincidence in the cessation of crime in the area. It became increasingly more evident that the Pirates had been responsible for the wave of burglaries. The psychology of Solly's intermediate position was extremely complicated. It was a game of cat and mouse. The police were ready to pounce if he made a mistake and revealed too much, perhaps providing enough evidence to arrest and possibly convict a Pirate. Actually, it resembled closely the Ketman institution[1] which is an outgrowth of the psychological war between the Russian administrators and native intelligentsia of the occupied countries behind the "Iron Curtain." The adversaries act roles in a gruesome drama. Each side strictly conforms to a ritualistic code of speech and behavior, knowing full well that it is a masquerade, except that the penalty for removing the mask at the wrong time is death. This very element of danger makes the game so fascinating. Psychological subtleties of the highest order are attained in order to gain a victory within the straight and narrow limits of the rules, which become almost institutionalized through constant practice.

Solly, then, was employing "Ketman tactics" against the police. Although the officers were aware of it, there was little that could be done. Both sides were constrained by the psychodynamics of the social process. Solly did contribute information on the location of stolen cars which had been abandoned by thieves, who probably were Pirates in the first place. Their recovery enhanced the reputation of the patrolmen for good observation and alert police work. Believing that they had elicited from the gang a "hot tip" of a loft scheduled to be burglarized that night, the crew of the radio car covering Madison Avenue and _____ Street (the address of the supposed target) was ordered to give it plenty of attention in order to catch the burglars in action. Unfortunately, the ability to "handle" Solly was overestimated. The burglary did take place, but it occurred at _____ Street and Avenue of the Americas in the flower market. Lulu (not Solly) had secreted himself in the building Friday afternoon and had spent a quiet weekend opening a well filled safe from which he took two thousand dollars. However, eventually the concentration on Solly paid off because he supplied the lead through which the case was finally broken.

4. BLACKY, LEADER AND BUFFOON

Blacky was the last and most peculiar of the group in power. Most of the time he played the clown, the butt of all the gang's earthy humor, which often took a brutal turn. In the rougher horseplay of the Pirates, Blacky was usually forced to run away to avoid a good drubbing. But Blacky was supreme in the domain of sex, the field where the others were sadly lacking. This may have been due to their lower class attitude toward girls and sex, which seems to be much more casual and matter-of-fact than that of the general middle class adolescent group. But casual or not, they looked to Blacky for leadership in matters relating to the opposite sex. For this special purpose he was the ruler and director. Therefore, in spite of his anomalous role in the other functions of the gang, he can be classified as a leader.

Girls hardly ever were allowed to stand around the headquarters stoop during the bull sessions, which took up so much time in the life of the gang. But when the gang broke up into two's and three's to leave headquarters, then girls became a normal and powerful interest. This was Blacky's province. He had a mistress and a "stable" of three or four girls who catered to him. He made these girls available to his special friends in the gang. In fact, he attempted to ingratiate himself with Patrolman C. by offering him a date with his girl friend. Where he hid this special "sex appeal" was a mystery. Rather dull and unprepossessing in appearance, he must have had some secret attraction that girls, but not policemen, could perceive. From talks with his associates, it was learned that Blacky was the "front man" who picked up girls at the week-end dances that they frequently attended. It was from this situation that a chain of events was set off which finally led to the demise of the Pirates. Strangely enough, each leader, except Paulie, played an unconscious part in the destruction of the gang.

SUMMARY

The division of power allowed completely different personality types to function efficiently. . . . In this way, the clash of rivals was avoided because each had a measure of autonomy to satisfy him. Flexibility resulted from the variety of talents brought to bear on problem situations. Translating the theory of Pareto into gang terms, it was evident that the comparatively large number of positions open at the top levels permitted a circulation of the elite.

The arrows on the chart showing normal lines of communication indicate some reasons for the continued success and growth of the gang. They demonstrate that every one in the gang had some degree of power to prove to himself that he was a man. The leaders controlled the average rank and file member, but even the lowest member could lord it over the aspiring Corner Boys, who were willing to endure any amount of hazing as long as they were permitted to stay in the vicinity of the admired Pirates.

Two psychological and symbolic patterns are of deep interest to students of group dynamics. One has already been described; any member could assert his superiority over Blacky, one of the leaders. The second device, which served the dual purpose of establishing an hierarchy and manipulating the masses, was the established use of the headquarters' stoop by the power group. The leaders assembled on the higher steps; the ordinary members congregated on the sidewalk at a physically lower level. It was symbolic of their superior status for the leaders to stay on top. Blacky was never sure of his place there because someone would be certain to chase him off the steps, and down the block. When he returned he would find someone else in his place. The stoop gave them a psychological advantage in their dealings with representatives of other street gangs who came for conferences with them. When the radio car pulled up, the gang leaders finally had to come off the stoop to gather around the car. That is, all, except Paulie. He hated everything connected with the police, with good reason, because he had definitely cast his lot with those whose life would be spent warring against the police.

· · ·

[The Pirates'] plan of action was strategically contrived to gain power, wealth, and expansion of the gang's criminal activities (i.e., burglaries, robberies, larcenies). Paulie chose the targets and disposed of the loot at a profit; Lulu planned the tactics and details of procedure; Solly contributed diplomacy; Blacky provided recreation for their leisure. Perhaps unwittingly, they were using this scheme to establish legitimacy.

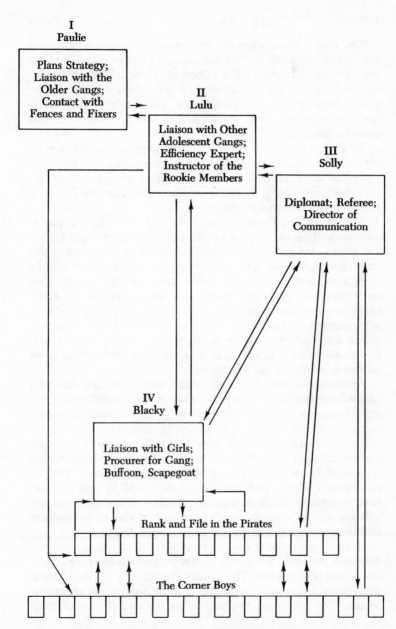

Table 1. Diagram of the Gang Power Structure.

The four leaders were the vanguard that led the gang and the fellow travelers toward the seizure of power and fulfilled the dual role of elite and intellectual. Their advanced knowledge of techniques and theory of crime, their clever diplomacy, their pragmatic intelligence, their calculating avoidance of apprehension, demonstrated intellectuality in this specific situation.

In their possession were material instruments of power, including, it was discovered later, an elaborate set of burglar's tools and several autos. Superior ability to that of rival gangs, and the interlocking role structure could be classified as nonmaterial instruments of power.

Ordinarily, legitimacy is achieved by working for public approval. Here we find an extremely interesting variation on the theme, revealing the political acumen of the Pirates. For most gangs contact with the police is anathema. In middle class neighborhoods the boys feel that they are stigmatized as ruffians by constant attention from the police. In lower class sections the police are an enemy in perpetual war with the delinquent gangs. As we have shown, the Pirates rose above this deep-seated almost instinctive class prejudice and by the use of diplomacy made an attempt to turn a dangerous situation to their own advantage.

Again it was the class and ethnic distribution of that part of the city that made this plan feasible. In a middle class environment the Mayor and the Police Commissioner, as public servants, would soon be deluged with letters and telephone calls, demanding to know why the police were either constantly harassing a group of fine young men, or badgering a bunch of known hoodlums but making no arrests. The inconsistency of the two complaints is typical of middle class interpretations which depend on whether or not the boys are related to the complainants or whether the complainants' children are at odds with the gang in question.

In the lower class a similar situation calls forth an entirely different reaction. Even where the policeman may be hated, his power is respected. The symbolic authority of his uniform inculcates a respectful attitude at least among the older residents. The officer on the post is an important part of their

daily life. He appears whenever one of the numerous am-
bulance calls is sent out; he settles the family fight; he gives
the young wrongdoers another chance. Who delivers the baby
in the absence of the doctor? Who carries home the drunken
husband? To whom are they forced to turn for help and re-
dress? The patrolman on post. Immigrants regard him with
the eyes of the old world. Jewish and Italian elders often doff
their hats when addressing the policeman. For the Puerto
Ricans he is a major point of contact with the strange new
world of New York. To the Irish who may have come from a
village in which the priest and the constable were the two
most important officials, the police officer is "one of their own
kind." For all these reasons the policeman patrolling a beat
on a lower class street has a lot more leeway and importance.
There is no tradition in the neighborhood for making complaints about the police.

The masses that the leaders of the Pirates wished to manip-
ulate were the rank and file of the gang, the Corner Boys,
representatives of other gangs, and those boys on _____
Street who did not belong to the gangs. Subtle symbolic techniques were employed which imparted psychological significance to the spatial arrangements of the headquarters' stoop.
Blacky's role as scapegoat for the gang provided a convenient
safety valve to divert the latent hostility from the real leaders.
The cumulative impact of these techniques of mass manip-
ulation resulted in a show of power and success which tended
to make other gangs submissive to the Pirates. As the Pirates
held power in spite of occasional attempts to dislodge them,
there was a gradual acceptance by rival groups of their
hegemony. This change in attitude was the final corroboration
that the Pirates had institutionalized their control over the
delinquent youth in the area.

So much for the power structure of the gang. Its history,
viewed from any angle, probably would yield sociological in-
sights that justify continuation of this analysis. We have seen
how the Pirates flourished much to the consternation of Patrolman C. and his partner, who were eager to put an end to
the gang's career. Rival gangs realized the strength of the
Pirates' position and looked to them for leadership. This was

most apparent in the case of "The Corner Boys" who were younger and less experienced in handling the various complications of delinquent group subculture. Directing his campaign aganst the Pirates to a more vulnerable point, Patrolman C. gave lots of attention to the Corner Boys, much to their discomfiture. Gradually, they moved into the protective shadow of the older gang and became an auxiliary to them. One day they all gathered at headquarters and at a prearranged signal, exhibited their wrists. Tattooed neatly in blue letters was the name "Corner Boys." Their pride was apparent. Now they were real men!

Lulu welcomed these new recruits and started to train them. Some mornings, at about three or four A.M., Lulu was spotted riding around with one or two Corner Boys. Although it was obvious that they were preparing to burglarize some loft, they could never be caught with enough evidence to justify an arrest.

Each tour of duty, Patrolman C., with his partner, visited _____ Street to show the gang that they were on duty and to check street conditions. The Pirates had a lot of information about criminal activities in the neighborhood which sometimes alerted the radio car partners to problems demanding police action. The mysterious underground channels of communication in criminal circles deserve a serious study. It was amazing how fast they knew details of crimes before the cases had even been reported to the police.

On Sundays, the gang dressed up in "formal" attire and attended church. For most of them it was the large Catholic Church on _____ Street. But even the presence of this imposing house of worship located so near their headquarters did not ameliorate their delinquent attitudes toward life and society. An extraordinary feature of this close proximity to the church was that it served to reinforce the gang's tendency to interpret events from the point of view of power relations, manipulating others, and "fixing" a case. For example, their respect for religion and the clergy was expressed in such admiring terms as "Father R. is a swell guy. He's a real powerhouse. He can get anything he wants around here." In certain respects their attitude was justified by the facts of lower class

life. Priests in such neighborhoods did exercise strong practical influence in every-day affairs. Sometimes, when called
upon for help by a member of their parish, they might intercede with the police to gain another chance for some mis-
creant of "tender" years.

The large Boys' Club in the neighborhood should have been
another socializing force for the adolescents in the community. But, here again, the boys defined the situation in terms
of their own distorted values. Did the Club have a boxing
ring? Fine! That meant fighting was approved. Only why confine it to the ring? They indulged in "free-for-alls" inside and
outside the Club buildings, which necessitated frequent calls
for police assistance to restore order. Were there regular meeting rooms? Good! The Pirates often met in the building for
conferences; but they used the boiler room, not the meeting
room, to hold their sessions.

The beginning of the end for the Pirates came, innocently
enough, at a dance held at the ＿＿＿ Church. Blacky, leading
the way, in his special domain, danced with a very attractive
girl. Her escort resented Blacky's attentions to her. A fight
ensued which was quickly brought under control, but the
damage had been done. To avenge Blacky, four or five car-
loads of Pirates set out the next night for Mulberry Street.
They were unable to make contact with the enemy. Retaliation was swift. A few nights later an auto with lights off raced
through ＿＿＿ Street and sprayed the Pirates with bullets
which fortunately did not hit anyone. They, in turn, with the
"feel" possessed by most gang youths had "made" the car as
it approached and had instinctively sought cover while mentally photographing the automobile. For days after this event,
the Pirates systematically scoured the city, riding up and down
the side streets in several automobiles searching for the as-
sailants' vehicle. One day they came to Patrolman C. and reported that they were sure that they had spotted the car on
＿＿＿ Street.

By some strange process of reasoning they had turned to
the policemen, their deadly enemy, for help in coping with
this crisis. The two patrolmen accompanied them on their
time off to the street where the auto had been seen. Unfor-

tunately, the car was gone. Upon checking the license number which the gang had noted, it was discovered that the car was not stolen and belonged to someone in Queens. This slight effort on their behalf made a deep impression on the gang and separated the partners from the general class of policemen in the gang's classification of external inimical forces.

Solly finally capitulated and disclosed the first definite information that could be used. In confidence and with requests to tell no one the source of knowledge, he intimated that Lulu had an arsenal of guns concealed somewhere. Lulu had rented these guns for twenty-five dollars to a gang who were robbing drug and liquor stores in Queens. Did Solly inform because he was grateful for the helping hand? Or was it a subtle device of power politics to eliminate a rival for control of the gang? Was there an undercover struggle for power in the gang of which the police were unaware? It was never discovered. But if this actually was the case, Solly miscalculated gravely the ultimate result of his action.

Events moved rapidly from this point on. Patrolman C. and his partner debated: (1) whether to search Lulu's autos to see if he had the guns concealed there, (2) whether to immediately inform the detectives, (3) whether to wait to see if this was another false trail as the others had been. Ultimately, the decision was made to investigate discreetly to see what they could turn up in the way of corroboration. The denouement was to come several days later. Patrolman C., this time with a rookie for a partner—his regular was off duty—had proceeded to _____ Street to check up on the Pirates. He observed Lulu walking east. As usual, Lulu sensed the presence of the police 'car even with his back turned to it. Equally acute, Patrolman C. saw that Lulu quickly put his hand inside his jacket and then sauntered on with exaggerated nonchalance. C., normally suspicious, but now doubly so, because of the recent disclosures about Lulu's activities, jumped to the conclusion that Lulu had just concealed a gun in his lumber jacket.

Lulu was "escorted" into the radio car. In response to the question of what he had concealed in his jacket, Lulu answered, "Nothing! You can search me if you want to." An immediate search revealed nothing. With his characteristic confidence, Patrolman C. refused to admit the possibility that Lulu was right and that his own intuition could be wrong. He immediately took command of the situation and ordered everyone out of the car. (Patrolman C. habitually ordered even other policemen who were his theoretical equals, and surprisingly enough, they usually followed his directions.) He then searched the street and the radio car thoroughly. Under the seat of the car he found a fully loaded revolver. Lulu, even under such pressure, watched carefully by two alert patrolmen next to him, had managed to conceal the gun under the seat as he entered.

In the station house, he at first conducted himself with his customary aplomb, until a detective of the old school decided that Lulu's breezy manner of answering questions insulted the hallowed dignity of the police department. As an impulsive reaction to the disrespect of a young hoodlum, the detective slapped Lulu once. An amazing thing then occurred, something that could never have been predicted. Lulu, on such slight provocation, broke down completely in the face of superior power. Gone was the pride, the panache, that had distinguished Lulu from the other Pirates. He confessed readily to approximately thirty burglaries, to lending and renting his guns to robbers who were later picked up, to systematically stealing cars including both his Cord and Chevrolet, and to forging the registrations.

Demoralized as he was, however, he still remained true to the gang code of loyalty. He refused to implicate any one in the immediate group. Sociologically, they were without doubt, as members of the same primary group, coconspirators and accomplices, as well as accessories after the fact. Legally, it was another matter. The rest of the Pirates were not technically connected with this arrest. A glimpse of the real Lulu was revealed as he was being lodged in the cell by the arresting officer, Patrolman C. With deadly hatred, Lulu turned to him and said, "C., I had you in the sight of my rifle one hundred times, up there on the roof. Now I know I should have pulled the trigger."

Lulu was sentenced to prison for a term of three to five years, on charges which included unlawful possession of dangerous weapons, burglary, larceny, conspiracy. His enforced leave of absence was the death blow to the gang even though on previous occasions it had firmly withstood the arrests of minor members. Without Lulu, their general, the Pirates lost their cohesiveness and a powerful integrating figure. The gang's effectiveness appeared to diminish rapidly.

POSTSCRIPT

The postscript is of interest because it throws light on the fate of the Corner Boys. About a year after the events described above, a patrolman found a teen-ager wandering along Third Avenue after midnight. The officer stopped him, questioned him, and receiving unsatisfactory answers, ordered him to get home. This adolescent happened to be Van, a prominent member of the Corner Boys gang. Van walked slowly away with that peculiar gait of the experienced gang boy which flaunts his defiance of authority but stops just short of irritating the policeman to a point that might invite rougher handling. The police officer followed casually just to make sure that Van, whom he had sized up as a potential burglar, did not remain in the neighborhood. Suddenly, for no apparent reason, Van stopped, turned, and shouted in a belligerent manner, "You wouldn't be so tough without that nightstick. Take off the uniform and fight like a man!"

This abrupt metamorphosis from a craven young hoodlum to the contemptuous, arrogant brawler was stunning to the policeman. Before the officer could take any punitive action, Van ran over to an auto which had cautiously approached the scene of action; he entered and the car roared away. Other Corner Boys were in the car. They were in the vicinity for possible use as a getaway car in case Van had "pulled a job." The point to be stressed here is the psychology of the gang which forced Van, even in a desperate situation, to play the big shot, to prove he was a man, as soon as he realized that his behavior was being measured by the rest of his gang.

This incident added to other predatory forays of the Corner

Boys . . . showed that the Pirates had lost their power to the "up and coming" Corner Boys. In terms of the theory of power it might be said that the Pirates had been defeated in war by the police. As a result the gang leadership had been dispersed and the members were demoralized. Theoretically, a revolutionary situation was thus created. A power vacuum ensued and the ambitious Corner Boys, still relatively untouched by the blow to the older group of Pirates, stepped in and took over without opposition.

On Drug Use and
Delinquent Subcultures

DRUG USE[1] has been described as a "retreatist" reaction of youngsters who are "double failures" in relation to both legitimate and illegitimate opportunities.[2] It has also been attributed to deep personality disturbance, including weak ego structure, inadequately functioning superego, and inadequate sex identity.[3] Regardless of how it has been conceptualized however, drug use among juveniles apparently is a subcultural phenomenon. For the confirmed addict, identity with a particular group is likely to be less important than is acquisition of the drug and participation in the subculture generally. Studies conducted in Chicago and New York suggest a close developmental affinity between drug use and delinquent gangs in terms of the types of neighborhoods in which both are found and the group context within which both so often occur. This is not to say that gangs and drug use inevitably are related. There is evidence that many gangs reject "hard" narcotics use and that boys who become users are less centrally involved in the gang and its activities than are other members. Once a user becomes an addict he is likely to drift away from nonusers, perhaps cliquing with other heavy users within the gang, or leaving the gang altogether to join with others whose life has become oriented around drug use. But there is much experimentation with "kicks" in most gangs, and some—perhaps those with severe personality and social handicaps, perhaps Cloward and Ohlin's "double failures"—become addicted and move into the subculture of drug use. The contrast in drug use patterns among gangs is illustrated by the fact that, in the recent Chicago study, except for one gang in which drug use was the principal activity of the group, addiction was virtually unknown, despite a high incidence of marihuana use.[4] One gang of boys, who smoked "pot" almost to a man, included a single addict—a boy who floated uncertainly in and out of the gang, his status in the gang varying inversely with his addiction cycle.

The Chicago study suggests, also that gangs characterized by extensive heavy drug use differ fundamentally in subcultural orientation from those which are oriented primarily toward conflict or criminal activity. The "pill poppers," as the drug-using group in this study was known, drank heavily, smoked pot (marihuana), and occasionally injected heroin in the blood stream. Their main "kicks," however, were derived from cheap and readily available synthetic drugs in pill form, and from "far-out" experiences shared by various members and relived on countless occasions until they were virtually legendary.[5]

Stealing was functional to the support of this way of life. Fighting was regarded as "square," even under the most provocative circumstances.[6] These white boys shared the preoccupation of Finestone's Negro "Cats" with "kicks" and with maintaining their "cool," but their conception of "hustles" to support this way of life was less elaborated and rationalized than was that of the "Cats."[7] These differences may be more apparent than real, due to difference in the populations studied and in research method. Finestone's subjects were somewhat older than the white boys comprising the "pill poppers" studied by Short and Strodtbeck.

The selection by Kobrin and Finestone presents the basic research out of which the "Cats, Kicks, and Color" article emerged. It represents, also, one of the most systematic studies of drug use ever undertaken in a major U.S. city.

DRUG ADDICTION AMONG YOUNG PERSONS IN CHICAGO

A REPORT OF A STUDY OF THE PREVALENCE, INCIDENCE, DISTRIBUTION, AND CHARACTER OF DRUG USE AND ADDICTION IN CHICAGO DURING THE YEARS, 1947–53

Solomon Kobrin and Harold Finestone

INTRODUCTION

Examined in the course of the study were the records of 6,384 drug users compiled by the Chicago Police Department; the Juvenile Court of Cook County; the Boys' Court Branch and the Psychiatric Institute of the Municipal Court of Chicago; the Cook County Hospital; the Federal Narcotics Hospital at Lexington, Ky. (Chicago admissions); the Federal Parole and Probation Service; the John Howard Association; the Illinois State Department of Public Welfare

Research Report, 1965, Vol. 2, No. 10; based on a reissue of a 1953 summary report of an unpublished study of the drug addiction problem in Chicago during the years 1947–53, on file at the Institute for Juvenile Research. Material on "Implications for Prevention and Treatment" has been deleted. The study was conducted from 1950 to 1953 under the joint sponsorship of the Institute for Juvenile Research and the Chicago Area Project, and was financed by a grant from the National Institute of Mental Health (3M–9030). The research was organized by the late Clifford R. Shaw, head of the Sociology Department at the Institute for Juvenile Research. As the services dealing with juvenile offenders; the United Charities, Catholic Charities, Jewish Charities, and Lutheran Charities of Chicago; the Cook County Department of Welfare; and the Chicago Welfare Department. The Chicago Board of Education cooperated in a special effort to determine the prevalence of drug use among high school students.

In addition, a large body of data was obtained through extensive interviewing of 84 young drug addicts. These interviews were obtained under conditions permitting frank disclosure of addict activity and experience, and comprise over 6,000 pages of transcribed material.[1]

The findings of the investigation are presented in four sections: (1) the number of drug users in the city's population, together with the trends in both the prevalence and the age distribution of the addict group; (2) a presentation of selected social characteristics of addicted persons; and (3) an appraisal of some of the forces operating to account for the diffusion of heroin use to the younger age group;

---

study's designated Principal Investigator he provided its theoretical orientation and overall supervision. I was the Project Director and Harold Finestone the Codirector. The Institute for Juvenile Research contributed the services of several of its research workers as well as office space for the study staff.

The principal purpose of the study was to provide some factual and empirical basis for estimating the number of persons in the addicted group during the period covered, as well as their distribution by age, sex, race, and community; and for ascertaining some of the more salient features of the young drug user's experience as he moved toward addict status.

Guidance in the analysis of the data and the preparation of this report was provided by Henry D. McKay of the Institute staff. His experience and sagacity in the analysis of the demographic correlates of social problems was invaluable. I wish to acknowledge the indispensable contribution of the late A. Gilmore DuVal, a member of the study staff, whose skill in the arts of persuasion induced public officials to open doors and files for untrammelled research use. The feat was the more remarkable in a time of acute apprehension over disclosure of official practice. Finally, we salute the young men and women, caught up in the harried and agonized existence of the junkie, who were willing to give more to their interviews than a strict *quid pro quo* for the money payment required.

and (4) some implications of the findings for prevention and treatment. The materials of the first two sections are presented in summary form, with major findings stated in topical sentence form.

NUMBER OF DRUG USERS

A. *It is estimated that there are in Chicago today approximately 5,000 habitual users of addicting and other proscribed drugs.* This number constitutes slightly more than one-tenth of I per cent of the city's population, or approximately 14 known addicts per 10,000 population. Included in this estimate are persons using opiates such as heroin, synthetic compounds with addicting properties, and such other drugs as cocaine and marijuana used together with opiates. Only those individuals whose case records contained positive evidence of heroin use, or the use of synthetic opiates were included. Those recorded as users of marijuana only were excluded from the count. The estimate is based upon a thorough search of all the available court, police, hospital, and social agency records. The completeness of the count based on official records was checked by using drug addicts in two sample areas to compile a list of addicts known to them. All but the youngest were also found in police and court records, suggesting habitual users of heroin in the city during the period covered were known to enforcement and other official agencies.[2]

B. *Available statistics reveal that the number of drug users in Chicago has increased significantly during the past decade.* While a count of the probable number of drug users in the city 10 years ago comparable in completeness and accuracy to that made on the present group was not available, police statistics furnish some clues. The average number of persons arrested annually for violation of the narcotic drug laws during the period 1937–1941 was 340. The annual average in the period 1947–1951, when narcotic drugs were more readily available, was 701. Although the police were probably more vigorous in arresting drug law violators during the recent period than they were 10 years ago, the large increase in the average number arrested annually probably cannot be accounted for solely on this basis.[3]

C. *The recent increase in the number of drug users in Chicago has occurred principally among teen-agers and young adults.* About one-third of the known drug users in the city at the end of 1952 were under 21 years of age. In 1943 one-tenth, and in 1932 one-fiftieth, of the known drug users fell in this age group. Slightly more than one-half of the known-user group in 1952 were under 26 years of age. In 1932 this age group constituted only 10 per cent of the total. The average number of persons under 26 years of age arrested annually for violation of the narcotic drug laws in the period 1937–1941 was 74. The annual average in this age group in the period 1947–1951 was 380. This represents a fivefold increase. In contrast, for all persons above 25 years of age the average number arrested annually for drug law violations during the period 1947–1951 showed an increase over the 1937–1941 period of only 21 per cent.[4]

In addition, data on first admissions of Chicago residents to the Federal Narcotics Hospital at Lexington, Kentucky, indicate an increase in the under-21 age group from a total of four in the 1937–1941 period to a total of 357 during the 1947–1951 period. First admissions of Chicago residents under 25 years of age increased from 24 during 1937–1941 to 840 during 1947–1951. Also, during 1937–1941 the group under 25 years of age constituted only 8.5 per cent of the total group of Chicago admissions, but made up 56.8 per cent of the total in the later period. In the earlier period the group under 21 years of age constituted a mere 1.4 per cent of the total Chicago admissions, while in the 1947–1951 period it rose to over 24 per cent of the Chicago residents admitted to the hospital.[5]

SELECTED SOCIAL CHARACTERISTICS
OF DRUG USERS

A. *Of those persons with official records as drug users, approximately 90 per cent used heroin. The balance are*

*recorded as users of nonaddicting drugs, principally mari-
juana.*[6] This finding raises the question of the definition of
addiction. The present study used the definition provided
by the more recent medical and pharmacological research,
which establishes a distinction between physiological dependence and emotional dependence upon drugs. Addicting
drugs are here regarded as those which establish not only
emotional dependence in the user, but physical dependence
as well. The use of opiates, including heroin, creates a
marked physical dependence upon the drug as evidenced
by the extreme symptoms of illness following withdrawal
of the opiate. In contrast, even extreme habituation to marijuana use produces only a craving for continued dosage of
the drug without symptoms of sharp physical distress.[7]
Moderate use of marijuana, probably widespread among
certain groups in the population, produces effects of approximately the same kind as does moderate use of alcohol.
In the same sense the use of cocaine by itself is also nonaddicting. At the present time cocaine is generally used in
combination with heroin.[8]

B. *Most of the city's users of illicit drugs were born in
Chicago or spent most of their first 20 years of life in this
city if born elsewhere.* For the most part, Chicago's drug
users are also the children of migrants to the city. This
finding suggests that the social experiences promoting drug
addiction in the person are probably similar to those underlying other social problems related to urbanization.

C. *The highest concentrations of drug users are found in
the communities displaying the highest rates of Juvenile
Court delinquents, of Boys' Court cases, of tuberculosis, and
of infant mortality. These are the communities of lowest income in the city.* Over half the known drug users in the
city reside in only five of the city's 75 community areas
(Oakland, Douglas, Near South, Grand Boulevard, and
Washington Park). Of the Police Narcotics Bureau cases,
91 per cent reside in 15 community areas containing only
25 per cent of the city's population. Of the narcotics cases
which came before the Boys' Court, 96 per cent reside in

these 15 community areas.[9] The distribution of the drug addict problem in relation to the distribution of income in the city's population is shown in Table 1.

D. *With few exceptions known drug users engage in delinquency in more or less systematic form. Contrary to the widely held view that the delinquency of the young addict is a consequence principally of addiction, it was found that delinquency both preceded and followed addiction to heroin.* Persons who became heroin users were found to have engaged in delinquency in a group-supported and habitual form either prior to their use of drugs or simultaneously with their developing interest in drugs. There was little evidence of a consistent sequence from drug use without delinquency to drug use with delinquency. Three observations may be made about the effect of addiction upon the delinquent behavior of the person: (1) The pressure of need for money to support his addiction impels the user to commit violations with greater frequency and with less caution than formerly. (2) Delinquents after becoming addicted to heroin do not engage in types of delinquency in which they are not already skilled. The postaddict delinquent, in other words, does not generally engage in more serious crimes than those he committed prior to his addiction. (3) Delinquents who as preaddicts tended to engage in riotous behavior such as street fighting and gang attacks tend after addiction to abandon this kind of activity. Three elements are probably responsible for the change: (a) the sedative effect of the opiate; (b) the desire to avoid attracting the attention of public and police; and (c) the tendency for adolescents to become quieter in their conduct as they approach maturity.

E. *Many of Chicago's heroin users, at the present time, appear to be at the beginning of their careers as drug addicts. In the absence of effective methods for curing persons of their addiction, it may be reasonably expected that this group, comprised as it is of a high proportion of younger persons, will continue as drug users in our population for a long time.* According to addicts' own statements

TABLE I. *Percentage Distribution of Individuals Dealt with for Violation of Narcotic Drug Laws in Chicago and Average Median Income for Quintiles of Chicago Population, When Community Areas are Ranked by Rates of Police Narcotics Bureau Offenders*

Quintiles of Population	Percentage Distribution of Individuals Dealt with for Violation of Narcotic Drug Laws by Three Official Agencies			Average Median Income (1950 U.S. Census)
	Police Narcotics Bureau[a]	Boys' Court[b]	Juvenile Court[c]	
Areas of Highest Rates	88.3	88.3	86.6	$2,229
Areas of Next Highest Rates	8.8	8.8	8.9	3,458
Areas of Intermediate Rates	1.9	1.9	1.9	3,734
Areas of Next Lowest Rates	0.8	0.8	2.6	3,835
Areas of Lowest Rates	0.2	0.2	0.0	4,329
All City Areas	100.0	100.0	100.0	3,956 (median)

[a]December, 1950—February, 1953
[b]1945–1951
[c]1947–1951

available in police records, approximately three-quarters of the heroin-using group have been addicted for less than 4 years. One-third of the group has been addicted for less than 2 years.[10]

F. *While the drug-using group is preponderantly male, 17 per cent of the known drug users are female.* This ratio represents a much higher proportion of females than may be found in the general criminal population. The female segment of the addicted group appears to be made up of persons older than those found in the male segment. This is indicated by the fact that females were, on the whole, addicted for a longer period of time than were the males, the ratio of each sex addicted for less than 4 years being 65 per cent for the males and 46 per cent for the females. Over 80 per cent of the males were addicted for less than 7 years, while only 55 per cent of the females fell in this category. Or, to put the matter another way, over 26 per cent of the females were addicted for more than 10 years as compared to 8 per cent of the males.

THE SPREAD OF HEROIN USE IN CHICAGO

The account of the spread of heroin presented here is directed to the problem of its spread among young males. The data from which the findings were derived are made up, for the most part, of the voluminous body of interview material referred to above. Hence, it should be borne in mind that the observations which follow apply not to the entire population of opiate addicts in Chicago, whose characteristics were statistically described in the preceding section, but to the young male segment of this population whose addiction is of relatively recent origin.

The fact that the spread of heroin to younger persons was confined almost exclusively·to a small number of communities raises the question as to what features of the social life of these areas were specifically involved in a change of this character. Analysis of the interview materials of this study, together with other studies of the problem, suggests an answer.

The areas of greatest concentration of heroin users were found to be also the areas of highest rates of other social problems.[11] As is well known, these problems are, among others, low family income, low social status, deteriorated housing, a high proportion of recent migrants to the city, absence of effective community organization, high rates of adult crime, and an absence of effective family and community control over the conduct of young persons.[12]

For the young male in these communities the social environment comes to be dominated by what has been called "street corner society."[13] This term has come into use in recent years to describe the street gangs which abound in certain quarters of the city. The use of the expression "society" in connection with such gangs is meant to suggest that all members of street gangs share a distinctive set of ideas and attitudes, much as would, say, the members of "cafe society." It is, moreover, a society in the sense that a large enough number of young persons have participated in it over a long enough period of time so that it exists independently of particular persons entering or leaving its ranks.

This society flourishes in those communities where the traditional influences and controls over the conduct of the youth group tends to be weak and uncertain. In such communities all young persons either participate in or are exposed to the activities of street groups and share in some measure the attitudes of this society. In the face of counteracting pressures for conformity to the norms of the wider society, of varying degrees of effectiveness, some youngsters merely dabble in street society, taking on only some of its superficial traits; others participate fully but for relatively short periods; and still others become full-fledged members and ultimately the bearers and agents of its code and its culture.

The central feature of this society and its body of practices, or "culture," is the support it gives to behavior which is generally inconsistent with the norms of conventional society, and often openly hostile to many of its expectations.

This orientation on the part of street boys is expressed in a variety of ways, but is most clearly and dramatically manifested in delinquency, and in the search for and exploitation of "kick."

The sequence of experiences suggesting the nature of group activity among street boys, and the setting in which they are introduced to drug use, is provided in the following interview excerpt:

Well, I was living on L-Street. . . . There wasn't too much to do. We'd just sit around and go to dances, things like that, go to the park. Didn't have nothing to do. There was a place over here on Madison Street where you used to get some wine. . . . We used to get drunk off that, get crazy, stack chicken coops up on the street car tracks about ten high, set them on fire, watch them burn, watch them street cars line up. We'd do such as all that. Just nothing to do, just roam around and go looking, go over to South Water market, take fruit, help somebody on a truck, just something to be doing. Wasn't nothing happening at school so we just decided we wouldn't go to school on some days; we'd go out and have fun. We'd go over there on Madison and get some wine and get drunk and go swimming and just do everything. . . . We used to hang on the corner, wouldn't work. We were going to high school and didn't want to do that so we wanted to loaf around. So we stood on the corner all day and waited for the man to come by, vegetable truck or something come by and we'd take a watermelon and sit down and eat that and wait for the pop man to come by. Hardly ever went home. We just stayed up all night. We'd sit on the corner. We'd talk all night long. . . . Sometimes we didn't go home for two days maybe. . . . And then there's all sorts of guys that hang on the corner. There's big guys, they're talking all that big-time talk. The girls they got, they're this, and she's that; well, you're curious. Well, they talk about all the clothes their girls buy them. She bought him a shirt and quite naturally you want to get you a girl now, you're ready to go out and see what's going on, and you say, "Well, I'm going to get me a girl, I'm going to try it on my girl." And sometimes it'd work, sometimes it don't. . . .

. . . Half the time I guess he [older boys who initiated informant and other younger boys into delinquency] wouldn't be telling the truth no way. He probably would be making it up

half of it as he go along. They don't know any better. It just
sounds exciting. So they believe every word. Well, then they
think he's a great guy, he's been to the joint [prison], yeah, he
knows everything. They probably come up and ask him a question, "How do you do this?" "How do you do that?" Just like
he was a teacher or something. He would sit down and tell
them all kinds of things. . . . He would tell them what to use
and you go in this way and watch out for the police and who to
watch out for and all such things as that. Well, he'd be on the
corner taking watermelons and things like that, breaking into
a few places, strong-arming, he'd probably take a few guys
with him and they'd go strong-arm somebody and they'd make
some money and come back and tell this guy he's all right, you
know. . . .

. . . We'd be sitting on the corner and some guy would come
by and he'd probably say, "Well, he looks like money." He'll
hand pick a few guys and tell them, "Come on." Well, everybody
would want to go. Most of the times I would go with him, you
know. I don't know if he took a liking to me or not. Every time
I'd always go out with him and we'd catch a few guys. Well,
he would strong-arm them, he would hold them because he's
the muscle man and then the other guys would run all in his
pockets.

. . . Sometimes he's got $15, $8, sometimes you don't get
nothing but a dollar. Then sometimes you almost get caught,
and it scares you to death; you don't even go out with him no
more for quite a while, you're scared to death. . . . You find out
later on that you just can't do everything he's doing the way
he does. You catch on, you know, to a way to steal that's more
convenient to you, anyway. And then you start snatching pocketbooks, that's about the next easiest thing. You go around the
hospital [boy's neighborhood was located near Chicago's West
Side Medical Center], you snatch women's pocketbooks and you
do that a certain number of times, and it seems as you go on
it looks like you graduate, you know, you learn the ropes, you
know. Then you go from there, now you want to burglarize,
you've got to be big now, you're ready to burglarize. . . .

. . . I mean, now you come down to the crowd that I hung
with, well, after the other kids started breaking off, I guess they
just got tired of stealing or something, I don't know what, there
was about twelve of us left. Well, we always stood together,
we always had a motto that we always were going to steal, it's

in the blood, you can't help it, you're just born to steal. That was your excuse all the time. There was a tavern and this guy Duke [leader referred to above] knew the bartender over there and we broke in there one night and we got whiskey and stuff. It was easy; there wasn't nothing to it. The guy [bartender] left the door half open and all you had to do was kick it down. Well, that was about the biggest job any of us did. . . . We was running all over the neighborhood selling the whiskey bottle by bottle.

. . . Some of the older boys was smoking reefers [marijuana cigarettes]. "What's that, what's that?" "Oh, that ain't for you. You're square, you don't know what's happening. You're too young. I'll get put in jail messing with you." . . . Well, then you get to smoking. . . . You say, "You high?" "Yeah, I'm high." You start smoking it and then you really get crazy. Then you wonder, "Well, this ain't like wine. I ain't going to mess with no wine. I'm going to smoke reefers. I want to be a reefer-head. All the big boys is reefer-heads." They just do what the big boys do. Now he smokes reefers, now he's hep, now he goes for himself. Now he'll begin to talk to girls. . . . Then you mess around and you go on, well then you meet with some guy, you see him stand up scratching on the corner, nodding, he looks crazy, you know, and you wonder what it is. . . . Then some guys are talking about, well if I tried this [marijuana] I'll try anything. Yeah, I'll try anything to get high on. I'm game, he's game. . . . Then some guy, he'll come along and turn one fellow on [induce him to use a drug]. He'll come back and he'll say, "I had some stuff to put in your arm, made you feel real nice, you know, you get real high. Never felt nothing like this, you know." . . . "What is it, a needle? No, I don't put no needle in my arm." You're scared. They say, "Well, you're square, you don't know what's happening." . . . I say, "No, I don't want to mess around." They say, "Oh, I'm going to stop running with you, you don't know what's happening." . . . I say, "Well I'll try it one time. One time and that's it. I ain't trying no more." He go and he probably give you a half of a cap. I got a half a cap and I couldn't even see.

The notion of the "kick" as used in these groups refers both to excitement and stimulation as a class of experiences, including delinquency itself; and to the physical intoxication obtained through the use of stimulants. Participants in these groups achieve personal recognition competitively through success in either or both of these activities. For example, one informant described the setting in which he attempted to play the role of the junkie even before he was addicted:

See, we [he and his friend] had a heated basement and we had a bed down there and we used to live down there together. So when I moved up there, well, the guys up west were faster and I started hanging around with them. I had a car at that time, I had a '37 Plymouth. I used to go around there and a couple of guys used to jump in the car and they always used to be high, they'd always be knocked out, laying in the back [of the car]. So I played the part that I was a big junkie, too, you know. If they were playing it, well, I was playing it, you know. I told myself I would try it every now and then, but I would never get like some of them because they had no interest in nothing; they just lay in the back of the car for six or seven hours, just lay there in the back of the car. So I used to be up west in front of Jim's and Potsy's [a tavern and restaurant, respectively]. I used to go there all the time and Louie [his friend] used to come there and always used to give me stuff for nothing. I used to give it to the junkies there, and I used to take maybe a little taste or something, half a thing [capsule] or a quarter of a thing, and then I used to give the rest away.

Success in the exploitation of "kicks" entails willingness to experiment with new drugs whose effects and properties are not precisely known to the user, and a capacity to communicate to his associates his perceptions of the more subtle effects of the intoxication. Another informant suggests the readiness of persons in these groups to learn about new and strange drugs, and to try the "kick" they produce, in the following excerpt:

And so as the things went on we went to smoking pot [marijuana]. I mean, they pass it on to their friends. I mean, girls, boys, you know. Always had a group of us running together. We always hang at the drug store and we all smoke pot together, you understand. And then up pops somebody, and he'll say, "Well, here, sip a little wine and smoke a little pot." Well, so that was a great kick, drink a little wine and smoke some pot, smoked more pot than we drink wine, you know. And here's a fellow coming in, he wants to introduce a new drug, you know. He'll say, "Well, since you're smoking pot, why don't you try some nembutols, you know." I said, "Nembutols? I don't know what those are." So he says, "It's a narcotic, too." I said, "Well, I never heard of it. What do it do to you?" He said, "It makes you high, it makes you real high, it makes you higher than pot." I said, "You mean to tell me it makes me higher than this stuff that I'm smoking?" He said, "Man, that's nowhere. You should try some of this."

These corner groups may be generally differentiated from the gangs or "crowds" of more conventionally oriented adolescents which may be found in other segments of society. Self-determined groupings remain a phenomenon of adolescence, and give rise principally to the more ordinary, if sometimes troublesome, problems of learning and filling well-established adult roles. While individual instances of breakdown in the socialization process do occur among conventional adolescents, such deviations are not, generally, a product of the norms which belong, distinctively, to the adolescent groups themselves, as is true in street corner society.

Street-corner groups in disorganized areas appear to vary in the degree to which they combine, through time, the double interest in delinquency and "kicks." Among many groups of delinquents in the past, the only "kick" explored or achieved was that deriving from the excitement and stimulation of delinquency itself.[14] Some of the materials of this study suggest that in recent years street groups have embarked on a more persistent and extreme exploration of intoxicants, although there is some evidence that in some communities wine and beer have been extensively used for many years by pubertal boys in such street groups to achieve intoxication. Again, other evidence indicates that, in the past, members of street groups avoided intoxicants where these were frowned upon by the cultural practices of the ethnic groups inhabiting their communities. In any event, a strong interest in the use of intoxicants among street gang boys appears now to be more widespread.

Further, it is possible that the rapid and extensive penetration of heroin into those neighborhoods of the city where its use is most concentrated is related to certain distinctive social features of these areas. Without exception, such areas are characterized by high density of a recently arrived and largely unsettled population. This situation creates for a family area an almost unparalleled anonymity of the person and confusion of moral standards. The following excerpt describes the sale of marijuana cigarettes by a boy too young to be admitted to a poolroom, and who professed a respectful attitude toward his pious and hard-working mother:

Well, I had to make a little money so I peddled it [marijuana] and smoked it, too. I peddled it for around about a year and a half, maybe two years until I was fourteen, but then I started using the needle. [How would you peddle the stuff?] Well, all my friends around they know me and I would sell it. I wouldn't deal in the house because my mother she's religious, but she didn't know what I was doing and she always stuck up for me because she thought I was a good boy. But I was good around the house because I'd give her a few dollars for food for the baby, but I couldn't spare too much. My father, he wouldn't give her nothing, so the little I gave her she like for me to give her, and she'd go to church every Sunday, religious. She didn't go out and didn't drink, didn't smoke or nothing, didn't curse, didn't beat me; but my father did. See, and so I started swinging [peddling] around there and everybody would come to me around the poolroom. I wouldn't be in the poolroom because I was too young, but I hang around the poolroom in the summer, and they'd come up to me and ask me have I got any reefers, and I tell them I did and I sell it to them. They buy two, three, four; some of them buy it by the can. And that's when I started with it.

Thus, unlike other low-income areas, in which residents tend to have a modicum of knowledge about the business and conduct of their neighbors, the areas of high concentration of heroin users are populated by individuals who tend to remain true strangers to one another. Clearly, it is relatively easy for the adult drug peddler bent on introducing drugs to young people to operate in such areas with minimum risk of detection.

Although no person reared in communities with an established adolescent street culture can avoid being affected by its practices, almost all young persons in these communities are also subject to pressures for conformity to the norms of the wider society. Many of the youngsters in these communities who engage in delinquency from time to time or who occasionally become intoxicated do not develop extensive criminal careers, and relatively few become either professional criminals or addicts. The fact of the matter is that the isolation of street boys from the norms, the practices, and the interests of the encompassing conventional society is never absolute. Most likely to remain delinquents or drug users are those who by virtue of their personal histories are least responsive to the expectations of conventional society. Thus, the problem of the differences between those who do and those who do not become drug addicts in the world of the street boy may be regarded as a problem of the differences in life history among individuals, with each life history constituting a unique equation of forces. No attempt was made to determine in a systematic way the character of such individual differences, since the focus of this study was on the group aspects of the drug addiction problem.

To a large degree the corner boy shares the ordinary interests of his age mates everywhere, despite the differences in the way these interests are expressed. For example, the corner boy is usually as concerned with girls, clothes, and popular forms of recreation and sports as is any middle-class high school boy. True, he may have scant regard for the respectable forms of courtship, dress in more extreme violation of the canons of conventional taste, and get into fights at dances, movies, or skating rinks, or when he and his gang engage an opposing team in a game of baseball or basketball. But the fact that they do participate in such activities is in itself warrant for assuming the average street boy to be accessible to most of the influences which determine the behavior of boys. This assumption is further supported by the fact that most street boys tend to terminate their delinquent activity when they enter adulthood. It is thus necessary to visualize the situation for the young person in our disorganized urban areas as made up of two elements: the adolescent street society with its emphasis on conflict, excitement, stimulation, "kicks"; and counteracting pressures for conformity emanating, even if weakly, from the family, school, and church.

It is thus a principal finding of this study that the introduction of the opiate, heroin, to such groups in these communities was facilitated by an established, pre-existing interest in the use of stimulants and intoxicants, and by the opportunity to experiment freely with new drugs. It is a mistake to assume that the practice of using heroin erupted without warning, like some mysterious plague, among a youth group to which such activity was alien. Equally fallacious is the widely accepted notion that the introduction of heroin was accomplished solely by the "pusher" who gives "free samples" to "hook" his victim and prospective customer. In truth, heroin may have been introduced initially by older persons motivated by a desire for profit, but it was "pushed," and vigorously, by the frenetic search of the street corner boy for newer, stranger, and more status-giving intoxicants. In such a situation, interest in heroin or any other drugs arises only when they are first defined as desirable and valuable by intimate associates whose views are meaningful to the potential user. In most instances the youth who is now addicted to heroin was first a user of alcohol or of marijuana, neither of which is generally addicting. The tragedy of his situation lies in the fact that by historical accident, and the active intercession of those who smuggle and distribute heroin, a drug with the addicting properties of the opiates was made available.

The rapidity of heroin diffusion through these communities was due to the fact that the new users were, for the most part, adolescents. As is well known, the urban adolescent is exceptionally vulnerable to epidemics of bizarre and unconventional behavior. Briefly, this susceptibility arises from the fact that being neither child nor adult, with the certainties either status might provide, the adolescent tends to be restless in his activity and unstable in his emotional states. Moreover, in periods following social upheavals like

wars this restlessness, often apparent in the entire population, becomes intensified in the adolescent group, usually
leading to a greater frequency and persistence of bizarre
behavior. Such behavior tends to sweep through the entire
youthful population in the form of fads, typically around
modes of dress or speech, and sometimes affecting manners
and morals. This development was exemplified in the "flap-
per" era following the first world war.

Among most young persons contagions of novel behavior
are limited both in duration and consequences. Ordinarily,
young persons move within a few short years into the
routines of established careers and rapidly acquire the traits
of conventional adults.

However, in those segments of urban society where an
extreme loss of control over the conduct of young persons
tends to occur, where group-supported forms of antisocial
activity tend to get established, and where career prospects
of a valued conventional type are in any case relatively less
available, the ravages of adolescent unrest are far more
drastic. Here social contagions, whether merely fads or more
drastic innovations in modes of behavior, seem to spread
more rapidly, go farther, and remain unchecked for longer
periods.

The epidemic character of the spread of heroin in these
communities accounts not only for the rapidity of its diffusion, but for the relatively large numbers of adolescent males
who became users. The norms of street-centered society
constitute a significant aspect of the social environment for
adolescent males in these communities. Consequently, the
practices of street groups affect even those youngsters who
are only marginally involved in their activities. The non-
rational character of such behavior is well known;[15] for the
restless and uncertain adolescent mere exposure to the enthusiasm of peers for some bit of novel, unconventional, or
bizarre behavior assures its adoption. The more restless and
uncertain the person, the greater will be his susceptibility.

However, the fact that a species of social contagion was
responsible for the rapid diffusion of heroin among adolescents in the city's underprivileged areas does not mean that

we may confidently anticipate the disappearances of heroin use. The true fad passes quickly from the scene because it is peripheral to the basic interests and values of the group, and is accepted largely for its novelty in situations where novelty as such is an established social value. The enthusiasm for heroin, on the other hand, was in large part a response to its genuine effectiveness in achieving an extreme and uncommon state of intoxication, an interest lying close to the heart of the value scheme of the street culture. The very manner in which older boys discussed the heroin "kick" evoked a desire in younger boys to use the drug. The following excerpt suggests the kind of situations in which heroin was defined as desirable, as well as the subsequent discovery by the new user that heroin intoxication produces an extreme "high."

. . . So kids used to tell me, older boys, I used to hear them talk about it [heroin], you know. I'd be around and I'd get an ear full. I wouldn't be in the conversation, you know, just off from them. Just in hearing distance. They'd say, "Yeah, man, that's a gone kick." So-and-so and so-and-so about stuff [heroin]. This about stuff, that about stuff. All I could hear was stuff. Well, I wanted stuff. So I was tight [friendly] with one of the boys, and I said, "Man, what's happening with stuff?" He told me, "Well, look, stuff is no good. I mean it's not good for you to use." I mean he begged me. He wouldn't even tell me what's happening, you know. So one time I catches him without any money to get him some stuff. He's sick. He wants money. So he says, "You got any money?" I said, "Yeah, I got some money." He said, "Loan me a couple of dollars." I said, "How many dollars?" He said, "Three." I said, "For what?" He said, "So I can make up." I said, "Make up? What do you mean?" He said, "Get high; I'm sick man." I said, "What you talking about, man?" He said, "You know I'm hooked, I'm sick, man." I said, "I'll loan you three [dollars], but depending that you get me high." He said, "Okay, I'll do that." So I goes with him . . . and he goes and connects [makes a purchase of drugs]. I waits around the corner for him. I don't know where he went. He come back. So he brings me two [capsules]. I takes it in the hallway and I snort them. I roll me a dollar bill and I snort them. I never snorted before . . . I gets high, I gets real twisted, I'm feeling nice. I never had no kick like that before.

Thus, while the element of novelty accounted for the relatively rapid spread of heroin among adolescents, the use of this drug has been partially incorporated into the street culture because it performs a vital function in relation to its value scheme.

TABLE 2. *Number of Arrests by Month Recorded by Chicago Police Narcotics Bureau for the Period, December, 1950 through February, 1953 for the 17–20 Age Group*

Month		Number of Arrests	Month		Number of Arrests
December,	1950	155	January,	1952	139
January,	1951	177	February,	"	117
February,	"	168	March,	"	113
March,	"	199	April,	"	66
April,	"	154	May,	"	100
May,	"	136	June,	"	95
June,	"	96	July,	"	131
July,	"	182	August,	"	147
August,	"	110	September,	"	127
September,	"	105	October,	"	93
October,	"	142	November,	"	111
November,	"	120	December,	"	99
December,	"	83	January,	1953	109
			February,	"	109

This evaluation of the place of heroin in the practices of young males in the city's disorganized areas is supported by an examination of the trend in arrests for violation of narcotics laws during the 27-month period, November, 1950–February, 1953. Arrests for the entire group, as well as for the 17- to 20-year-old group, remained relatively constant during the last year and a half of this period. It appears reasonable to anticipate, therefore, that as long as heroin is available, and in the absence of drastic change in the general features of street-centered adolescent society, new heroin users recruited from among young persons in these groups will continue to enter and swell the size of the addict

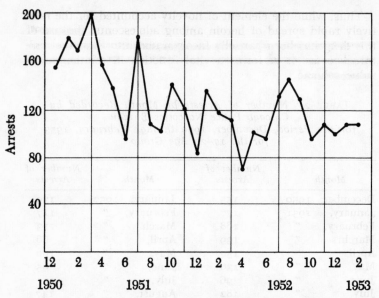

Number of Arrests by Month Recorded by
Chicago Police Narcotics Bureau for the Period,
Dec., 1950 to Feb., 1953, for the 17-20 Age Group.

Both a straight line ($y = 156.5 - 2.39 x$) and a second degree parabola ($y = 114 - 2.4 x + 0.2 x^2$) were fitted to the above data. Despite great fluctuations from month to month in 1951, there was a definite tendency for the number of arrests to decline. During 1952 and the early months of 1953, the fluctuations though still pronounced tended to balance off about a horizontal plane. This suggests a stabilizing in the average number of monthly arrests.

population. On the other hand, there is little reason to expect heroin use to spread to groups of young persons which have not already shown a marked interest in the use of intoxicants. For such persons both the kind and quantity of intoxicants used by most young persons, as well as the meaning of the experience of intoxication, will continue to be determined by prevailing norms.[16]

Part II

Theories and Data Concerning Delinquent Subcultures

Cultural and Social
Structural Explanations

SOCIOLOGICAL theories concerning delinquent subcultures grew out of earlier attempts to explain the characteristics and the social distribution of gangs. These, in turn, were related to research and speculation concerning structural and growth processes of cities and the influence of different, and sometimes conflicting, cultures in the American melting pot. As noted in the introductory chapter, it was Albert Cohen who first attempted to draw these several strands of research and thinking together into a theory to account for the generation and the maintenance of the "delinquent subculture," as distinguished from the task of accounting for why a particular boy, or group of boys, was delinquent. Cohen's theory has had a major impact on more recent research and theory in this area. The "reaction formation" formulation concerning the origin of the delinquent subculture has been seriously questioned by data from some studies,[1] and a good deal of attention has focused on attempts to delineate and account for a variety of subcultures. The latter task has been only partially successful, however, and much remains to be done in relating particular social structures and processes to particular patterns of behavior. The selections which follow are indicative of the type of research which has been done, and document the need for more and better research in this area.

The division of articles into those which are addressed on the one hand to cultural and social structural factors, and on the other to those which focus on group process in explanation of gang behavior, is somewhat arbitrary. Structural and cultural conditions provide the context within which group interaction occurs, and group processes provide the mechanisms by which structural and cultural conditions become "translated" into behavior. These points of view ought surely to be considered as complementary to one another, rather than as mutually exclusive. In any case, such is the intention in the present volume.

LOWER CLASS CULTURE AS A GENERATING MILIEU OF GANG DELINQUENCY

Walter B. Miller

THE ETIOLOGY of delinquency has long been a controversial issue, and is particularly so at present. As new frames of reference for explaining human behavior have been added to traditional theories, some authors have adopted the practice of citing the major postulates of each school of thought as they pertain to delinquency, and going on to state that causality must be conceived in terms of the dynamic interaction of a complex combination of variables on many levels. The major sets of etiological factors currently adduced to explain delinquency are, in simplified terms, the physiological (delinquency results from organic pathology), the psychodynamic (delinquency is a "behavioral disorder" resulting primarily from emotional disturbance generated by a defective mother-child relationship), and the environmental (delinquency is the product of disruptive forces, "disorganization," in the actor's physical or social environment).

This paper selects one particular kind of "delinquency"[1]—law-violating acts committed by members of adolescent street corner groups in lower class communities—and attempts to show that the dominant component of motivation underlying these acts consists in a directed attempt by the actor to adhere to forms of behavior, and to achieve standards of value as they are defined within that community. It takes as a premise that the motivation of behavior in this situation can be approached most productively by attempting to understand the nature of cultural forces impinging on the acting individual

From the *Journal of Social Issues*, 14 (Summer, 1958), 5–19. Reprinted by permission.

as they are perceived *by the actor himself*—although by no means only that segment of these forces of which the actor is consciously aware—rather than as they are perceived and evaluated from the reference position of another cultural system. In the case of "gang" delinquency, the cultural system which exerts the most direct influence on behavior is that of the lower class community itself—a long-established, distinctively patterned tradition with an integrity of its own— rather than a so-called "delinquent subculture" which has arisen through conflict with middle class culture and is oriented to the deliberate violation of middle class norms.

The bulk of the substantive data on which the following material is based was collected in connection with a service-research project in the control of gang delinquency. During the service aspect of the project, which lasted for three years, seven trained social workers maintained contact with twenty-one corner group units in a "slum" district of a large eastern city for periods of time ranging from ten to thirty months. Groups were Negro and white, male and female, and in early, middle, and late adolescence. Over eight thousand pages of direct observational data on behavior patterns of group members and other community residents were collected; almost daily contact was maintained for a total time period of about thirteen worker years. Data include workers' contact reports, participant observation reports by the writer—a cultural anthropologist—and direct tape recordings of group activities and discussions.[2]

FOCAL CONCERNS OF LOWER CLASS CULTURE

There is a substantial segment of present-day American society whose way of life, values, and characteristic patterns of behavior are the product of a distinctive cultural system which may be termed "lower class." Evidence indicates that this cultural system is becoming increasingly distinctive, and that the size of the group which shares this tradition is increasing.[3] The lower class way of life, in common with that of all distinctive cultural groups, is characterized by a set of focal concerns—areas or issues which command widespread

CHART 1. *Focal Concerns of Lower Class Culture*

Area	Perceived Alternatives (State, Quality, Condition)	
1. *Trouble:*	law-abiding behavior	law-violating behavior
2. *Toughness:*	physical prowess, skill; "masculinity"; fearlessness, bravery, daring	weakness, ineptitude; effeminacy; timidity, cowardice, caution
3. *Smartness:*	ability to outsmart, dupe, "con"; gaining money by "wits"; shrewdness, adroitness in repartee	gullibility, "con-ability"; gaining money by hard work; slowness, dull-wittedness, verbal maladroitness
4. *Excitement:*	thrill; risk, danger; change, activity	boredom; "deadness," safeness; sameness, passivity
5. *Fate:*	favored by fortune, being "lucky"	ill-omened, being "unlucky"
6. *Autonomy:*	freedom from external contraint; freedom from superordinate authority; independence	presence of external contraint; presence of strong authority; dependency, being "cared for"

and persistent attention and a high degree of emotional involvement. The specific concerns cited here, while by no means confined to the American lower classes, constitute a distinctive *patterning* of concerns which differs significantly, both in rank order and weighting from that of American middle class culture. The following chart presents a highly schematic and simplified listing of six of the major concerns of lower class culture. Each is conceived as a "dimension" within which a fairly wide and varied range of alternative behavior patterns may be followed by different individuals under different situations. They are listed roughly in order of the degree of *explicit* attention accorded each, and, in this sense represent a weighted ranking of concerns. The "perceived alternatives" represent polar positions which define certain parameters within each dimension. As will be explained in more detail, it is necessary in relating the influence of these "concerns" to the motivation of delinquent behavior to specify *which* of its aspects is oriented to, whether orientation is *overt* or *covert, positive* (conforming to or seeking the aspect), or *negative* (rejecting or seeking to avoid the aspect).

The concept "focal concern" is used here in preference to the concept "value" for several interrelated reasons: (1) It is more readily derivable from direct field observation. (2) It is descriptively neutral—permitting independent consideration of positive and negative valences as varying under different conditions, whereas "value" carries a built-in positive valence. (3) It makes possible more refined analysis of subcultural differences, since it reflects actual behavior, whereas "value" tends to wash out intracultural differences since it is colored by notions of the "official" ideal.

Trouble

Concern over "trouble" is a dominant feature of lower class culture. The concept has various shades of meaning; "trouble" in one of its aspects represents a situation or a kind of behavior which results in unwelcome or complicating involvement with official authorities or agencies of middle class society. "Getting into trouble" and "staying out of trouble" represent major issues for male and female, adults and children. For men, "trouble" frequently involves fighting or sexual adventures while drinking; for women, sexual involvement with disadvantageous consequences. Expressed desire to avoid behavior which violates moral or legal norms is often based less on an explicit commitment to "official" moral or legal standards than on a desire to avoid "getting into trouble," e.g., the complicating consequences of the action.

The dominant concern over "trouble" involves a distinction of critical importance for the lower class community—that between "law-abiding" and "nonlaw-abiding" behavior. There is a high degree of sensitivity as to where each person stands in relation to these two classes of activity. Whereas in the middle class community a major dimension for evaluating a person's status is "achievement" and its external symbols, in the lower class, personal status is very frequently gauged along the law-abiding-nonlaw-abiding dimension. A mother will evaluate the suitability of her daughter's boyfriend less on the basis of his achievement potential than on the basis of his innate "trouble" potential. This sensitive awareness of the opposition of "trouble-producing" and "nontrouble-producing" behavior represents both a major basis for deriving status distinctions, and an internalized conflict potential for the individual.

As in the case of other focal concerns, which of two perceived alternatives—"law-abiding" or "nonlaw-abiding"—is valued varies according to the individual and the circumstances; in many instances there is an overt commitment to the "law-abiding" alternative, but a covert commitment to the "nonlaw-abiding." In certain situations, "getting into trouble" is overtly recognized as prestige-conferring; for example, membership in certain adult and adolescent primary groupings ("gangs") is contingent on having demonstrated an explicit commitment to the law-violating alternative. It is most important to note that the choice between "law-abiding" and "nonlaw-abiding" behavior is still a choice *within* lower class culture; the distinction between the policeman and the criminal, the outlaw and the sheriff, involves primarily this one dimension; in other respects they have a high community of interests. Not infrequently brothers raised in an identical cultural milieu will become police and criminals, respectively.

For a substantial segment of the lower class population "getting into trouble" is not in itself overtly defined as prestige-conferring, but is implicitly recognized as a means to other valued ends, e.g., the covertly valued desire to be "cared for" and subject to external constraint, or the overtly valued state of excitement or risk. Very frequently "getting into trouble" is multi-functional, and achieves several sets of valued ends.

Toughness

The concept of "toughness" in lower class culture represents a compound combination of qualities or states. Among its most important components are physical prowess, evidenced both by demonstrated possession of strength and endurance and athletic skill; "masculinity," symbolized by a distinctive complex of acts and avoidance (bodily tatooing; absence of sentimentality; nonconcern with "art," "literature," conceptualization of women as conquest objects, etc.); and bravery in the face of physical threat. The model for the "tough guy"—hard, fearless, undemonstrative, skilled in physical combat—is represented by the movie gangster of the thirties, the "private eye," and the movie cowboy.

The genesis of the intense concern over "toughness" in lower class culture is probably related to the fact that a significant proportion of lower class males are reared in a predominantly female household, and lack a consistently present male figure with whom to identify and from whom to learn essential components of a "male" role. Since women serve as a primary object of identification during preadolescent years, the almost obsessive lower class concern with "masculinity" probably resembles a type of compulsive reaction-formation. A concern over homosexuality runs like a persistent thread through lower class culture. This is manifested by the institutionalized practice of baiting "queers," often accompanied by violent physical attacks, an expressed contempt for "softness" or frills, and the use of the local term for "homosexual" as a generalized pejorative epithet (e.g., higher class individuals or upwardly mobile peers are frequently characterized as "fags" or "queers"). The distinction between "overt" and "covert" orientation to aspects of an area of concern is especially important in regard to "toughness." A positive overt evaluation of behavior defined as "effeminate" would be out of the question for a lower class male; however, built into lower class culture is a range of devices which permit men to adopt behaviors and concerns which in other cultural milieux fall within the province of women, and at the same time to be defined as "tough" and manly. For example, lower class men can be professional short-order cooks in a diner and still be regarded as "tough." The highly intimate circumstances of the street corner gang involve the recurrent expression of strongly affectionate feelings towards other men. Such expressions, however, are disguised as their opposite, taking the form of ostensibly aggressive verbal and physical interaction (kidding, "ranking," roughhousing, etc.).

Smartness

"Smartness," as conceptualized in lower class culture, involves the capacity to outsmart, outfox, outwit, dupe, "take," "con" another or others, and the concomitant capacity to avoid being outwitted, "taken," or duped oneself. In its essence, smartness involves the capacity to achieve a valued entity—material goods, personal status—through a maximum use of mental agility and a minimum use of physical effort. This capacity has an extremely long tradition in lower class culture, and is highly valued. Lower class culture can be characterized as "non-intellectual" only if intellectualism is defined specifically in terms of control over a particular body of formally learned knowledge involving "culture" (art, literature, "good" music, etc.), a generalized perspective on the past and present conditions of our own and other societies, and other areas of knowledge imparted by formal educational institutions. This particular type of mental attainment is, in general, overtly disvalued and frequently associated with effeminacy; "smartness" in the lower class sense, however, is highly valued. The lower-class child learns and practices the use of this skill in the street corner situation. Individuals continually practice duping and outwitting one another through recurrent card games and other forms of gambling, mutual exchanges of insults, and "testing" for mutual "con-ability." Those who demonstrate competence in this skill are accorded considerable prestige. Leadership roles in the corner group are frequently allocated according to demonstrated capacity in the two areas of "smartness" and "toughness"; the ideal leader combines both, but the "smart" leader is often accorded more prestige than the "tough" one—reflecting a general class respect for "brains" in the "smartness" sense.[4]

The model of the "smart" person is represented in popular media by the card shark, the professional gambler, the "con" artist, the promoter. A conceptual distinction is made between two kinds of people: "suckers," easy marks, "lushes," dupes, who work for their money and are legitimate targets of exploitation; and sharp operators, the "brainy" ones, who live by their wits and "getting" from the suckers by mental adroitness.

Involved in the syndrome of capacities related to "smartness" is a dominant emphasis in lower class culture on ingenious aggressive repartee. This skill, learned and practiced in the context of the corner group, ranges in form from the widely prevalent semiritualized teasing, kidding, razzing, "ranking," so characteristic of male peer group interaction, to the highly ritualized type of mutual insult interchange known as "the dirty dozens," "the dozens," "playing house," and other terms. This highly patterned cultural form is practiced on its most advanced level in adult male Negro society, but less polished variants are found throughout lower class culture—practiced, for example, by white children, male and female, as young as four or five. In essence, "doin' the dozens" involves two antagonists who vie with each other in the exchange of increasingly inflammatory insults, with incestuous and perverted sexual relations with the mother a dominant theme. In this form of insult interchange, as well as on other less ritualized occasions for joking, semiserious, and serious mutual invective, a very high premium is placed on ingenuity, hair-trigger responsiveness, inventiveness, and the acute exercise of mental faculties.

Excitement

For many lower class individuals the rhythm of life fluctuates between periods of relatively routine or repetitive activity and sought situations of great emotional stimulation. Many of the most characteristic features of lower class life are related to the search for excitement or "thrill." Involved here are the highly prevalent use of alcohol by both sexes and the widespread use of gambling of all kinds—playing the numbers, betting on horse races, dice, cards. The quest for excitement finds what is perhaps its most vivid expression in the highly patterned practice of the recurrent "night on the town." This practice, designated by various terms in different areas ("honky-tonkin'"; "goin' out on the town"; "bar hoppin'"), involves a patterned set of activities in which alcohol, music, and sexual adventuring are major components. A group or individual sets out to "make the rounds" of various bars or night clubs. Drinking continues progressively throughout the evening. Men seek to "pick up" women, and women play the risky game of entertaining sexual advances. Fights between men involving women, gambling, and claims of physical prowess, in various combinations, are frequent consequences of a night of making the rounds. The explosive potential of this type of adventuring with sex and aggression, frequently leading to "trouble," is semiexplicitly sought by the individual. Since there is always a good likelihood that being out on the town will eventuate in fights, etc., the practice involves elements of sought risk and desired danger.

Counterbalancing the "flirting" with danger" aspect of the "excitement" concern is the prevalence in lower class culture of other well established patterns of activity which involve long periods of relative inaction, or passivity. The term "hanging out" in lower class culture refers to extended periods of standing around, often with peer mates, doing what is defined as "nothing," "shooting the breeze," etc. A definite periodicity exists in the pattern of activity relating to the two aspects of the "excitement" dimension. For many lower class individuals the venture into the high risk world of alcohol, sex, and fighting occurs regularly once a week, with interim periods devoted to accommodating to possible consequences of these periods, along with recurrent resolves not to become so involved again.

Fate

Related to the quest for excitement is the concern with fate, fortune, or luck. Here also a distinction is made between two states—being "lucky" or "in luck," and being unlucky or jinxed. Many lower class individuals feel that their lives are subject to a set of forces over which they have relatively little control. These are not directly equated with the supernatural forces of formally organized religion, but relate more to a concept of "destiny," or man as a pawn of magical powers. Not infrequently this often implicit world view is associated with a conception of the ultimate futility of directed effort towards a goal: if the cards are right, or the dice good to you, or if your lucky number comes up, things will go your way; if luck is against you, it's not worth trying. The concept of performing semimagical rituals so that one's "luck will change" is prevalent; one hopes that as a result he will move from the state of being "unlucky" to that of being "lucky." The element of fantasy plays an important part in this area. Related to and complementing the notion that "only suckers work" (Smartness) is the idea that once things start going your way, relatively independent of your own effort, all good things will come to you. Achieving great material rewards (big cars, big houses, a roll of cash to flash in a fancy night club), valued in lower class as well as in other parts of American culture, is a recurrent theme in lower class fantasy and folk lore; the cocaine dreams of Willie the Weeper or Minnie the Moocher present the components of this fantasy in vivid detail.

The prevalence in the lower class community of many forms of gambling, mentioned in connection with the "excitement" dimension, is also relevant here. Through cards and pool which involve skill, and thus both "toughness" and "smartness"; or through race horse betting, involving "smartness"; or through playing the numbers, involving predominantly "luck," one may make a big killing with a minimum of directed and persistent effort within conventional occupational channels. Gambling in its many forms illustrates the fact that many of the persistent features of lower class culture are multi-functional—serving a range of desired ends at the same time. Describing some of the incentives behind gambling has involved mention of all of the focal concerns cited so far—Toughness, Smartness, and Excitement, in addition to Fate.

Autonomy

The extent and nature of control over the behavior of the individual—an important concern in most cultures—has a special significance and is distinctively patterned in lower class culture. The discrepancy between what is overtly valued and what is covertly sought is particularly striking in this area. On the overt level there is a strong and frequently expressed resentment of the idea of external controls, restrictions on behavior, and unjust or coercive authority. "No one's gonna push *me* around," or "I'm gonna tell him he can take the job and shove it. . . ." are commonly expressed sentiments. Similar explicit attitudes are maintained to systems of behavior-restricting rules, insofar as these are perceived as representing the injunctions, and bearing the sanctions of superordinate authority. In addition, in lower class culture a close conceptual connection is made between "authority" and "nurturance." To be restrictively or firmly controlled is to be cared for. Thus the overtly negative evaluation of superordinate authority frequently extends as well to nurturance, care, or protection. The desire for personal independence is often expressed in such terms as "I don't need *nobody* to take care of me. I can take care of myself!" Actual patterns of behavior, however, reveal a marked discrepancy between expressed sentiment and what is covertly valued. Many lower class people appear to seek out highly restrictive social environments wherein stringent external controls are maintained over their behavior. Such institutions as the armed forces, the mental hospital, the disciplinary school, the prison or correctional institution, provide environments which incorporate a strict and detailed set of rules defining and limiting behavior, and enforced by an authority system which controls and applies coercive sanctions for deviance from these rules. While under the jurisdiction of such systems, the lower class person generally expresses to his peers continual resentment of the coercive, unjust, and arbitrary exercise of authority. Having been released, or having escaped from these milieux, however, he will often act in such a way as to insure recommitment, or choose recommitment voluntarily after a temporary period of "freedom."

Lower class patients in mental hospitals will exercise considerable ingenuity to insure continued commitment while voicing the desire to get out; delinquent boys will frequently "run" from a correctional institution to activate efforts to return them; to be caught and returned means that one is cared for. Since "being controlled" is equated with "being cared for," attempts are frequently made to "test" the severity or strictness of superordinate authority to see if it remains firm. If intended or executed rebellion produces swift and firm punitive sanctions, the individual is reassured, at the same time that he is complaining bitterly at the injustice of being caught and punished. Some environmental milieux, having been tested in this fashion for the "firmness" of their coercive sanctions, are rejected, ostensibly for being too strict, actually for not being strict enough. This is frequently so in the case of "problematic" behavior by lower class youngsters in the public schools, which generally cannot command the coercive controls implicitly sought by the individual.

A similar discrepancy between what is overtly and covertly desired is found in the area of dependence-independence. The pose of tough rebellious independence often assumed by the lower class person frequently conceals powerful dependency cravings. These are manifested primarily by obliquely expressed resentment when "care" is not forthcoming rather than by expressed satisfaction when it is. The concern over autonomy-dependency is related both to "trouble" and "fate." Insofar as the lower class individual feels that his behavior is controlled by forces which often propel him into "trouble" in the face of an explicit determination to avoid it, there is an implied appeal to "save me from myself." A solution appears to lie in arranging things so that his behavior will be coercively restricted by an externally imposed set of controls strong enough to forcibly restrain his inexplicable inclination to get in trouble. The periodicity observed in connection with the "excitement" dimension is also relevant here; after involvement in trouble-producing behavior (assault, sexual adventure, a "drunk"), the individual will actively seek a locus of imposed control (his wife, prison, a restrictive job); after a given period of subjection to this control, resentment against it mounts, leading to a "break away" and a search for involvement in further "trouble."

FOCAL CONCERNS OF THE LOWER CLASS ADOLESCENT STREET CORNER GROUP

The one-sex peer group is a highly prevalent and significant structural form in the lower class community. There is a strong probability that the prevalence and stability of this type of unit is directly related to the prevalence of a stabilized type of lower class child-rearing unit—the "female-based" household. This is a nuclear kin unit in which a male parent is either absent from the household, present only sporadically, or, when present, only minimally or inconsistently involved in the support and rearing of children. This unit usually consists of one or more females of child-bearing age and their offspring. The females are frequently related to one another by blood or marriage ties, and the unit often includes two or more generations of women, e.g., the mother and/or aunt of the principal child-bearing female.

The nature of social groupings in the lower class community may be clarified if we make the assumption that it is the *one-sex peer unit* rather than the two-parent family unit which represents the most significant relational unit for both sexes in lower class communities. Lower class society may be pictured as comprising as set of age-graded one-sex groups which constitute the major psychic focus and reference group for those over twelve or thirteen. Men and women of mating age leave these groups periodically to form temporary marital alliances, but these lack stability, and after varying periods of "trying out" the two-sex family arrangement, gravitate back to the more "comfortable" one-sex grouping, whose members exert strong pressure on the individual *not* to disrupt the group by adopting a two-sex household pattern of life.[5] Membership in a stable and solidary peer unit is vital to the lower class individual precisely to the extent to which a range of essential functions—psychological, educational, and others, are not provided by the "family" unit.

The adolescent street corner group represents the adolescent variant of this lower class structural form. What has been called the "delinquent gang" is one subtype of this form, defined on the basis of frequency of participation in law-violating activity; this subtype should not be considered a legitimate unit of study per se, but rather as one particular variant of the adolescent street corner group. The "hanging" peer group is a unit of particular importance for the adolescent male. In many cases it is the most stable and solidary primary group he has ever belonged to; for boys reared in female-based households the corner group provides the first real opportunity to learn essential aspects of the male role in the context of peers facing similar problems of sex-role identification.

The form and functions of the adolescent corner group operate as a selective mechanism in recruiting members. The activity patterns of the group require a high level of intragroup solidarity; individual members must possess a good capacity for subordinating individual desires to general group interests as well as the capacity for intimate and persisting interaction. Thus high "disturbed" individuals, or those who cannot tolerate consistently imposed sanctions on "deviant" behavior cannot remain accepted members; the group itself will extrude those whose behavior exceeds limits defined as "normal." This selective process produces a type of group whose members possess to an unusually high degree both the *capacity* and *motivation* to conform to perceived cultural norms, so that the nature of the system of norms and values oriented to is a particularly influential component of motivation.

Focal concerns of the male adolescent corner group are those of the general cultural milieu in which it functions. As would be expected, the relative weighting and importance of these concerns pattern somewhat differently for adolescents than for adults. The nature of this patterning centers around two additional "concerns" of particular importance to this group—concern with "belonging," and with "status." These may be conceptualized as being on a higher level of abstraction than concerns previously cited, since "status" and "belonging" are achieved *via* cited concern areas of Toughness, etc.

Belonging

Since the corner group fulfills essential functions for the individual, being a member in good standing of the group is of vital importance for its members. A continuing concern over who is "in" and who is not involves the citation and detailed discussion of highly refined criteria for "in-group" membership. The phrase "he hangs with us" means "he is accepted as a member in good standing by current consensus;" conversely, "he don't hang with us" means he is not so accepted. One achieves "belonging" primarily by demonstrating knowledge of and a determination to adhere to the system of standards and valued qualities defined by the group. One maintains membership by acting in conformity with valued aspects of Toughness, Smartness, Autonomy, etc. In those instances where conforming to norms of this reference group at the same time violates norms of other reference groups (e.g., middle class adults, institutional "officials"), immediate reference group norms are much more compelling since violation risks invoking the group's most powerful sanction: exclusion.

Status

In common with most adolescents in American society, the lower class corner group manifests a dominant concern with "status." What differentiates this type of group from others, however, is the particular set of criteria and weighting thereof by which "status" is defined. In general, status is achieved and maintained by demonstrated possession of the valued qualities of lower class culture—Toughness, Smartness, expressed resistance to authority, daring, etc. It is important to stress once more that the individual orients to these concerns *as they are defined within lower class society;* e.g., the status-conferring potential of "smartness" in the sense of scholastic achievement generally ranges from negligible to negative.

The concern with "status" is manifested in a variety of ways. Intragroup status is a continued concern, and is derived and tested constantly by means of a set of status-ranking activities; the intragroup "pecking order" is constantly at issue. One gains status within the group by demonstrated superiority in Toughness (physical prowess, bravery, skill in athletics and games such as pool and cards), Smartness (skill in repartee, capacity to "dupe" fellow group members), and the like. The term "ranking," used to refer to the pattern of intragroup aggressive repartee, indicates awareness of the fact that this is one device for establishing the intragroup status hierarchy.

The concern over status in the adolescent corner group involves in particular the component of "adultness," the intense desire to be seen as "grown up," and a corresponding aversion to "kid stuff." "Adult" status is defined less in terms of the assumption of "adult" responsibility than in terms of certain external symbols of adult status—a car, ready cash, and, in particular, a perceived "freedom" to drink, smoke, and gamble as one wishes and to come and go without external restrictions. The desire to be seen as "adult" is often a more significant component of much involvement in illegal drinking, gambling, and automobile driving than the explicit enjoyment of these acts as such.

The intensity of the corner group member's desire to be seen as "adult" is sufficiently great that he feels called upon to demonstrate qualities associated with adultness (Toughness, Smartness, Autonomy) to a much greater degree than a lower class adult. This means that he will seek out and utilize those avenues to these qualities which he perceives as available with greater intensity than an adult and less regard for their "legitimacy." In this sense the adolescent variant of lower class culture represents a maximization or an intensified manifestation of many of its most characteristic features.

Concern over status is also manifested in reference to other street corner groups. The term "rep" used in this regard is especially significant, and has broad connotations. In its most frequent and explicit connotation, "rep" refers to the "toughness" of the corner group as a whole relative to that of other groups; a "pecking order" also exists among the several corner groups in a given interactional area, and there is a common perception that the safety or security of the group and all its members depends on maintaining a solid "rep" for toughness vis-à-vis other groups. This motive is most frequently advanced as a reason for involvement in gang fights: "We *can't* chicken out on this fight; our rep would be shot!"; this implies that the group would be relegated to the bottom of the status ladder and become a helpless and recurrent target of external attack.

On the other hand, there is implicit in the concept of "rep" the recognition that "rep" has or may have a dual basis— corresponding to the two aspects of the "trouble" dimension. It is recognized that group as well as individual status can be based on both "law-abiding" and "law-violating" behavior. The situational resolution of the persisting conflict between the "law-abiding" and "law-violating" bases of status comprises a vital set of dynamics in determining whether a "delinquent" mode of behavior will be adopted by a group, under what circumstances, and how persistently. The determinants of this choice are evidently highly complex and fluid, and rest on a range of factors including the presence and perceptual immediacy of different community reference-group loci (e.g., professional criminals, police, clergy, teachers, settlement house workers), the personality structures and "needs" of group members, the presence in the community of social work, recreation, or educational programs which can facilitate utilization of the "law-abiding" basis of status, and so on.

What remains constant is the critical importance of "status" both for the members of the group as individuals and for the group as a whole insofar as members perceive their individual destinies as linked to the destiny of the group, and the fact that action geared to attain status is much more acutely oriented to the fact of status itself than to the legality or illegality, morality or immorality of the means used to achieve it.

LOWER CLASS CULTURE AND THE MOTIVATION OF DELINQUENT BEHAVIOR

The customary set of activities of the adolescent street corner group includes activities which are in violation of laws and ordinances of the legal code. Most of these center around assault and theft of various types (the gang fight; auto theft; assault on an individual; petty pilfering and shoplifting; "mugging"; pocketbook theft). Members of street corner gangs are well aware of the law-violating nature of these acts; they are not psychopaths, nor physically or mentally "defective"; in fact, since the corner group supports and enforces a rigorous set of standards which demand a high degree of fitness and personal competence, it tends to recruit from the most "able" members of the community.

Why, then, is the commission of crimes a customary feature of gang activity? The most general answer is that the commission of crimes by members of adolescent street corner groups is motivated primarily by the attempt to achieve ends, states, or conditions which are valued, and to avoid those that are disvalued within their most meaningful cultural milieu, through those culturally available avenues which appear as the most feasible means of attaining those ends.

The operation of these influences is well illustrated by the gang fight—a prevalent and characteristic type of corner group delinquency. This type of activity comprises a highly stylized and culturally patterned set of sequences. Although details vary under different circumstances, the following events are generally included. A member or several members of group A "trespass" on the claimed territory of group B. While there they commit an act or acts which group B defines as a violation of its rightful privileges, an affront to their honor, or a challenge to their "rep." Frequently this act involves advances to a girl associated with group B; it may occur at a dance or party; sometimes the mere act of "trespass" is seen as deliberate provocation. Members of group B then assault members of group A, if they are caught while still in B's territory. Assaulted members of group A return to their "home" territory and recount to members of their group details of the incident, stressing the insufficient nature of the provocation ("I just *looked* at her! Hardly even said anything!"), and the unfair circumstances of the assault ("About *twenty* guys jumped just the *two* of us!"). The highly colored account is acutely inflammatory; group A, perceiving its honor violated and its "rep" threatened, feels obligated to retaliate in force. Sessions of detailed planning now occur; allies are recruited if the size of group A and its potential allies appears to necessitate larger numbers; strategy is plotted, and messengers dispatched. Since the prospect of a gang fight is frightening to even the "toughest" group members, a constant rehearsal of the provocative incident or incidents and the essentially evil nature of the opponents accompanies the planning process to bolster possibly weakening motivation to fight. The excursion into "enemy" territory sometimes results in a full scale fight; more often group B cannot be found, or the police appear and stop the fight, "tipped off" by an anonymous informant When this occurs, group members express disgust and disappointment; secretly there is much relief; their honor has been avenged without incurring injury; often the anonymous tipster is a member of one of the involved groups.

The basic elements of this type of delinquency are sufficiently stablized and recurrent as to constitute an essentially ritualized pattern, resembling both in structure and expressed motives for action classic forms such as the European "duel," the American Indian tribal war, and the Celtic clan feud. Although the arousing and "acting out" of individual aggressive emotions are inevitably involved in the gang fight, neither its form nor motivational dynamics can be adequately handled within a predominantly personality-focused frame of reference.

It would be possible to develop in considerable detail the processes by which the commission of a range of illegal acts is either explicitly supported by, implicitly demanded by, or not materially inhibited by factors relating to the focal concerns of lower class culture. In place of such a development, the following three statements condense in general terms the operation of these processes:

1. Following cultural practices which comprise essential elements of the total life pattern of lower class culture automatically violates certain legal norms.
2. In instances where alternate avenues to similar objectives are available the nonlaw-abiding avenue frequently provides a relatively greater and more immediate return for a relatively smaller investment of energy.
3. The "demanded" response to certain situations recurrently engendered within lower class culture involves the commission of illegal acts.

The primary thesis of this paper is that the dominant component of the motivation of "delinquent" behavior engaged in by members of lower class corner groups involves a positive effort to achieve states, conditions, or qualities valued within the actor's most significant cultural milieu. If "conformity to immediate reference group values" is the major component of motivation of "delinquent" behavior by gang members, why is such behavior frequently referred to as negativistic, malicious, or rebellious? Albert Cohen, for example, in *Delinquent Boys* (Glencoe: Free Press, 1955) describes behavior which violates school rules as comprising elements of "active spite and malice, contempt and ridicule, challenge and defiance." He ascribes to the gang "keen delight in terrorizing 'good' children, and in general making themselves obnoxious to the virtuous." A recent national conference on social work with "hard-to-reach" groups characterized lower class corner groups as "youth groups in conflict with the culture of their (*sic*) communities." Such characterizations are obviously the result of taking the middle class community and its institutions as an implicit point of reference.

A large body of systematically interrelated attitudes, practices, behaviors, and values characteristic of lower class culture are designed to support and maintain the basic features of the lower class way of life. In areas where these differ from features of middle class culture, action oriented to the achievement and maintenance of the lower class system may violate norms of middle class culture and be perceived as deliberately nonconforming or malicious by an observer strongly cathected to middle class norms. This does not mean, however, that violation of the middle class norm is the dominant component of motivation; it is a by-product of action primarily oriented to the lower class system. The standards of lower class culture cannot be seen merely as a reverse function of middle class culture—as middle class standards "turned upside down"; lower class culture is a distinctive tradition many centuries old with an integrity of its own.

From the viewpoint of the acting individual, functioning within a field of well-structured cultural forces, the relative impact of "conforming" and "rejective" elements in the motivation of gang delinquency is weighted preponderantly on the conforming side. Rejective or rebellious elements are inevitably involved, but their influence during the actual commission of delinquent acts is relatively small compared to the influence of pressures to achieve what is valued by the actor's most immediate reference groups. Expressed awareness by the actor of the element of rebellion often represents only that aspect of motivation of which he is explicitly conscious; the deepest and most compelling components of motivation—adherence to highly meaningful group standards of Toughness, Smartness, Excitement, etc.—

are often unconsciously patterned. No cultural pattern as well-established as the practice of illegal acts by members of lower class corner groups could persist if buttressed primarily by negative, hostile, or rejective motives; its principal motivational support, as in the case of any persisting cultural tradition, derives from a positive effort to achieve what is valued within that tradition, and to conform to its explicit and implicit norms.

ILLEGITIMATE MEANS, ANOMIE, AND DEVIANT BEHAVIOR

Richard A. Cloward

The theory of anomie has undergone two major phases of development, as exemplified by the work of Durkheim and Merton. In this paper a third phase is outlined. As currently stated, the theory focusses on pressures toward deviant behavior arising from discrepancies between cultural goals and approved modes of access to them. It focusses, in short, upon variations in the availability of legitimate means. One may also inquire, however, about variations in access to success-goals by illegitimate means. The latter emphasis may be detected in the work of Shaw, McKay, Sutherland, and others in the "cultural transmission" and "differential association" tradition. By taking into account differentials in access to success-goals both by legitimate and by illegitimate means, the theory of anomie may be extended to include seemingly unrelated theories of deviant behavior now contained in the traditional literature of criminology.

THIS PAPER[1] represents an attempt to consolidate two major

From the *American Sociological Review*, 24 (April, 1959), 164–176. Reprinted by permission of the American Sociological Association.

sociological traditions of thought about the problem of deviant behavior. The first, exemplified by the work of Emile Durkheim and Robert K. Merton, may be called the anomie tradition.[2] The second, illustrated principally by the studies of Clifford R. Shaw, Henry D. McKay, and Edwin H. Sutherland, may be called the "cultural transmission" and "differential association" tradition.[3] Despite some reciprocal borrowing of ideas, these intellectual traditions developed more or less independently. By seeking to consolidate them, a more adequate theory of deviant behavior may be constructed.

DIFFERENTIALS IN AVAILABILITY OF LEGITIMATE MEANS: THE THEORY OF ANOMIE

The theory of anomie has undergone two major phases of development. Durkheim first used the concept to explain deviant behavior. He focussed on the way in which various social conditions lead to "overweening ambition," and how, in turn, unlimited aspirations ultimately produce a breakdown in regulatory norms. Robert K. Merton has systematized and extended the theory, directing attention to patterns of disjunction between culturally prescribed goals and socially organized access to them by *legitimate* means. In this paper, a third phase is outlined. An additional variable is incorporated in the developing scheme of anomie, namely, the concept of *differentials in access to success-goals by illegitimate means*.[4]

Phase I: Unlimited Aspirations and the Breakdown of Regulatory Norms

In Durkheim's work, a basic distinction is made between "physical needs" and "moral needs." The importance of this distinction was heightened for Durkheim because he viewed physical needs as being regulated automatically by features of man's organic structure. Nothing in the organic structure, however, is capable of regulating social desires; as Durkheim put it, man's "capacity for feeling is in itself an insatiable and bottomless abyss."[5] If man is to function without "friction," "the passions must first be limited. . . . But since the individual has no way of limiting them, this must be done by some force exterior to him." Durkheim viewed the collective order as the external regulating force which defined and ordered the goals to which men should orient their behavior. If the collective order is disrupted or disturbed, however, men's aspirations may then rise, exceeding all possibilities of fulfillment. Under these conditions, "de-regulation or anomy" ensues: "At the very moment when traditional rules have lost their authority, the richer prize offered these appetites stimulates them and makes them more exigent and impatient of control. The state of de-regulation or anomy is thus further heightened by passions being less disciplined precisely when they need more disciplining." Finally, pressures toward deviant behavior were said to develop when man's aspirations no longer matched the possibilities of fulfillment.

Durkheim therefore turned to the question of *when* the regulatory functions of the collective order break down. Several such states were identified, including sudden depression, sudden prosperity, and rapid technological change. His object was to show how, under these conditions, men are led to aspire to goals extremely difficult if not impossible to attain. As Durkheim saw it, sudden depression results in deviant behavior because "something like a declassification occurs which suddenly casts certain individuals into a lower state than their previous one. Then they must reduce their requirements, restrain their needs, learn greater self-control. . . . But society cannot adjust them instantaneously to this new life and teach them to practice the increased self-repression to which they are unaccustomed. So they are not adjusted to the condition forced on them, and its very prospect is intolerable; hence the suffering which detaches them from a reduced existence even before they have made trial of it." Prosperity, according to Durkheim, could have much the same effect as depression, particularly if upward changes in economic conditions are abrupt. The very abruptness of these changes presumably heightens aspirations beyond possibility of fulfillment, and this too puts a strain on the regulatory apparatus of the society.

According to Durkheim, "the sphere of trade and industry . . . is actually in a chronic state [of anomie]." Rapid technological developments and the existence of vast, unexploited markets excite the imagination with the seemingly limitless possibilities for the accumulation of wealth. As Durkheim said of the producer of goods, "now that he may assume to have almost the entire world as his customer, how could passions accept their former confinement in the face of such limitless prospects?" Continuing, Durkheim states that "such is the source of excitement predominating in this part of society. . . . Here the state of crisis and anomie [are] constant and, so to speak, normal. From top to bottom of the ladder, greed is aroused without knowing where to find ultimate foothold. Nothing can calm it, since its goal is far beyond all it can attain."

In developing the theory, Durkheim characterized goals in the industrial society, and specified the way in which unlimited aspirations are induced. He spoke of "dispositions . . . so inbred that society has grown to accept them and is accustomed to think them normal," and he portrayed these "inbred dispositions": "It is everlastingly repeated that it is man's nature to be eternally dissatisfied, constantly to advance, without relief or rest, toward an indefinite goal. The longing for infinity is daily represented as a mark of moral distinction. . . ." And it was precisely these pressures to strive for "infinite" or "receding" goals, in Durkheim's view, that generate a breakdown in regulatory norms, for "when where is no other aim but to outstrip constantly the point arrived at, how painful to be thrown back!"

Phase II: Disjunction Between Cultural Goals and Socially Structured Opportunity

Durkheim's description of the emergence of "overweening ambition" and the subsequent breakdown of regulatory norms constitutes one of the links between his work and the later development of the theory by Robert K. Merton. In his classic essay, "Social Structure and Anomie," Merton suggests that goals and norms may vary independently of each other, and that this sometimes leads to malintegrated states. In his view, two polar types of disjunction may occur: "There may develop a very heavy, at times a virtually exclusive, stress upon the value of particular goals, involving comparatively little concern with the institutionally prescribed means of striving toward these goals. . . . This constitutes one type of malintegrated culture."[6] On the other hand, "A second polar type is found where activities originally conceived as instrumental are transmuted into self-contained practices, lacking further objectives. . . . Sheer conformity becomes a central value." Merton notes that "between these extreme types are societies which maintain a rough balance between emphases upon cultural goals and institutionalized practices, and these constitute the integrated and relatively stable, though changing societies."

Having identified patterns of disjunction between goals and norms, Merton is enabled to define anomie more precisely: "Anomie [may be] conceived as a breakdown in the cultural structure, occurring particularly when there is an acute disjunction between cultural norms and goals and the socially structured capacities of members of the group to act in accord with them."

Of the two kinds of malintegrated societies, Merton is primarily interested in the one in which "there is an exceptionally strong emphasis upon specific goals without a corresponding emphasis upon institutional procedures." He states that attenuation between goals and norms, leading to anomie or "normlessness," comes about because men in such societies internalize an emphasis on common success-goals under conditions of varying access to them. The essence of this hypothesis is captured in the following excerpt: "It is only when a system of cultural values extols, virtually above all else, certain *common* success-goals for the population at large while the social structure rigorously restricts or completely closes access to approved modes of reaching these goals *for a considerable part of the same population,* that deviant behavior ensues on a large scale." The focus, in short, is on the way in which the social structure puts a strain upon the cultural structure. Here one may point to diverse structural differentials in access to culturally approved goals by legitimate means, for example, differentials of age, sex, ethnic status, and social class. Pressures for anomie or normlessness vary from one social position to another, depending on the nature of these differentials.

In summary, Merton extends the theory of anomie in two principal ways. He explicitly identifies types of anomic or malintegrated societies by focussing upon the relationship between cultural goals and norms. And, by directing attention to patterned differentials in the access to success-goals by legitimate means, he shows how the social structure exerts a strain upon the cultural structure, leading in turn to anomie or normlessness.

Phase III: The Concept of Illegitimate Means

Once processes generating differentials in pressures are identified, there is then the question of how these pressures are resolved, or how men respond to them. In this connection, Merton enumerates five basic categories of behavior or role adaptations which are likely to emerge: conformity, innovation, ritualism, retreatism, and rebellion. These adaptations differ depending on the individual's acceptance or rejection of cultural goals, and depending on his adherence to or violation of institutional norms. Furthermore, Merton sees the distribution of these adaptations principally as the consequence of two variables: the relative extent of pressure, and values, particularly "internalized prohibitions," governing the use of various illegitimate means.

It is a familiar sociological idea that values serve to order the choices of deviant (as well as conforming) adaptations which develop under conditions of stress. Comparative studies of ethnic groups, for example, have shown that some tend to engage in distinctive forms of deviance; thus Jews exhibit low rates of alcoholism and alcoholic psychoses.[7] Various investigators have suggested that the emphasis on rationality, fear of expressing aggression, and other alleged components of the "Jewish" value system constrain modes of deviance which involve "loss of control" over behavior.[8] In contrast, the Irish show a much higher rate of alcoholic deviance because, it has been argued, their cultural emphasis on masculinity encourages the excessive use of alcohol under conditions of strain.[9]

Merton suggests that differing rates of ritualistic and innovating behavior in the middle and lower classes result from differential emphases in socialization. The "rule-oriented" accent in middle-class socialization presumably disposes persons to handle stress by engaging in ritualistic rather than innovating behavior. The lower-class person, contrastingly, having internalized less stringent norms, can violate conventions with less guilt and anxiety.[10] Values, in other words, exercise a canalizing influence, limiting the choice of deviant adaptations for persons variously distributed throughout the social system.

Apart from both socially patterned pressures, which give rise to deviance, and from values, which determine choices of adaptations, a further variable should be taken into account: namely, *differentials in availability of illegitimate means*. For example, the notion that innovating behavior may result from unfulfilled aspirations and imperfect socialization with respect to conventional norms implies that illegitimate means are freely available—as if the individual, having decided that "you can't make it legitimately," then simply turns to illegitimate means which are readily at hand whatever his position in the social structure. However, these means may not be available. As noted above, the anomie theory assumes that conventional means are differentially distributed, that some individuals, because of their social position, enjoy certain advantages, which are denied to others. Note, for example, variations in the degree to which members of various classes are fully exposed to and thus acquire the values, education, and skills which facilitate upward mobility. It should not be startling, therefore, to find similar variations in the availability of illegitimate means.

Several sociologists have alluded to such variations without explicitly incorporating this variable in a theory of deviant behavior. Sutherland, for example, writes that "an inclination to steal is not a sufficient explanation of the genesis of the professional thief."[11] Moreover, "the person must be appreciated by the professional thieves. He must be appraised as having an adequate equipment of wits, front, talking-ability, honesty, reliability, nerve and determination." In short, "a person can be a professional thief only if he is recognized and received as such by other professional thieves." But recognition is not freely accorded: "Selection and tutelage are the two necessary elements in the process of acquiring recognition as a professional thief. . . . A person cannot acquire recognition as a professional thief until he has had tutelage in professional theft, *and tutelage is given only to a few persons selected from the total population.*" Furthermore, the aspirant is judged by high standards of performance, for only "a very small percentage of those who start on this process ever reach the stage of professional theft." The burden of these remarks—dealing with the processes of selection, induction, and assumption of full status in the criminal group—is that motivations or pressures toward deviance do not fully account for deviant behavior. The "self-made" thief—lacking knowledge of the ways of securing immunity from prosecution and similar techniques of defense—"would quickly land in prison." Sutherland is in effect pointing to differentials in access to the role of professional thief. Although the criteria of selection are not altogether clear from his analysis, definite evaluative standards do appear to exist; depending on their content, certain categories of individuals would be placed at a disadvantage and others would be favored.

The availability of illegitimate means, then, is controlled by various criteria in the same manner that has long been ascribed to conventional means. Both systems of opportunity are (1) limited, rather than infinitely available, and (2) differentially available depending on the location of persons in the social structure.

When we employ the term "means," whether legitimate or illegitimate, at least two things are implied: first, that there are appropriate learning environments for the acquisition of the values and skills associated with the performance of

a particular role; and second, that the individual has opportunities to discharge the role once he has been prepared. The
term subsumes, therefore, both *learning structures* and *opportunity structures*.

A case in point is recruitment and preparation for careers
in the rackets. There are fertile criminal learning environments for the young in neighborhoods where the rackets
flourish as stable, indigenous institutions. Because these environments afford integration of offenders of different ages,
the young are exposed to "differential associations" which
facilitate the acquisition of criminal values and skills. Yet
preparation for the role may not insure that the individual
will ever discharge it. For one thing, more youngsters may
be recruited into these patterns of differential association
than can possibly be absorbed, following their "training," by
the adult criminal structure. There may be a surplus of con-
tenders for these elite positions, leading in turn to the necessity for criteria and mechanisms of selection. Hence a certain
proportion of those who aspire may not be permitted to engage in the behavior for which they have been prepared.

This illustration is similar in every respect, save for the
route followed, to the case of those who seek careers in the
sphere of legitimate business. Here, again, is the initial
problem of securing access to appropriate learning environments, such as colleges and postgraduate school of business.
Having acquired the values and skills needed for a business
career, graduates then face the problem of whether or not
they can successfully discharge the roles for which they have
been prepared. Formal training itself is not sufficient for occupational success, for many forces intervene to determine
who shall succeed and fail in the competitive world of business and industry—as throughout the entire conventional
occupational structure.

This distinction between learning structures and opportunity structures was suggested some years ago by Sutherland. In 1944, he circulated an unpublished paper which
briefly discusses the proposition that "criminal behavior is
partially a function of opportunities to commit specific classes
of crimes, such as embezzlement, bank burglary, or illicit

heterosexual intercourse."[12] He did not, however, take up the problem of differentials in opportunity as a concept to be systematically incorporated in a theory of deviant behavior. Instead, he held that "opportunity" is a necessary but not sufficient explanation of the commission of criminal acts, "since some persons who have opportunities to embezzle, become intoxicated, engage in illicit heterosexual intercourse or to commit other crimes do not do so." He also noted that the differential association theory did not constitute a full explanation of criminal activity, for, notwithstanding differential association, "it is axiomatic that persons who commit a specific crime must have the opportunity to commit that crime." He therefore concluded that "while opportunity may be partially a function of association with criminal patterns and of the specialized techniques thus acquired, *it is not determined entirely in that manner,* and consequently differential association is not the sufficient cause of criminal behavior" (emphasis not in original).

In Sutherland's statements, two meanings are attributed to the term "opportunity." As suggested above, it may be useful to separate these for analytical purposes. In the first sense, Sutherland appears to be saying that opportunity consists in part of learning structures. The principal components of his theory of differential association are that "criminal behavior is learned," and, furthermore, that "criminal behavior is learned in interaction with other persons in a process of communication." But he also uses the term to describe situations conducive to carrying out criminal roles. Thus, for Sutherland, the commission of a criminal act would seem to depend upon the existence of two conditions: differential associations favoring the acquisition of criminal values and skills, and conditions encouraging participation in criminal activity.

This distinction heightens the importance of identifying and questioning the common assumption that illegitimate means are freely available. We can now ask (1) whether there are socially structured differentials in access to illegitimate learning environments, and (2) whether there are differentials limiting the fulfillment of illegitimate·roles. If differentials exist and can be identified, we may then inquire about their consequences for the behavior of persons in different parts of the social structure. Before pursuing this question, however, we turn to a fuller discussion of the theoretical tradition established by Shaw, McKay, and Sutherland.

DIFFERENTIALS IN AVAILABILITY OF ILLEGITIMATE MEANS: THE SUBCULTURE TRADITION

The concept of differentials in availability of illegitimate means is implicit in one of the major streams of American criminological theory. In this tradition, attention is focussed on the processes by which persons are recruited into criminal learning environments and ultimately inducted into criminal roles. The problems here are to account for the acquisition of criminal roles and to describe the social organization of criminal activities. When the theoretical propositions contained in this tradition are reanalyzed, it becomes clear that one underlying conception is that of variations in access to success-goals by illegitimate means. Furthermore, this implicit concept may be shown to be one of the bases upon which the tradition was constructed.

In their studies of the ecology of deviant behavior in the urban environment, Shaw and McKay found that delinquency and crime tended to be confined to delimited areas and, furthermore, that such behavior persisted despite demographic changes in these areas. Hence they came to speak of "criminal tradition," of the "cultural transmission" of criminal values.[13] As a result of their observations of slum life, they concluded that *particular importance must be assigned to the integration of different age-levels of offenders.* Thus:

> Stealing in the neighborhood was a common practice among the children and approved by the parents. Whenever the boys got together they talked about robbing and made more plans for stealing. I hardly knew any boys who did not go robbing. The little fellows went in for petty stealing, breaking into freight cars, and stealing junk. The older guys did big jobs like stick-up, burglary, and stealing autos. The little fellows admired the "big shots" and longed for the day when they could get into the big racket. Fellows

who had "done time" were the big shots and looked up to and gave the little fellow tips on how to get by and pull off big jobs.[14]

In other words, access to criminal roles depends upon stable associations with others from whom the necessary values and skills may be learned. Shaw and McKay were describing deviant learning structures—that is, alternative routes by which people seek access to the goals which society holds to be worthwhile. They might also have pointed out that, in areas where such learning structures are unavailable, it is probably difficult for many individuals to secure access to stable criminal careers, even though motivated to do so.[15]

The concept of illegitimate means and the socially structured conditions of access to them were not explicitly recognized in the work of Shaw and McKay because, probably, they were disposed to view slum areas as "disorganized." Although they consistently referred to illegitimate activities as being organized, they nevertheless often depicted high-rate delinquency areas as disorganized because the values transmitted were criminal rather than conventional. Hence their work includes statements which we now perceive to be internally inconsistent, such as the following:

> This community situation [in which Sidney was reared] was not only disorganized and thus ineffective as a unit of control, but it was characterized by a high rate of juvenile delinquency and adult crime, not to mention the widespread political corruption which had long existed in the area. Various forms of stealing and many organized delinquent and criminal gangs were prevalent in the area. These groups exercised a powerful influence and tended to create a community spirit which not only tolerated but actually fostered delinquent and criminal practices.[16]

Sutherland was among the first to perceive that the concept of social disorganization tended to obscure the stable patterns of interaction among carriers of criminal values. Like Shaw and McKay, he had been influenced by the observation that lower-class areas were organized in terms of both conventional and criminal values, but he was also impressed that these alternative value systems were supported by patterned systems of social relations. He expressly recognized that crime, far from being a random, unorganized activity, was typically an intricate and stable system of human arrangements. He therefore rejected the concept of "social disorganization" and substituted the concept of "differential group organization."

The third concept, social disorganization, was borrowed from Shaw and McKay. I had used it but had not been satisfied with it because the organization of the delinquent group, which is often very complex, is social disorganization only from an ethical or some other particularistic point of view. At the suggestion of Albert K. Cohen, this concept has been changed to differential group organization, with organization for criminal activities on one side and organization against criminal activities on the other.[17]

Having freed observation of the urban slum from conventional evaluations, Sutherland was able to focus more clearly on the way in which its social structure constitutes a "learning environment" for the acquisition of deviant values and skills. In the development of the theory of "differential association" and "differential group organization," he came close to stating explicitly the concept of differentials in access to illegitimate means. But Sutherland was essentially interested in learning processes, and thus he did not ask how such access varies in different parts of the social structure, nor did he inquire about the consequences for behavior of variations in the accessibility of these means.[18]

William F. Whyte, in his classic study of an urban slum, advanced the empirical description of the structure and organization of illegitimate means a step beyond that of Sutherland. Like Sutherland, Whyte rejected the earlier view of the slum as disorganized:

It is customary for the sociologist to study the slum district in terms of "social disorganization" and to neglect to see that an area such as Cornerville has a complex and well-established organization of its own. . . . I found that in every group there was a hierarchical structure of social relations binding the individuals to one another and that the groups were also related hierarchically to one another. Where the group was formally organized into a political club, this was immediately apparent, but for informal groups it was no less true.[19]

Whyte's contribution to our understanding of the organization of illegitimate means in the slum consists primarily in showing that individuals who participate in stable illicit enterprise do not constitute a separate or isolated segment of the community. Rather, these persons are closely integrated with the occupants of conventional roles. In describing the relationship between racketeers and politicians, for example, he notes that "the rackets and political organizations extend from the bottom to the top of Cornerville society, mesh with one another, and integrate a large part of the life of the district. They provide a general framework for the understanding of the actions of both 'little guys' and 'big shots.' "[20] Whyte's view of the slum differs somewhat from that conveyed by the term "differential group organization." He does not emphasize the idea that the slum is composed of two different systems, conventional and deviant, but rather the way in which the occupants of these various roles are integrated in a single, stable structure which organizes and patterns the life of the community.

The description of the organization of illegitimate means in slums is further developed by Solomon Kobrin in his article, "The Conflict of Values in Delinquency Areas."[21] Kobrin suggests that urban slum areas vary in the degree to which the carriers of deviant and conventional values are integrated with one another. Hence he points the way to the development of a "typology of delinquency areas based on variations in the relationship between these two systems," depicting the "polar types" on such a continuum. The first type resembles the integrated areas described in preceding paragraphs. Here, claims Kobrin, there is not merely structural integration between carriers of the two value systems, but reciprocal participation by each in the value system of the other. Thus:

Leaders of [illegal] enterprises frequently maintain membership in such conventional institutions of their local communities as churches, fraternal and mutual benefit societies and political parties. . . . Within this framework the influence of each of the two value systems is reciprocal, the leaders of illegal enterprise participating in the primary orientation of the conventional elements in the population, and the latter, through their participation in a local power structure sustained in large part by illicit activity, participating perforce in the alternate, criminal value system.

Kobrin also notes that in some urban slums there is a tendency for the relationships between carriers of deviant and conventional values to break down. Such areas constitute the second polar type. Because of disorganizing forces such as "drastic change in the class, ethnic, or racial characteristics of its population," Kobrin suggests that "the bearers of the conventional culture and its value system are without the customary institutional machinery and therefore in effect partially demobilized with reference to the diffusion of their value system." At the same time, the criminal "value system remains implicit" since this type of area is "characterized principally by the absence of systematic and organized adult activity in violation of the law, despite the fact that many adults in these areas commit violations." Since both value systems remain implicit, the possibilities for effective integration are precluded.

The importance of these observations may be seen if we ask how accessibility of illegal means varies with the relative integration of conventional and criminal values from one type of area to another. In this connection, Korbrin points out that the "integrated" area apparently constitutes a "training ground" for the acquisition of criminal values and skills.

The stable position of illicit enterprise in the adult society of the community is reflected in the character of delinquent conduct on the part of children. While delinquency in all high rate areas is intrinsically disorderly in that it is unrelated to official programs for the education of the young, in the [integrated community] boys may more or less realistically recognize the potentialities for personal progress in local society, through access to delinquency. In a general way, therefore, delinquent activity in these areas constitutes a training ground for the acquisition of skill in the use of violence, concealment of offense, evasion of detection and arrest, and the purchase of immunity from punishment. Those who come to excel in these respects are frequently noted and valued by adult leaders in the rackets who are confronted, as are the leaders of all income-producing enterprises, with problems of the recruitment of competent personnel.

With respect to the contrasting or "unintegrated area," Kobrin makes no mention of the extent to which learning structures and opportunities for criminal careers are available. Yet his portrayal of such areas as lacking in the articulation of either conventional or criminal values suggests that the appropriate learning structures—principally the integration of offenders of different age levels—are not available. Furthermore, his depiction of adult violative activity as "unorganized" suggests that the illegal opportunity structure is severly limited. Even if youngsters were able to secure adequate preparation for criminal roles, the problem would appear to be that the social structure of such neighborhoods provides few opportunities for stable, criminal careers. For Kobrin's analysis—as well as those of Whyte and others before him—leads to the conclusion that illegal opportunity structures tend to emerge in lower-class areas only when stable patterns of accommodation and integration arise between the carriers of conventional and deviant values. Where these values remain unorganized and implicit, or where their carriers are in open conflict, opportunities for stable criminal role performance are more or less limited.[22]

Other factors may be cited which affect access to criminal roles. For example, there is a good deal of anecdotal evidence which reveals that access to the upper echelons of organized racketeering is controlled, at least in part, by ethnicity. Some ethnic groups are found disproportionately in the upper ranks and others disproportionately in the lower. From an historical perspective, as Bell has shown, this realm has been successively dominated by Irish, East-European Jews, and more recently, by Italians.[23] Various other ethnic groups have been virtually excluded or at least relegated to lower-echelon positions. Despite the fact that many rackets (especially "policy") have flourished in predominantly Negro neighborhoods, there have been but one or two Negroes who have been known to rise to the top in syndicated crime. As in the conventional world, Negroes are relegated to the more menial tasks. Moreover, access to elite positions in the rackets may be governed in part by kinship criteria, for various accounts of the blood relations among top racketeers indicate that nepotism is the general rule.[24] It has also been noted that kinship criteria sometimes govern access to stable criminal roles, as in the pickpocket.[25] And there are, of course, deep-rooted sex differentials in access to illegal means. Although women are often employed in criminal vocations—for example, thievery, confidence games, and extortion—and must be employed in others—such as prostitution—nevertheless females are excluded from many criminal activities.[26]

Of the various criteria governing access to illegitimate means, class differentials may be among the most important. The differentials noted in the preceding paragraph—age, sex, ethnicity, kinship, and the like—all pertain to criminal activity historically associated with the lower class. Most middle- or upper-class persons—even when interested in following "lower-class" criminal careers—would no doubt have difficulty in fulfilling this ambition because of inappropriate preparation. The prerequisite attitudes and skills are more easily acquired if the individual is a member of the lower class; most middle- and upper-class persons could not easily unlearn their own class culture in order to learn a new one. By the same token, access to many "white collar" criminal roles is closed to lower-class persons. Some occupations afford abundant opportunities to engage in illegitimate activity; others offer virtually none. The businessman, for example, not only has at his disposal the means to do so, but, as some studies have shown, he is under persistent pressure to employ illegitimate means, if only to maintain a competitive advantage in the market place. But for those in many other occupations, white collar modes of criminal activity are simply not an alternative.[27]

SOME IMPLICATIONS OF
CONSOLIDATED APPROACH TO
DEVIANT BEHAVIOR

It is now possible to consolidate the two sociological traditions described above. Our analysis makes it clear that these traditions are oriented to different aspects of the same problem: differentials in access to opportunity. One tradition focusses on legitimate opportunity, the other on illegitimate. By incorporating the concept of differentials in access to *illegitimate* means, the theory of anomie may be extended to include seemingly unrelated studies and theories of deviant behavior which form a part of the literature of American criminology. In this final section, we try to show how a consolidated approach might advance the understanding of both rates and types of deviant conduct. The discussion centers on the conditions of access to *both* systems of means, legitimate and illegitimate.

The Distribution of Criminal Behavior

One problem which has plagued the criminologist is the absence of adequate data on social differentials in criminal activity. Many have held that the highest crime rates are to be found in the lower social strata. Others have suggested that rates in the middle and upper classes may be much higher than is ordinarily thought. The question of the social distribution of crime remains problematic.

In the absence of adequate data, the theorist has sometimes attacked this problem by assessing the extent of pressures toward normative departures in various parts of the social structure. For example, Merton remarks that his "primary aim is to discover how some social structures exert a definite pressure upon certain persons in the society to engage in non-conforming rather than conforming conduct."[28] Having identified structural features which might be expected to generate deviance, Merton suggests the presence of a correlation between "pressures toward deviation" and "rate of deviance."

But whatever the differential rates of deviant behavior in the several social strata, and we know from many sources that the official crime statistics uniformly showing higher rates in the lower strata are far from complete or reliable, *it appears from our analysis that the greater pressures toward deviation are exerted upon the lower strata.* . . . Of those located in the lower reaches of the social structure, the culture makes incompatible demands. On the one hand they are asked to orient their behavior toward the prospect of large wealth . . . and on the other, they are largely denied effective opportunities to do so institutionally. *The consequence of this structural inconsistency is a high rate of deviant behavior.*[29]

Because of the paucity and unreliability of existing criminal statistics, there is as yet no way of knowing whether or not Merton's hypothesis is correct. Until comparative studies of crime rates are available the hypothesized correlation cannot be tested.

From a theoretical perspective, however, questions may be raised about this correlation. Would we expect, to raise the principal query, the correlation to be fixed or to vary depending on the distribution of access to illegitimate means? The three possibilities are (1) that access is distributed uniformly throughout the class structure, (2) that access varies inversely with class position, and (3) that access varies directly with class position. Specification of these possibilities permits a more precise statement of the conditions under which crime rates would be expected to vary.

If access to illegitimate means is *uniformly distributed* throughout the class structure, then the proposed correlation would probably hold—higher rates of innovating behavior would be expected in the lower class than elsewhere. Lower-class persons apparently experience greater pressures toward deviance and are less restrained by internalized prohibitions from employing illegitimate means. Assuming uniform access to such means, it would therefore be reasonable to predict higher rates of innovating behavior in the lower social strata.

If access to illegitmate means varies *inversely* with class position, then the correlation would not only hold, but might even be strengthened. For pressures toward deviance, including socialization that does not altogether discourage the use of illegitimate means, would coincide with the availability of such means.

Finally, if access varies *directly* with class position, comparative rates of illegitimate activity become difficult to forecast. The higher the class position, the less the pressure to employ illegitimate means; furthermore, internalized prohibitions are apparently more effective in higher positions. If, at the same time, opportunities to use illegitimate methods are more abundant, then these factors would be in opposition. Until the precise effects of these several variables can be more adequately measured, rates cannot be safely forecast.

The concept of differentials in availability of illegitimate means may also help to clarify questions about varying crime rates among ethnic, age, religious, and sex groups, and other social divisions. This concept, then, can be systematically employed in the effort to further our understanding of the distribution of illegitimate behavior in the social structure.

Modes of Adaptation: The Case of Retreatism

By taking into account the conditions of access to legitimate *and* illegitimate means, we can further specify the circumstances under which various modes of deviant behavior arise. This may be illustrated by the case of retreatism.[30]

As defined by Merton, retreatist adaptations include such categories of behavior as alcoholism, drug addiction, and psychotic withdrawal. These adaptations entail "escape" from the frustrations of unfulfilled aspirations by withdrawal from conventional social relationships. The processes leading to retreatism are described by Merton as follows: "[Retreatism] arises from continued failure to near the goal by legitimate measures and from an inability to use the illegitimate route because of internalized prohibitions, *this process occurring while the supreme value of the success-goal has not yet been renounced.* The conflict is resolved by abandoning *both* precipitating elements, the goals and means. The escape is complete, the conflict is eliminated and the individual is asocialized."[31]

In this view, a crucial element encouraging retreatism is

internalized constraint concerning the use of illegitimate means. But this element need not be present. Merton apparently assumed that such prohibitions are essential because, in their absence, the logic of his scheme would compel him to predict that innovating behavior would result. But the assumption that the individual uninhibited in the use of illegitimate means becomes an innovator presupposes that successful innovation is only a matter of motivation. Once the concept of differentials in access to illegitimate means is introduced, however, it becomes clear that retreatism is possible even in the absence of internalized prohibitions. For we may now ask how individuals respond when they fail in the use of *both* legitimate and illegitimate means. If illegitimate means are unavailable, if efforts at innovation fail, then retreatist adaptations may still be the consequence, and the "escape" mechanisms chosen by the defeated individual may perhaps be all the more deviant because of his "double failure."

This does not mean that retreatist adaptations cannot arise precisely as Merton suggests: namely, that the conversion from conformity to retreatism takes place in one step, without intervening adaptations. But this is only one route to retreatism. The conversion may at times entail intervening stages and intervening adaptations, particularly of an innovating type. This possibility helps to account for the fact that certain categories of individuals cited as retreatists—for example, hobos—often show extensive histories of arrests and convictions for various illegal acts. It also helps to explain retreatist adaptations among individuals who have not necessarily internalized strong restraints on the use of illegitimate means. In short, retreatist adaptations may arise with considerable frequency among those who are failures in both worlds, conventional and illegitimate alike.[32]

Future research on retreatist behavior might well examine the interval between conformity and retreatism. To what extent does the individual entertain the possibility of resorting to illegitimate means, and to what extent does he actually seek to mobilize such means? If the individual turns to innovating devices, the question of whether or not he becomes a retreatist may then depend upon the relative accessibility of illegitimate means. For although the frustrated conformist seeks a solution to status discontent by adopting such methods, there is the further problem of whether or not he possesses appropriate skills and has opportunities for their use. We suggest therefore that data be gathered on preliminary responses to status discontent—and on the individual's perceptions of the efficacy of employing illegitimate means, the content of his skills, and the objective situation of illegitimate opportunity available to him.

Respecification of the processes leading to retreatism may also help to resolve difficulties entailed in ascertaining rates of retreatism in different parts of the social structure. Although Merton does not indicate explicitly where this adaptation might be expected to arise, he specifies some of the social conditions which encourage high rates of retreatism. Thus the latter is apt to mark the behavior of downwardly mobile persons, who experience a sudden breakdown in established social relations, and such individuals as the retired, who have lost major social roles.[33]

The long-standing difficulties in forecasting differential rates of retreatism may perhaps be attributed to the assumption that retreatists have fully internalized values prohibiting the use of illegitimate means. That this prohibition especially characterizes socialization in the middle and upper classes probably calls for the prediction that retreatism occurs primarily in those classes—and that the hobohemias, "drug cultures," and the ranks of the alcoholics are populated primarily by individuals from the upper reaches of society. It would appear from various accounts of hobohemia and skid row, however, that many of these persons are the products of slum life, and, furthermore, that their behavior is not necessarily controlled by values which preclude resort to illegitimate means. But once it is recognized that retreatism may arise in response to limitations on both systems of means, the difficulty of locating this adaptation is lessened, if not resolved. Thus retreatist behavior may vary with the particular process by which it is generated. The process described by Merton may be somewhat more characteristic of higher positions in the social structure where rule-oriented socialization is typical, while in the lower strata retreatism may tend more often to be the consequence of unsuccessful attempts at innovation.

SUMMARY

This paper attempts to identify and to define the concept of differential opportunity structures. It has been suggested that this concept helps to extend the developing theory of social structure and anomie. Furthermore, by linking propositions regarding the accessibility of *both* legitimate and illegitimate opportunity structures, a basis is provided for consolidating various major traditions of sociological thought on nonconformity. The concept of differential systems of opportunity and of variations in access to them, it is hoped, will suggest new possibilities for research on the relationship between social structure and deviant behavior.

CRITERIA OF STATUS
AMONG STREET GROUPS

Solomon Kobrin, Joseph Puntil, and Emil Peluso

AMONG major sociological theories advanced in the past decade to account for the emergence, persistence, location in the social structure, and normative content of subcultural delinquency, those of Cohen[1] and Cloward and Ohlin[2] probably have been most fruitful. On the formal side their principal virtue is their use of a soundly functional perspective and

This article previously appeared in the *Journal of Research in Crime and Delinquency,* Vol. 4 (January, 1967).

The assistance of Kenneth I. Howard and Henry D. McKay of the Institute for Juvenile Research in the analysis of the data of this study is gratefully acknowledged.

the parsimony with which the same limited set of factors is utilized to explain not only the location in the social structure of subcultural delinquency, but variations in its normative content as well.

Both the Cohen and the Cloward and Ohlin theories represent delinquent norms as a group elaborated response to problems which lower class boys share by virtue of their social class position. The problems are held to arise from the disjuncture between societal expectations of conventional forms of success and the training and resources required to equip lower class boys to meet such expectations. In Cohen's view the discrepancy leads to their depreciation at the hands of such middle class socializing agents as school teachers.[3] This experience, perceived as an attack on their self esteem, creates for the boys a shared need for defense which is met by a counterattack on middle class virtues, including law observance. The delinquency becomes prescriptive as, in time, it comes to constitute a basis of status in boys' groups, and therefore the grounds for the emergence of a subculture.

While Cloward and Ohlin accept Cohen's account of the manner in which a common solution of a shared problem leads to the formation of a delinquent subculture, they differ with him on the nature of the problem. This they see as resulting from the fact of reduced legitimate opportunity for lower class youth to achieve the common success goals of the wider culture. Using a comprehensive framework of theory for the analysis of deviant conduct, they characterize delinquent norms as a product of the collective withdrawal of legitimacy from the legal norms in the interest of solving the problem of goal frustration.[4] Thus, while Cohen views a drive for the restoration of self esteem as the dynamic force underlying the development of delinquent norms, for Cloward and Ohlin the drive to achieve the success goals of the culture powers the delinquent subculture.

Each theory accordingly offers a separate set of predictions respecting the types of delinquent subcultures which may be expected to develop in lower class urban communities. The Cohen theory predicts a generic type of "parent" delinquent subculture whose norms center on a concern with the prob-

reciated status. Variants of the subculture are
ed as an outcome of marginal differentiation and
zation based on the exploitation of relatively more
ble sources of status as adolescent groups advance in
. This process occasionally produces a semiprofessional
left variant, a conflict variant, or a drug using variant of
the delinquent subculture. However, the theory predicts that
the most common and expectable type is the parent subculture, whose major norm prescribes versatility respecting
various forms of delinquency.[5]

On the other hand, Cloward and Ohlin assert that while
all delinquent subcultures come into existence because of
limited access to *legitimate* opportunity, specific types of
delinquent subcultures result from variation in the extent
to which lower class boys have access to *illegitimate* opportunity. Thus, in communities characterized by politically protected organized crime there exists the fullest access to illegitimate opportunity, and the *criminal* type of delinquent
subculture predominates. In lower class communities marked
by the absence of both illegitimate and legitimate opportunity two other types of delinquent subculture are expected
to occur. The *conflict* type of street gang includes those boys
who, frustrated in their aspirations for a high money income,
and without effective access to illegitimate opportunity, shift
their status goals to prowess as street warriors. The *retreatist*
type of gang includes boys for whom illegitimate opportunity
is similarly unavailable. But unable to use violence because
of subjective inhibition, they resort to drug use as they seek
status in groups for which the cultivation of inner experience
constitutes a dominant value.[6]

Although the two are commonly contrasted as "status"
and "opportunity" theories respectively, the latter is in effect
a "status" theory as well, although radically different from
Cohen's. Both generally and specifically, the opportunity concept has reference to the net chances differentially available
to boys to win what they perceive to be satisfactory status.
However, as the Cloward and Ohlin typology of delinquent
subculture suggests, essential to the theory as well is the
concept of shifting status goals, whereby failure to gain an

initially preferred goal, under conditions specified in the theory, may result in its replacement by an alternative status goal. Each concept, opportunity and status goal, operates in the theory as a genuine variable. The Cloward and Ohlin explanation of the emergence of the delinquent subculture assumes a relative fixity of the status goal as determined by the general culture for a limited proportion of lower class boys, with the substitution of illegitimate for legitimate means in the effort to attain it. However, in facing the fact of limited availability of illegitimate as well as of legitimate opportunity, Cloward and Ohlin find that they must invoke variation in status goals as well as in types of opportunity in order to account for variety in the forms of the delinquent subculture. In so doing they open the way to a more general consideration of the dynamics of status as an important determinant of variation in delinquent subcultures.

In postulating the predominant form of the delinquent subculture in any given lower class community as a function of access to illegitimate opportunity, the Cloward and Ohlin theory also implicitly predicts the expectable order of prestige among street gangs exhibiting the delinquent styles characterizing variants of the subculture in communities affording specifiable degrees of access to such opportunity. The study reported here hypothesized that in communities in which illegitimate opportunity was relatively available those street gangs whose norms conformed most closely to the criminal variant of the delinquent subculture would enjoy the highest prestige. However, since the Cloward and Ohlin theory also postulates the shifting of status goals as a consequence of inability to attain those initially preferred, the study undertook in addition to ascertain, within the limits of the available data, the character of interaction between status goals and the opportunity to achieve them under conditions of accessible but limited legitimate as well as illegitimate opportunity.

THE COMMUNITY

The community selected for the investigation of these matters qualified on a number of grounds. As an inner-city low income community it had remained an area of first settlement for virtually all of the immigrant groups that came to the midwest metropolis in which it was located. During the four decades preceding the study the area's population was predominantly Italian in ethnic origin, and constituted the cultural base as well as the bastion of its political power in the city. In terms of the theory of cultural assimilation by which Cloward and Ohlin account for variation in the availability of illegitimate opportunity, the community was passing from the second to the third stage at the time of the study.[7] There had existed for some time a firmly established integration of the legitimate and illegitimate elements of the community, manifested in a locally acknowledged alliance between the political leadership and that of the city's gambling, vice, and other rackets. The process of out-migration by those who had achieved higher socioeconomic status by either the legitimate or illegitimate route was slowly under way, and new ethnic groups, principally Mexican and Negro, were beginning to move in.

METHOD OF STUDY

Four residents of the community employed by a locally sponsored community improvement and delinquency prevention program[8] as organizers and detached street gang workers furnished a complete census of all street gangs known to them by name and membership. Seventeen such groups were identified, ten with members ranging in age from fifteen to seventeen, and seven in the eighteen to twenty-five year group. Some groups included a few members whose ages fell above or below the typical range for their groups.

Because the activity pattern of street groups often remain amorphous and uncrystallized during the early adolescent years, the decision was made to focus the analysis on the seven groups in the eighteen to twenty-five age range. One of these groups was dropped from the analysis as it became evident that it was perceived with sharply reduced clarity by the subsequently invoked panel of participant informants. The remaining six were then viewed as constituting a network of mutually known and interacting groups functioning in a commonly perceived community context.

Four types of data respecting the network of older adolescent street groups were obtained from three panels of informants, two of which overlapped marginally in membership. The panel of four community agency staff members which had provided the initial census of street groups, interviewed together and required to arrive at a consensus, furnished a preliminary ranking of the prestige of the six groups and a description of their activity patterns, including a specification of their delinquent style, if applicable. They were then pressed to justify their rankings by making explicit the status criteria they had employed. Seven criteria were defined by the panel, four of which represented achieved status and three ascribed status. The second panel consisted of two core members of each of the six groups, each selected for his acknowledged leadership position in his own group, his knowledgeability concerning the street world of the community, and his articulateness. Interviewed separately and in random order, the twelve members of this panel independently ranked the six groups in order of prestige and furnished an independent description of the activity pattern of each.[9] The four criteria of achieved status defined by the first panel were then presented, each in the form of a simple three-point scale, and the informant requested to rate each group on each criterion, including his own.

The ratings of the groups on the ascribed criteria required the use of a third panel competent to make such judgments. The four judges constituting this panel were all life-long adult residents of the community. Two were the same staff members of the locally sponsored youth welfare organization referred to above; a third was a recently resigned staff member with qualifications similar to those of the first two. The fourth was a long time functionary of the monolithic political organization of the community whose business it was to muster out the vote at election time and to participate in decisions respecting the distribution of patronage.

This rather complex data generating procedure may be summarized in the following way: (1) The first panel of informants, consisting of four staff members of a locally sponsored youth welfare organization, described the activity patterns of the six groups, placed them in rank order of prestige, and defined the criteria of status on which they based their rankings. (2) The second panel, consisting of twelve group members, also described the activity patterns of the groups, placed them in rank order of prestige, and rated each group on the four criteria of achieved status defined by the first panel. (3) A third panel of qualified judges rated the groups on three criteria of ascribed status.

FINDINGS

Group Patterns

Four of the six groups in the network were found to possess a readily identifiable pattern of delinquency. The other two, although consistently characterized by informants as nondelinquent, were regarded as falling within the street group network. Both were described as organized around "social" interests such as maintaining clubrooms, dating, and promoting social dances. However, they differed from one another in the emphasis of their interests and in the pattern of their activities. Further, they not only differed widely in their prestige rank score but, as will be seen, in the status elements on which their prestige rested.

Each of the four delinquent groups exhibited a distinctive delinquent style, summarized in the following brief descriptions.

1. *Sophisticated delinquents.* The delinquent style of this group was characterized by infrequent but relatively lucrative theft. They were cautious in the planning and execution of their delinquencies, taking pains to avoid needless risk. They were highly knowledgeable regarding channels for the disposal of stolen goods and the resources available for protection in the event of detection. They characteristically included a Mexican or other low status boy on their "jobs" as a potential "fall guy" in case of later difficulty with the law. They were disdainful of delinquent activity which was petty or

which attracted undue attention. This group occasionally victimized persons who were without the power and status to defend themselves within their own community. For example, they once stole several hundred dollars in the burglary of a local store, whose proprietor, knowing the perpetrators and their family connections, declined to report the crime to the police. Other elements of their activity pattern included participation in sports, in which they consistently demonstrated their commitment to competitive success at any price by resorting to techniques of psychological warfare to overcome rivals. Informants pictured them as the commonly recognized elite group of the local street world. They came from well-connected families, had "plenty of clout," commanded good jobs through politics and the rackets when they worked, were well supplied with money, and were the first in their age group to own new automobiles. They were described as "just as tough as anybody else," but not inclined to go out of their way to prove it.

2. *Conspicuous delinquents.* The principal feature of the style of this group was a striving for high visibility in their delinquent acts. This they achieved principally through conflict: they were the local specialists in the community's occasional episodes of gang fighting. Their reputation among their peers rested solely on their accomplishments as fighters. This brought them a certain notoriety among teen-age gangs in distant sections of the metropolitan area, for which they were admired by their local peers. They did not, however, confine themselves to conflict, but engaged with at least equal consistency in property crimes. These included strong arm robbery as well as burglary. The group was characterized by swagger, assaultiveness, and recklessness. As one informant put it, "They didn't care what they did as long as it was a big deal." Other characteristics included a high proportion of lower status Mexican boys in their membership, residence in the local public housing project, sharp fluctuation in the frequency of activity involving the entire group, and an almost total disinterest in sports.

3. *Occupational delinquents.* The delinquent style of this group was defined by a high frequency of petty theft. In per-

sistence and regularity delinquent activity took on a routine rather than episodic character. The group was active during the night and slept days, often in movie houses or abandoned automobiles. They were described as "car crazy" and much of their theft was directed to the stripping and stealing of automobiles. They were known to "accept orders" for auto accessories placed by community residents. They did not, however, confine themselves to this type of theft, but stole anything which could be converted into cash. They were fully knowledgeable concerning local channels for protection when detected, and although they made extensive use of the "fix" they were relatively unsuccessful in staying the hand of the law. Two reasons were cited for this failure: local sources of protection would intercede for them for cash only, and they were chronically short of cash; and they had, as one informant put it, "worn out their welcome," i.e., they had been arrested and prosecuted so frequently that intervention in their behalf had become difficult even with cash payment. Other characteristics included a small and fluctuating membership made up principally of boys from the favored Italian group, but with a small admixture of Mexican boys; the illusion that their delinquent activities were effectively concealed from residents; and a disinterest in sports and in "social" activity. Their status in the community was suggested by the contemptuous remark of one adult informant: "Oh, them! They're just a bunch of thieves!"

   4. *Versatile delinquents.* As the designation suggests, the style of delinquency of this group was not unified around a clearly identifiable pattern. They exhibited elements of all three of the delinquent styles already described. Instances of sophisticated delinquency cited by informants characterized certain cliques within the groups, as did those of the conspicuous and occupational variety. Some of the information suggested that a few individuals had also experimented with drug use, although there was no evidence of resulting addiction. The picture presented provoked skepticism as to whether this was a group at all. But probing disclosed evidence that its membership was stable, that it had persisted through time,

and that its identity as a group was meaningful to themselves and to others.

5. *Unconventional nondelinquents.* This group was oriented to a "playboy" pattern. They maintained an attractive clubroom in which they spent a great deal of time "drinking and fooling with girls." Informants were somewhat impressed with the fact that they dated girls from the suburban communities to which the more successful and affluent residents of the community had been moving. They seemed even more impressed, however, with their possession of what one informant termed "shady power," by which he meant power whose sources were not clearly discernible to local residents. The members, all Italian in ethnic extraction, were reputed to have "good" political jobs deriving from their ties to "shady power."

6. *Respectable nondelinquents.* This group was uniformly judged to be the best organized in the entire network. They were described unpatronizingly as "respectable kids." There was, however, a touch of disdain in the mild respect accorded them, expressed in one informant's characterization of them as "do nothing kids." Moreover, they were derided for their occasional outbursts of honest civic zeal, as on the occasion when they took up a collection for Red Cross in the neighborhood. They were also described as the "best educated kids" in the neighborhood since it was customary for the members of the group to finish high school. They were devoted to sports, though this interest, in contrast to that of the sophisticated delinquents, lay in the enjoyment of play rather than in vanquishing opponents. Social activities were centered in the local parish church where they were permitted to participate in the communion service wearing their club jackets, and given clubroom space where they ran "closed" dances to which only those with invitations were admitted. As a club they were sponsored by a group which informants could identify only by their patronage of an ice cream parlor fronting for a bookie joint. Italian in ethnic background, the fathers of these boys were perceived by informants as holding tenured civil service jobs in local government, and consequently as

enjoying some independence from the control of local political leaders.

Prestige Rank of Groups

As noted, each of the twelve group member informants was asked, individually, to rank order each group, including his own, in what he perceived to be the local prestige hierarchy. A rank score for each group was then calculated, based on the simple procedure of multiplying the cumulated number of choices for each rank position by the reverse of its ordinal number, so that the first position received a weight of six, the second position a weight of five, etc.

TABLE 1.   *Group Prestige as Ranked by Member Informants*

Group	1st (6)	2nd (5)	3rd (4)	4th (3)	5th (2)	6th (1)	Rank Score
Sophisticated delinquents	10	2					70
Conspicuous delinquents	1	9	1	1			58
Unconventional nondelinquents		1	8	1	2		44
Versatile delinquents			2	5	3	2	31
Occupational delinquents	1		1	2	2	6	26
Respectable nondelinquents				3	5	4	23

NOTE: Average rank correlation between all pairs of raters: .680.

As in evident in Table 1, agreement respecting rank order, although expectedly not uniform, was sufficiently consistent to sustain the assumption that the six groups constituted a network unified around consensus concerning prestige rank. The high average correlation (.68) between all pairs of raters,

TABLE 2. *Prestige Rating of Own Group by Two
Raters from Each*

Prestige Rank	Group	Rater	1st	2nd	3rd	4th	5th	6th
1	Sophisticated delinquents	1	x					
		2	x					
2	Conspicuous delinquents	1		x				
		2		x				
3	Unconventional nondelinquents	1			x			
		2			x			
4	Versatile delinquents	1			x			
		2			x			
5	Occupational delinquents	1	x					
		2					x	
6	Respectable nondelinquents	1					x	
		2					x	

and the fact that the modal category for virtually each group falls on the diagonal, reflect the reality of a status order among the groups making up the network. There is, of course, the further critical question whether consensus regarding prestige rank stops, so to speak, at one's own doorstep. The final reality of a status order is its acceptance by participants in the form of deference to those they acknowledge as their superiors. If, for example, the raters from each group had consistently rated their own group first in prestige, the assertion that the network of groups in the neighborhood constituted a status order would be seriously compromised. As may be seen in Table 2, however, this was not in general the case, even though there is evidence of uncertainty in the middle of the array, and a stubborn refusal of the representatives of the groups lowest in prestige to acknowledge their ignominy in occupying the bottom position.

Criteria of Status

The primary interest in the group ranking operation performed by the local agency staff panel was not in their ratings but in the reasons they adduced for them. Interviewers present during the conferences in which the judgments of the four raters were advanced and defended noted that seven criteria of status were consistently and systematically invoked. These were fighting ability, organizational competence, sports competence, reputation in the sense of notoriety, ethnicity, residential location, and family power. Each appeared to be conceived of as an aspect of public image and was treated in a global manner as an attribute of the entire group, with interindividual variation in each attribute ignored. In treating the information so generated the assumption is made that the primary orientation of the adolescent group is to forms of achieved status, reflecting an equalitarian bias,[10] and a complementary tendency to call into question the legitimacy of the ascriptive forms of status more frequently stressed by adults.[11] It was for this reason, as noted above, that a separate panel of adult judges, familiar with the street life of the neighborhood, was used to rank the groups on ascriptive status criteria.

TABLE 3. Status Item Definitions and Score Values of Position on Rating Scale

Position on Rating Scale	Score Value	Ascribed Status Items				Achieved Status Items		
		Ethnic Identity	Family Power	Residential Location	Fighting Ability	Reputation	Org. Competence	Sports Competence
High	3	Italian only	Personal or kin involvement in political organization	Center of community: "Italian" streets	Aggressive posture: "looking for fights"	Known by name and "rep" in distant communities	Unity and discipline in all of group's interests	Ability to win despite athletic inferiority
Intermediate	2	Italian with small admixture of Mexican	No direct involvement, loyal to political organization	Streets occupied by both Italian and Mexican families	Capable of holding own when challenged	Known in adjacent communities	Unified only in episodes of delinquency	Technical competence with interest in recreational aspects
Low	1	Predominantly Mexican	No links to politics or rackets	Public housing project and "Mexican" streets at periphery of community	Avoid combat, cannot stand up to challenge	Known only in home community	Not unified in any of group's interests	Total disinterest and incompetence in sports

Examination of the list of criteria reveals that ethnicity, residential location, and family power constitute ascribed status characteristics, with the remaining four representing status of the achieved variety. As shown in Table 3, the seven criteria of status were defined on the basis of cues offered by the agency staff panel in the course of their conferences with interviewers. Their discussion also suggested that these status criteria were perceived and treated as varying across a three-point scale. Achieved status items were, therefore, presented to the twelve raters making up the street group panel, who were requested to assign a high (3), intermediate (2), or low (1) rating to each group on each of the four achieved status criteria. As noted above, the groups were rated on the three ascribed status criteria by a panel with special competence for the task.

Ratings on Status Criteria

Each status criterion for each group was given a total score based on the summed scores across raters, with total scores for each group constituting the basis for its rank ordering with respect to the given item. As in the case of the prestige ranking operation, a high degree of agreement existed among the judges (Tables 4 and 5), providing further evidence that the network of groups constituted a single status universe. The lowered reliability for ratings of family power may be attributed to the generally privileged nature of such information except for families having high public visibility in the community.

The findings respecting ratings on status criteria are probably best expressed in the form of a quasi-impressionistic status profile (Table 6), adequate to define gross but fundamental differences in the pattern of status elements related to the prestige rank of each group; and by a comparison of the rank of each group on each status criterion with its prestige rank (Table 7), and with its rank on both achieved and ascribed status.[12] The status profile was devised by trichotomizing the raw numerical score ranges and assigning each group on each item to a high, intermediate, or low category according to its raw score.

TABLE 4. *Achieved Status Scores*[a]

Group	1. Fighting Ability 3	2	1	Total
Conspicuous	11	1	0	35
Versatile	4	8	0	28
Sophisticated	3	9	0	27
Occupational	2	8	2	24
Unconventional	1	9	2	23
Respectable	0	7	5	19

Reliability: .92[b]

Group	2. Reputation 3	2	1	Total
Conspicuous	12	0	0	36
Unconventional	7	0	5	26
Sophisticated	6	0	6	24
Respectable	2	0	10	16
Occupational	1	0	11	14
Versatile	0	0	12	12

Reliability: .88

Group	3. Organizational Competence 3	2	1	Total
Respectable	11	1	0	35
Unconventional	9	3	0	33
Sophisticated	7	5	0	31
Versatile	2	9	1	25
Occupational	0	10	2	22
Conspicuous	1	5	6	19

Reliability: .94

Group	4. Sports Competence 3	2	1	Total
Sophisticated	11	1	0	35
Unconventional	3	9	0	27
Versatile	1	9	2	23
Respectable	0	9	3	21
Conspicuous	1	2	9	16
Occupational	0	4	8	16

Reliability: .84

[a]Scoring key: high, 3; intermediate, 2; low, 1.
[b]"Variance Form" reliability used throughout. Cf. R. C. Tryon, "Reliability and Behavior Domain Validity: Reformulation and Historical Critique," *Psychological Bulletin*, Vol. 54 (1957), 229–249.

TABLE 5. *Ascribed Status Scores*[a]

Group	1. Ethnic Identity			
	3	2	1	Total
Sophisticated	4	0	0	12
Respectable	4	0	0	12
Unconventional	2	2	0	10
Versatile	2	2	0	10
Occupational	1	3	0	9
Conspicuous	0	4	0	8

Reliability: .80

Group	2. Residential Location			
	3	2	1	Total
Sophisticated	4	0	0	12
Respectable	4	0	0	12
Unconventional	3	1	0	11
Occupational	3	1	0	11
Versatile	2	1	1	9
Conspicuous	0	1	3	5

Reliability: .89

Group	3. Family Power			
	3	2	1	Total
Sophisticated	4	0	0	12
Unconventional	1	3	0	9
Respectable	0	4	0	8
Versatile	1	1	2	7
Conspicuous	0	2	2	6
Occupational	0	0	4	4

Reliability: .65

[a]Methods for scoring and for measuring reliability are the same as those used in Table 4.

The two high prestige groups, the sophisticated delinquents and the conspicuous delinquents, contrast sharply in the kinds of status elements associated with their prestige rank. The former are high in all three of the ascribed status criteria, in but two of the four achieved status criteria, and intermediate

TABLE 6. Group Profiles of Prestige, Achieved Status and Ascribed Status

Ranked Items	Sophisticated Delinquents			Conspicuous Delinquents			Unconventional Non-delinquents			Versatile Delinquents			Occupational Delinquents			Respectable Non-delinquents		
	Hi	Int	Lo	Hi	Int	Lo	Hi	Int	Lo	Hi	Int	Lo	Hi	Int	Lo	Hi	Int	Lo
Prestige	X			X				X				X			X			X
Achieved status	X			X			X					X			X		X	
Fighting ability		X		X					X	X					X			X
Reputation		X		X				X				X			X			X
Org. competence	X					X	X				X				X	X		
Spts. competence	X					X		X			X				X			X
Ascribed status	X					X		X			X				X	X		
Ethnic identity	X					X		X			X				X	X		
Res. location	X					X	X				X		X			X		
Family power	X					X		X			X				X		X	

TABLE 7. *Rank Position of Groups by Prestige, Achieved Status and Ascribed Status*

Ranked Items	Soph. Dels.	Conspic. Dels.	Unconven. Nondels.	Vers. Dels.	Occu. Dels.	Resp. Nondels.
Prestige	1.0	2.0	3.0	4.0	5.0	6.0
Achieved status	1.0	3.0	2.0	5.0	6.0	4.0
Fighting ability	3.0	1.0	5.0	2.0	4.0	6.0
Reputation	3.0	1.0	2.0	6.0	5.0	4.0
Org. competence	3.0	6.0	2.0	4.0	5.0	1.0
Sports competence	1.0	5.5	2.0	3.0	5.5	4.0
Ascribed status	1.0	6.0	3.0	4.0	5.0	2.0
Ethnic identity	1.5	6.0	3.5	3.5	5.0	1.5
Residential location	1.5	6.0	3.5	5.0	3.5	1.5
Family power	1.0	5.0	2.0	4.0	6.0	3.0

in the other two. Although they also occupy the high sector in street prestige, the conspicuous delinquents are low in every criterion of status but two: fighting ability and reputation.

The status profile of the occupational delinquents, low in street prestige, is similar to that of the conspicuous delinquents in some important respects, although here, again, the contrasts are striking. Both score in the lower third of the range on the ascribed status items, with the exception of residential location for the occupational delinquent. However, the latter differ sharply from the conspicuous delinquents in falling in the lowest sector of the score range on every item of achieved status.

The contrast between the profiles of the occupational and the sophisticated delinquents is, with the exception of one item, complete. The former are lowest in virtually every category, the latter highest. The item forming the exception to the general picture of extreme contrast is that of residential location, in which the two groups are identical.

The group representing the versatile style of delinquency is characterized by a profile similar to those of the other three delinquent groups only with respect to its relative consistency. The consistency lies, however, in the uniformly intermediate position it occupies on all criteria of status with the exception of reputation, where it scores in the lowest third of the range.

Both nondelinquent groups differ from the four delinquent groups in presenting status profiles of marked irregularity. The unconventional nondelinquents, the "playboy" group, intermediate in street prestige, are intermediate in four of the seven status criteria. They were rated low in fighting ability, but high in organizational competence and residential location. On the other hand, the respectable nondelinquents, low in street prestige, were seen as high or intermediate in all of the ascribed status items. In achieved status they scored low in every category but organizational competence.

The contrasts and similarities in the patterns of status elements associated with the prestige ranking of the groups is evident in slightly more precise form in the status rank data of Table 7. The holders of top prestige rank, the sophisticated delinquents, and those in second place, the conspicuous delinquents, exhibit an interesting contrast in the kinds of status points they can afford to "give away" without thereby suffering serious loss in prestige rank. The sophisticated delinquents, in first place or tied for first place on all of the ascribed status items, rank third in three of the achieved items: fighting ability, reputation, and organizational competence. The conspicuous delinquents, on the other hand, maintain their second position in prestige rank despite their occupancy of last or next to last place on five of the seven status criteria. They are lowest on all the ascribed items and on two of the four achieved items, but occupy the first rank in fighting ability and reputation.

No such "trade off" of status points characterizes the occupational delinquents. They hold positions on all status items similar or adjacent to their prestige rank with the single exception, already noted, of rank in residential location, in which they are tied for third place with the unconventional nondelinquents. The prestige position of the versatile delinquents also seems concordant with position on all status items except reputation, in which they occupy last place, and fighting ability, where they occupy second place.

The two nondelinquent groups exhibit interesting differences in the distribution of their ranks across status items. The prestige rank of the unconventional group accords closely with its rank on individual status items, with the sole exception of fighting ability, in which they rank fifth. The respectables, however, last in prestige, are in first place or tied for first place in three of the seven status criteria, and rank higher in a fourth, family power, than both the conspicuous and the occupational delinquents. Indeed, the only status items in which their ranks match or approach their bottom (sixth) position in prestige rank are fighting ability (sixth), reputation (fourth), and sports competence (fourth).

The rank order correlations presented in Table 8 may suggest in more summary fashion the possible character of the relationships among the ranked items. Of particular interest is the fact that while the correlation between prestige and achieved status is expectedly high (.77), that between fight-

TABLE 8. Matrix of Intercorrelations Among Ranked Items (Rho)

Ranked Items	Achieved Status	Ascribed Status	Ethnic Identity	Residential Location	Family Power	Fighting Ability	Reputation	Organizational Competence	Sports Competence
Prestige	.09	.77	-.06	-.14	.43	.60	.60	-.31	.47
Ascribed status	.54		.97	.89	.89	-.54	-.09	.86	.81
Achieved status			.40	.31	.83	.03	.71	.31	.70
Ethnic identity				.87	.80	-.49	-.20	.86	.73
Residential location					.63	-.69	-.11	.77	.51
Family power						-.31	.26	.71	.93
Fighting ability							.14	-.83	-.16
Reputation								-.08	.04
Organizational competence									.59

ing ability and achieved status is unexpectedly low (.03). Achieved status rank is highly and positively related to rank on family power (.83), reputation (.71), and sports competence (.70). Achieved status has, however, a low (.31) association with rank on organizational competence, and a virtually nonexistent one with rank on fighting ability (.03). Thus, rank on achieved status is highly and positively associated with rank on only two of the four achieved status items, and betrays an even higher positive association with rank on family power.

That rank on ascribed status is highly and positively associated with rank on all three of the ascribed status items is not unexpected. It is striking, however, that the ascribed status ranking of the groups is also highly and positively associated with ranking on two of the achieved status criteria, organizational competence (.86) and sports competence (.81), but moderately negatively correlated (−.54) with fighting ability. Street prestige appears in general to be more closely associated with achievement than with ascription, with the single exception of organizational competence.[13]

The final observation respecting these data is based on an assumption that the criteria of achieved status fall into two distinguishable categories. Fighting ability and reputation may be regarded as oriented to distinctively adolescent values; organizational and sports competence as oriented to adult values. There can be little question with regard to the former two. Organizational competence seems clearly to reflect the adult interest in promoting in youth the capacity for planning and for rational action sustained over relatively long periods of time. Sports competence, while distinctively an area of primary adolescent interest and activity, carries the sanction and support, sometimes with immoderate enthusiasm, of the adult segment of the community.[14] At worst, little objection is customarily voiced regarding the preoccupation of youth with competitive sports.

When scores on fighting ability and reputation are averaged to obtain a single score for achieved status oriented to adolescent values, and a similar computation made for organizational and sports competence to obtain the score for achieved

TABLE 9. *Average Scores on Two Categories of Achieved Status Criteria by Ascribed Rank of Four Delinquent Groups*

Delinquent Group	Ascribed Status Rank	Value Orientation of Achieved Status Criteria	
		Adolescent (Fighting Ability and Reputation)	Adult (Organizational and Sports Competence)
Sophisticated	1	25.5	33.0
Versatile	2	20.0	24.0
Occupational	3	19.0	19.0
Conspicuous	4	35.5	17.5

TABLE 10. *Per Cent Distribution of Achieved Status Scores by Ascribed Status Rank of Four Delinquent Groups*

Delinquent Group	Ascribed Status Rank	Fighting Ability A	Reputation B	Per Cent of Total Score A + B	Organizational Competence C	Sports Competence D	Per Cent of Total Score C + D	Total Score	Per Cent
Sophisticated	1	27	24	43.6	31	35	56.4	117	100.0
Versatile	2	28	12	45.5	25	23	54.5	88	100.0
Occupational	3	24	14	50.0	22	16	50.0	76	100.0
Conspicuous	4	35	36	67.0	19	16	33.0	106	100.0

status oriented to adult values, the array of
relation to ascribed status rank for the four del
exhibits a suggestive pattern. As shown in T:
ranking group on ascribed status, the sophi
quents, have a distinctly higher score on adult
on adolescent oriented achievement criteria. The group ranking lowest on ascribed status, the conspicuous delinquents,
show a contrasting distribution: their score on adolescent
oriented criteria of achievement is almost twice as high as
their score on adult oriented criteria. Also evident is a de-
clining score on adult oriented achievement criteria in association with lowered ascriptive rank. The same is true for
adolescent oriented achievement, with a dramatic soaring of
the score in this area for the conspicuous delinquents, holding the lowest ascriptive status rank among the four delinquent groups.

The relationship of ascriptive status to the two types of
achieved status is also apparent when, as shown in Table 10,
the proportion of the total achieved status score for each
group assignable to adolescent and adult oriented values is
viewed in relation to ascribed status rank. The former varies
inversely with ascribed status rank; the latter directly.

DISCUSSION

The findings of the investigation confirm the prediction
implied by the Cloward and Ohlin theory that in a community
of the type here described, highest prestige among adolescent
street groups would be accorded the group whose norms conform most closely to the criminal variant of the delinquent
subculture, in this case the sophisticated delinquents. As
has been indicated, the theory is taken as asserting that the
predominant form of the delinquent subculture in any given
lower class community may be expected to reflect the stage
of cultural assimilation of its principal population group.
Since mixed forms may be encountered empirically, in which
the stage marked by a stable integration of criminal and conventional elements of the community is giving way to the
stage marked by the invasion of a new population group not

yet capable of reproducing this pattern, the conflict variant
of the subculture may be expected to occur simultaneously.
Hence, the existence in the community investigated of a
street gang, the conspicuous delinquents, whose style of delinquency was in fact that of the conflict group, is also taken
as confirmation of the Cloward and Ohlin theory. More precisely, in view of the continuing predominance of the old
ethnic group in the community's power structure, the theory
would also predict that the sophisticated delinquents would
outrank the conspicuous delinquents in street prestige, as was
found.

A further implication of the theory confirmed by the findings concerns its assertion of the integration of criminal and
conventional elements as a key feature of communities of the
type here involved. The inclusion in the mutually recognized
and interacting set of older street groups, sharing a common
status universe, of two nondelinquent groups is taken as representing a reflection in the adolescent world of the realities
of the local adult society. Moreover, the placement of the two
groups in the prestige hierarchy seems to distinguish in an
exemplary way an expected difference between a nondelinquent group with ties to the politics-rackets power complex
(the unconventional nondelinquents) and a nondelinquent
group predominantly oriented to the legitimate opportunity
structure (the respectable nondelinquents). The unconventional nondelinquents outranked in prestige not only the respectable nondelinquents, but two delinquent groups as well.
Further, informants' references to their access to "shady
power," power having low local visibility, seems to specify
ties to the more mobile and successful segment of the community's organized criminal element, and therefore involvement in the main direction of development in organized
crime: its transformation from small scale, locally controlled
activity to large scale rationally organized and administered
enterprise.[15]

There remain, however, two delinquent groups in the network, the occupational and versatile delinquents, whose
normative patterns include elements not fully predicted by
opportunity theory.

By all reasonable behavioral indexes the occupational delinquents exhibited a criminal pattern of delinquency within the meaning of the term as used in opportunity theory. Yet the close integration across age grades which the theory specifies as an essential condition for the emergence of the pattern is absent. By contrast, the pattern of the sophisticated delinquents seems solidly founded on precisely such ties, largely within a kinship framework. The theory seems not to have taken into account the possibility of an adolescent orientation to an adult reference group, the politics-rackets elite of the local society, with which there is no effective contact. That this may well have been the case for the occupational delinquents is suggested by a single feature of the group's ascriptive position: residential location. A number of the members of this relatively small group lived on the streets occupied by the Italian ethnic group, and were familiar with the personnel and procedures by which the machinery of enforcement and prosecution could be tempered.

However, as their family power rank indicates, and as confirmed by informants' descriptions of their families as "poor," they were accorded scant consideration from those who controlled local resources of political influence. These features of their situation probably precluded realistic access to illegitimate opportunity; opportunity theory would therefore predict a conflict pattern for this group as for the conspicuous delinquents, whose access to illegitimate opportunity was similarly restricted. The most salient difference between the two groups seems to lie in the existence, for the occupational delinquents, of *grounds for identification with the power elite of the neighborhood,* on the basis of a partial sharing of residential location.

Theories of reference group behavior suggest, among other things, that the choice of a reference group is frequently determined by the presence of some such common element of status, probably ascriptive status.[16] Furthermore, the excesses of petty theft to which the occupational delinquents were addicted, perceived in the community as a violation of elementary canons of judgment and taste, strongly suggest the parallel of gaucherie among the new rich with whom they share orientation to reference groups in which they have no membership. Both nouveau riche and our occupational delinquents, it is suggested, are dependent, for this reason, on inaccurate perceptions of norms they seek to incorporate.

These considerations imply a need for a somewhat fuller utilization of reference group theory as a means of unifying opportunity and status interpretations of delinquent subcultures. Status goals are, after all, largely determined by the kinds of reference groups to which an orientation is formed; adults as well as peers are included among the reference groups to which adolescents may be oriented; reference groups may or may not also constitute membership groups; and the location in specifiable segments of the social structure of any defined population is likely to determine the range of alternative reference groups to which access exists.[17] Insofar as opportunity theory is concerned with explaining variation in delinquent subcultures it must, as noted earlier, take into account shifts in status goals incident to achievement failure. To explain such shifts it is necessary to explain choice of reference group.[18]

As to the group exemplifying the versatile delinquent pattern, it may well be that it is in fact predicted by the provision in the Cloward and Ohlin theory for mixed forms of the delinquent subculture during transitional phases of the assimilation cycle. However, an unresolved issue concerns the question of whether the mixing of forms of the subculture is an attribute of the lower class community or of its delinquent groups. It seems most likely that in older adolescent groups, more homogeneous and stable in membership than younger groups, versatility in delinquent style reflects the diversity to be expected during periods of transition to new stages of assimilation on the part of lower class populations. Thus, while versatility in delinquency seems to accord with the observed facts, its foundations are not necessarily restricted to those postulated by Cohen. The versatile delinquent group in the network appeared to be oriented to each of the potential sources of achieved status available within the street milieu. Their pattern may perhaps best be interpreted as reflecting the fact that they were without a decisive status advantage of either the ascribed or the achieved kind.

On the other hand, informants' descriptions of the ten younger groups in the community strongly supported the Cohen and Short assertion regarding versatility in delinquent pattern at earlier age levels, and their supposition that specialization of pattern is most likely to occur only among older adolescent boys.[19]

As noted at the outset, opportunity theory makes the minimal assumption with respect to the dynamics of status that blocked aspirations tend to result in a shift of status goals. Further, such shifts are seen as essential in accounting for variations in delinquent subcultures. It is in this sense that opportunity theory also constitutes a status theory. The principal question posed by the data of the present investigation is whether the status goals ultimately fixed upon by various segments of the lower class male adolescent population may be accurately represented as the outcome of a series of aspirations successively blocked, relinquished, and substituted. The characteristics of the several delinquent styles found in the network of street groups suggest, instead, that they represent accommodation to available status niches within the local adolescent social subsystem. Each niche, further, seems peculiarly to accord with the origin of each group within the local adult social system.

The data of the study suggest that ascriptive position of a person within the relatively narrow confines of a local social system operates from the beginning to limit and ultimately to fix the kinds of status goals entertained.[20] The constraints of ascriptive position as a determinant of status goals may be conceptualized as originating in *types* of social resources differentially available at various points in a social system. Not the least of these resources are opportunities specifically to acquire the skills and experience requisite to the achievement of status goals indigenous to any ascriptive position actually occupied. At the same time it remains for the individual actor, through a process of uncertain and sometimes anguished experimentation, to discover just those status goals that accord with his resources. The crucial issue posed by the treatment of status dynamics in opportunity theory is the degree to which genuine commitment to inapposite status goals occurs on the part of the lower class adolescent male, such that he is peculiarly liable to blockage of aspirations. When account is taken of the pervasive ways in which ascriptive position molds expectation of achievement, the issue may be approached as a problem of the conditions under which status goals having little prospect of achievement arise for the young person. We need to know, also, the conditions under which an orientation to adult status goals in general are disavowed in favor of adolescent forms of status.

Only the most tentative answer to these questions is provided by the present analysis. It is suggested (1) that the greater the discrepancy between adult reference and membership groups available to the young person the greater will be his tendency to adopt status aspirations for which he does not possess the requisite social resources; and (2) that the higher the ascriptive position of the adolescent the more likely he is to emphasize those forms of achievement within the adolescent normative system that are cognate with adult values. While it is apparent that these two propositions are not unrelated, a discussion of their connections lies outside the purposes of this report.

SIGNIFICANT ADULTS, CARETAKERS, AND STRUCTURES OF OPPORTUNITY: AN EXPLORATORY STUDY

Ramon J. Rivera and James F. Short, Jr.

THE CHICAGO study of "Street Corner Groups and Patterns of Delinquency" had as its primary focus the generation of knowledge concerning gang delinquency.[1] The research was designed in such a way as to permit comparative study of observations and responses of Negro and white boys in each of the following categories: lower-class gang and nongang, and middle-class nongang. Boys in the gang categories were broadly representative of Chicago's "worst" during the period of study, particularly as concerns conflict, excessive consumption of alcohol, illicit sexual behavior, and property crimes of great variety. The YMCA of Metropolitan Chicago, through their Program for Detached Workers, was in effective contact with the gangs, having been directed to them by various community agencies and by field investigations which sought to

The research program of which this paper is a partial report was made possible by grants from the National Institute of Mental Health (research grants M-3301 and MH-01758 and training grant MH-08559), the Office of Juvenile Delinquency and Youth Development, the Ford Foundation, and the Research Committee of Washington State University. The authors are grateful for this support and for the cooperation of the Program for Detached workers, YMCA of Metropolitan Chicago. Some of the data which appear in this analysis were discussed in a paper presented at the annual meeting of the Pacific Sociological Association in 1964. This earlier version, "Significant Adults and Adolescent Adjustment: An Exploratory Study" was authored by James F. Short, Jr., Harvey Marshall, and Ramon J. Rivera. This article previously appeared in the *Journal of Research in Crime and Delinquency*, Vol. 4 (January, 1967).

locate representatives of major hypothesized "delinquent sub-cultures."

Lower class nongang boys were contacted through social agencies in the gang areas, such as YMCAs, Boys' Clubs, and Settlement Houses. Their nongang status was attested to by agency personnel and the detached workers. A measure of research control thus was obtained over "community factors" in selectivity for gang membership. Middle-class boys were chosen from HiY clubs in two areas of the city which, by conventional ecological criteria, justified this classification. We were directed to these clubs by YMCA personnel who agreed that these boys provided the best "contrast" groups in the city, so far as their class orientation was concerned. The white middle-class boys, especially, had the reputation of being the "cream of the YMCA crop."

These samples of Chicago adolescents have become the subjects of a series of special inquiries deriving mainly from current theory and speculation in the area of adolescent behavior, and delinquent behavior in particular. This paper represents a continuation of that series and has as its special point of interest the relationships existing between these youngsters and the world of adults which surrounds them.

ADULTS AND ADOLESCENTS:
SOME THEORETICAL CONSIDERATIONS

In 1937 this passage appeared in an article by Edward Reuter:

> An Adolescent world—an area of human experience lying between childhood and adulthood and in a measure apart from each —appears to be a phenomenon of our time and a product of our cultural organization. . . . As any other culture complex, it is essentially a system of collective definitions that creates a world apart.[2]

These sentences appeared in 1962 in a book by Ernest Smith:

> The exclusion of American youth from significant adult activities, combined with the widespread conflict between youth and

adults, leads to the withdrawal of youth from institutions sponsored or controlled by adults.[3]

. . . the underlying conflict of the two cultures—youth versus adult—is fundamental and may develop into crises as both parental exasperation and youth resentment accumulate.[4]

There is an obvious continuity in these passages, and the point of view represented—the "youth culture" perspective—received strong support between 1937 and 1962 in the relevant work of Benedict, Davis, Parsons, and Coleman.[5] In fact, the "youth culture" perspective can be described as the accepted and traditional mode of theorizing about adult-adolescent relationships in modern America. It is not unfair to label these works as contributions to a theory of *devisiveness.* The integration of adolescents and adults is viewed as an attribute of some societies, present during earlier, certainly more idyllic days, but clearly absent from the contemporary scene. Adolescents, in this view, are more adolescent than they used to be. They most certainly do *not* seem to be persons becoming adults and interacting with them in any meaningful way.

There have been occasional departures from this point of view. Nye, Withey and Douvan, Douvan and Kaye, and Elkin and Westley have, implicitly or directly, challenged the existence of a pervasive and continuing tension between adolescents and adults.[6] Our research on this problem, while cognizant of the "youth culture" perspective and its critics, was even more directly shaped by an attempt to evaluate and operationalize a theory which stems from a different tradition entirely—Cloward and Ohlin's "theory of differential opportunity."[7]

Briefly, this theory argues that the genesis of specialized types of delinquent adaptation lies, to an important degree, in differential exposure to structures of opportunity. The theory is familiar to criminologists and has been summarized in other project papers.[8] Cloward and Ohlin's use of such terms as "opportunity structures," "legitimate and illegitimate means," "role models," "integration of age levels," etc., clearly implies that somewhere within the institutional or informal social context of an adolescent's life there exist individuals who can offer or withhold keys to certain sectors of adult status. Presumably these individuals are often *adults*. An important question then becomes: Who are the older persons who function, for the adolescents, as mediators of the values and opportunities of the outside world?

Direct field observation, and continuing interviews with the detached workers, provided a valuable "window" through which we were able to observe the behavior of delinquent boys within the context of local community life. Very early in the project our attention was drawn to the relationships that existed between these adolescents and the adults who were part of their everyday world.[9] We began to explore the possibility of some type of community study (or series of studies) that would put us into direct contact with these individuals.

A survey of the literature suggested that an undertaking of this type would be almost unique in the field of juvenile delinquency.[10] It also suggested that such a study might prove *impossible* because of the "underlying conflict" between adolescents and adults so often referred to in the literature. We were faced with a curious dilemma. On one hand we had evidence (the observer and detached worker reports) which argued that adolescents quite frequently interacted with community adults; on the other hand were arguments that meaningful contact of this type was virtually nonexistent. The problem struck us as intriguing enough to warrant a modest investment of funds for research. This paper outlines the research strategy followed, and presents a number of findings from the study which ensued.

SECURING NOMINATIONS

We hoped to be able to locate and to interview samples of adults who were in effective contact with the boys. Initially, we considered straightforward community studies of selected areas, i.e., contacting every nth dwelling unit in a given neighborhood, and interviewing a sample of randomly selected local residents. This strategy was rejected, largely on the grounds that such a procedure could never guarantee that the adults contacted had any meaningful relationship with the boys. We were, of course, interested in the characteristics of community adults, but this interest was made selective by our conviction that primary attention should be directed to those older persons who figured significantly in the lives of our boys.

An alternate strategy was adopted, one that placed the major burden of sample selection *on the youngsters themselves.* Our solution was simply to encourage the boys to provide us with the names of those adults with whom they *regularly interacted.* (We assumed that the adolescents *would* know adults who could meet this criterion.) At the moment this decision was made, we were in the early stages of administering a personal interview to many of the youngsters involved in the program. The interview schedule was quickly adapted to include a sequence of items requesting from each boy, the names, addresses, and occupations of "the four adults with whom you have the most contact." We were primarily concerned with the character of adolescent-adult relations within the broad context of community life and, in line with this emphasis, a respondent's immediate family members were explicitly excluded from nomination. As it turned out (cf. Table 2 below), other boys were quick to fill this gap by nominating a large number of adult relatives of their peers. At the close of interviewing, relevant data (names, addresses, etc.) had been secured from 458 boys.

Each boy had been asked for four names, and the sheer volume of adults identified by this procedure, together with our limited financial resources, dictated a narrowing of research interests to a more manageable number of potential respondents. The basic design of the overall study suggested the appropriateness of selecting a sample of adults from each of the six categories which had guided the initial choice of adolescents in this study (NG, NLC, etc.). Since the gang and lower-class control youngsters were selected from the same areas of the city, we could easily match the gang samples with their appropriate LC controls and thus compare the characteristics and responses of adults nominated by gang and nongang boys in the *same* neighborhood.

Accordingly, two lower-class communities (Negro and white) were selected on the basis of the delinquency involvement of the gang boys and because of the relative richness of supporting material from other sources of data collection.[11] Our limited selection of middle-class adolescents yielded two groups (Negro and white) and two communities which seemed fairly representative, given our previous experience with these categories of urban adolescents. Our attention was thus centered on four Chicago communities, the adolescents within them, and the adults who had captured their attention.

NOMINEES AND SAMPLES FOR THE SIX GROUPS

Table 1 indicates the name and size of each group of adolescents selected to generate respondents for the adult interviews. Each boy had been asked to nominate four adults, and the third column of the table indicated, at least for nongang boys, that this request was generally followed by the adolescents. We might pause to underline the significance of this point. *The boys seemed to have little difficulty in nominating adults beyond their family circles with whom they were in regular contact.* These data, if taken as rough indicators of age-grade integration, suggest that integration of this type *is* characteristic of the communities selected, although it is somewhat *less pronounced* among boys who are members of delinquent gangs.

TABLE 1. *The Nomination Process*

Status of Nominators (Adolescents)	N	Total Number of Adult Nominations	Mean Number of Nominations Per Adolescent
NG—Rattlers	33	105	3.2
NLC—Market St. Y.	15	59	3.9
NMC—Omegas	12	44	3.7
WG—Pizza Grill	19	59	3.1
WLC—St. Paul Settlement	45	176	3.9
WMC—Admirals Hi-Y	34	136	4.0

The table also documents a second point, which was seriously to modify our research strategy. Altogether, a total of 158 adolescents offered a total of 579 adult nominations. Even allowing for *multiple* nominations—i.e., the fact that more than one boy in a group may have nominated the *same* adult—the adolescents had generated six samples of adults that offered more potential respondents than we could afford to interview. However, the fact that a large number of multiple nominations had been received suggested a tactic for reducing the case loads for our interviewers and, hopefully, for enhancing the relevance of the study.

The tactic was a simple one. Each sample of adults was stratified into two categories: the names of those persons who had been nominated by more than one boy were placed in a special group, those adults nominated only once were grouped separately. We set out to interview *every* adult who was a multiple nominee, plus randomly selected adults nominated by only one boy in each of the six groups. At this point our samples had become frankly purposive, the selection procedure depending largely on the relative salience of a given adult for a given group of adolescents. Our departure from conventional sampling procedures, imposed mainly by reasons of economy, was made more palatable by the realization that the solution accepted would maximize, for this study, the probability that we would be interviewing those adults who were important to *a number* of boys within the original groups of adolescents.

Locating multiple nominees proved to be a relatively simple task. Since more than one boy had volunteered the name and address, we were provided with a built-in check on the accuracy of our identifying information. The check was a welcome corrective device, especially in the lower-class areas where youngsters were apt to be hazy about the precise addresses of the adults they had nominated. The problems we encountered tracking down respondents in these communities are suggested by the following exchange that occurred as a Negro gang boy nominated a girl named "Dee Dee."

Interviewer: Under what circumstances do you see Dee Dee?

Respondent: Mostly I see her in a restaurant on Market and Rockford. I dance with her.

Interviewer: Does Dee Dee have a job?

Respondent: She a prostitute.

Interviewer: Where does she live?

Respondent: I don't know. (Probe) Somewhere on Rockford. The 1200 block.

Dee Dee was nominated only once, but she was among those randomly selected for interviews in the NG adult sample. We never managed to locate her (she had apparently moved from the neighborhood). At the height of our search we had the active cooperation of the Rattlers (the gang from which her nomination came) and a number of Dee Dee's former colleagues, but all to no avail.

Instances of vagueness concerning names and addresses were relatively common, and they seemed to be most prevalent among lower-class (G and LC) boys.

CHARACTERISTICS OF THE RESPONDENTS

Interviews were successfully completed with 146 adults. A high proportion of these persons (85%) either lived or worked in the communities where the boys themselves had been found. Another 11% had lived or worked there at one time, but at the moment of their interview they were located elsewhere in the city. The boys had not been asked to limit their choices to neighborhood adults, but, given an opportunity to define the scope of their adult contacts, most of the youngsters had restricted themselves to older persons in their immediate milieu.

Table 2 presents additional data describing the adult respondents. The mean number of (adolescent) nominations per (adult) respondent, ranging from 1.3 to 2.5, directly reflects our effort to enhance the representation of *multiple nominees*, i.e., adults nominated by more than one boy. The median ages of the six categories of respondents ranges between 35 and 47 years. These figures do not demonstrate a consistent pattern by race or class or gang status, but it is

TABLE 2. *Selected Characteristics of Adults Interviewed, by Race, Class and Gang Status of Nominators*

Status of Nominators	Adequate Interviews	Mean Number of Nominations Per Interview	Median Age of Adults Interviewed	Percent of Adults Who Are Female	Percent of Adults with Adolescents in Their Household	Percent of Adults Who Occupy "Caretaker" Roles
NG	23	2.2	45	47.8	40.9	9.1
NLC	20	2.5	45	45.0	52.6	60.0
NMC	20	1.3	39	50.0	60.0	20.0
WG	27	1.5	35	22.2	22.2	18.5
WLC	23	1.5	41	43.5	50.0	31.8
WMC	33	1.3	47	24.2	51.5	42.4

interesting to note that the adolescent nominators (who are roughly 16–17 years of age) did *not* concentrate their choices within a young adult age category (e.g., 20–29 yrs.). Typically, they selected persons who were more mature. At first glance this finding suggests a hopeful note for it implies that these youngsters may have been open to the influence of more *experienced* members of the civilian labor force. Presumably, these would be individuals well situated to advise adolescents on existing career opportunities and the contemporary realities of the world of work.

The fourth column of the table presents the percent of each category of adults who are female. The column has a special relevance. Most discussions of the social organization of the American Negro community emphasize the prevalance of female dominance within the typical Negro household.[12] Here we shift our attention from the immediate family to the wider community and examine the relative dominance of females within the adult milieu of these adolescents. A glance at the column of figures tells us that females constitute a *minority* of the respondents for each group; within this overall pattern we also note that females are more often found in the Negro samples than in the white.

The next column of the table presents the proportion of adult respondents with adolescent members in their own households. Perusal of the completed interviews indicates that this designation ordinarily identifies adults who come to the attention of the boys in the normal course of interaction between a youngster and his age mates. The boys come to know parents of friends, adult relatives of girl(s) they date, boarders at friends' homes, and older persons (with teen-agers of their own) whose interest in adolescents have led them to volunteer work with Boy Scout troops, etc. These are adult-adolescent relationships, to be sure, but they represent a particular *type* of relationship—one that is made available to youngsters by virtue of their own peer relationships. Very often these adults are relatives of the other young people he knows.

The preceding category of respondent suggests the appropriateness of examining the distribution of a related (and occasionally overlapping) type of adult nominee. These would be adults who come to the attention of adolescents in a more *formal* or *more strictly institutional setting.* Borrowing from Gans,[13] we shall call them *caretakers;* in the context of this report, the term caretaker will be used to refer to any adult who, in the course of his ordinary daily activities, comes into contact with adolescents *as a representative of some larger adult-dominated institution that is formally committed to guide or to change the behavior of youth.* The proportion of caretakers in each sample of adolescents appears in the final column of Table 2. As we examine this column of figures, we note also the specific types of caretakers contacted (see Table 3), and the significance of their activities on the local community scene.

A. Types of Caretakers

Table 3 lists the specific caretaker roles that were identified within each group of adult respondents. Initially we might observe that there were more than a few such persons; on an overall basis almost one-third (30%) of the 146 adults interviewed could be classified as occupants of caretaker roles. Their functions can be summarized as follows:

Caretaker Roles	Percent As A Proportion of All Caretakers	Percent As A Proportion of the Combined Samples
Detached worker and other YMCA and youth center personnel	40%	12%
High school teachers and related personnel	27	8
Clergy and related personnel	20	6
Boy Scout personnel	7	2
Other	7	2
	101%[a]	30%

[a]Higher than 100% because one adult was coded into two categories.

TABLE 3. "Caretaker" Roles of Community Adults Nominated by Adolescents; by Status of Nominators

			Status of Nominators		
NG	NLC	NMC	WG	WLC	WMC
Detached worker (9)[a]	Girl's secretary, YMCA (7)	Physical director, YMCA (2)	Detached worker (5)	Program director, St. Paul	Executive secretary, YMCA (5)
Minister (1)	Phys. ed. programmer, YMCA (6)	Physical director, YMCA (1)	Asst. director, youth club (1)	Teacher and athletic coach (3)	Teacher and chairman, phys. ed. department (3)
	Program director, youth club	Group worker, YMCA (1)	Community relations aide, Chicago public housing (1)	Teacher (2)	Assistant scoutmaster (2)
	Group worker youth club (3)	Teacher (1)	Counselor, Chicago youth advisors (1)[b]	Teacher (1)	School counselor (2)
	Administrative assistant, YMCA (3)		Lawyer (1)[c]	Teacher (1)	Minister (2)
	Executive secretary YMCA (2)				Minister and pastor of youth (1)

Game room instructor, youth club (2)	Minister (1)	Minister and pastor of youth (1)
Porter, YMCA (1)		Minister (1)
Secretary, youth club, (1)		Priest (1)
Teacher (1)		Scoutmaster (1)
Teacher (1)		Teacher and high school band director (1)
		Sunday school teacher and member, boy scout troop committee (1)
Teacher (1)		Teacher (1)
		Straight life group worker (1)[d]

[a] Numbers in parens indicate the number of boys nominating this adult.
[b] This organization provides voluntary counseling services for adolescents on probation or parole.
[c] This adult has defended several of the WG boys in court.
[d] A religious organization aimed at guiding the moral development of adolescents.

The proportion of YMCA and other Youth Center personnel in these samples comes as no surprise. The study, after all, originally located its youngsters through agencies such as these, and it stands to reason that when the boys were asked to nominate "significant" adults, a number of them would refer us back to the staff of their local youth center. Perhaps it is noteworthy that there were not *more* such nominations. That is, given our method of *locating* youngsters, the fact that *only* 12% of *all* adult respondents were agency personnel may strike some as surprising. Thus the proportion may be viewed as rather large, or rather small, depending on one's point of view.

Smaller clusters of caretaker roles can be identified with other major institutional settings. Thus we find additional groups of adult respondents whose relationship with children would seem to flow primarily from their positions as teachers (27% of all caretakers), religious figures (20% of all caretakers), and Scouting personnel (7% of all caretakers). The *significance* of adolescent exposure to these specialized adult roles, and the more basic question of their *availability* to young persons, is likely to vary from community to community and, *within* communities, from adolescent group to adolescent group. These questions are addressed below.

B. Caretakers: Their Availability and Significance

At this point it is appropriate to ask: What does the *presence* of caretakers (and the *types* of caretakers who *are* present) tell us about the communities that were surveyed in Chicago? Let us begin with a NG–NLC neighborhood—the Market Street area.

Market Street is overwhelmingly Negro and largely dilapidated. To the typical caretaker, it offered what amounted to a textbook example of a neighborhood gone to seed. Caretakers existed, and in large numbers. Did the boys notice them?

The nongang boys did. Sixty % of the NLC adults interviewed were caretakers, a figure that is about 50% larger than the comparable proportion of NG adult respondents. The difference is considerable and readers are reminded that these nominations were offered by boys who lived in the *same* community. It is also useful to remember that the Detached Worker Program was specifically *aimed* at those young persons who were felt to be largely ignored by conventional caretaker agencies. The fact that nine NG boys (27% of the Rattlers) nominated their Worker as a "significant" adult, and that only *one* other caretaker appears in the NG adult sample suggests that the YMCA's motives were not entirely illusionary. It is also instructive to examine the *types* of caretakers interviewed from the NLC nominations, if only to underline their absence from the NG adult sample.

Thus we note, within the group of NLC adult respondents, nine YMCA or Youth Center caretakers and three school teachers. Together these individuals collected 34 nominations from the boys, which amounts to 58% of all the nominations that the NLC offered to our interviewers. Our NLC comparison group, then, is heavily dominated by institutionalized roles, and their adult incumbents actually seem to have "captured" the loyalty of their "clients"—*given all of their adult contacts to choose from, the NLC boys tended to nominate their caretakers*. The contrast with NG boys is striking.

We find a somewhat similar picture if we examine the number and the type of caretakers interviewed in our low-status white categories. WLC adult respondents more often represent institutionalized roles, but in this case the margin over the WG group of adults is only 13%. More instructive are the specific caretaker roles which appear in each sample.

WG boys nominated caretakers who exist *to answer the special needs of boys who are in trouble*. We find a detached worker, a lawyer, and a probation officer, as well as a civic emmissary (Community Relations Aide) assigned to a neighborhood that needs "help." Other adolescents (WLC) in the same community nominate their teachers, a minister, and the officers of their local recreation centers. In this comparison it appears that the types of caretakers who become salient to groups of adolescent boys reflect the degree to which they are in "trouble."

The middle-class groups present quite different profiles. NMC adults are seldom caretakers, but they are often community adults *with teen-age children of their own.* The group of WMC adult respondents is also weighted in this direction, but it does include a sizeable number of clergymen, teachers, and scouting personnel. The picture presented by the WMC adult sample is close to that offered by Elkin and Westley in their study of a Canadian suburb.[14] Control of the environment and protection of adolescents from disruptive events is a task shared *jointly* by parents and caretakers. For the NMC group it is the *parents* of group members (rather than caretakers) who predominate in this particular type of community context.

A final point should be made concerning the presence of caretakers. Relative to the educational and income characteristics of the entire civilian labor force, *professional caretakers tend to be persons of high socioeconomic status.* The Duncan SES scale, for example, ranks teachers, group workers and clergymen along with lawyers, engineers and real estate agents, at the "top of the heap"—that is, at the ninth or tenth decile in an SES ranking of all American occupations.[15] (See Table 4.)

The significance of this fact for low-status youngsters should not be overlooked. Groups of adolescents in urban slums which act to maximize contact with caretakers, are likely also to maximize exposure to individuals *qualified to serve as role models for a middle-class way of life.* Table 5 contains relevant data.

Section A of the table presents the mean (Duncan SES) decile rank of all adult respondents who are caretakers. Not unexpectedly, the mean ranks are quite high, ranging between 8.7 and 10.0.[16] Other community adults tend to be much lower in status; on an overall basis a margin of 3.6 deciles separates caretaker roles from other community adult respondents. This differential in adult status is especially characteristic of lower-class communities, and it is most obvious in communities that are Negro.

Since the number and the proportion of caretakers varies across categories, their net contribution to the SES "mix" of a community varies as well. Part B of the table takes this factor into account, comparing the SES rank of all adult

TABLE 4.   *Selected Occupations by Decile Rank and Socioeconomic Index*

Occupation	Decile	Socioeconomic Index
Lawyer	10	93
Electrical engineer	10	84
Accountant	10	78
Teacher	10	70
Recreation or group worker	10	67
Social worker (except group)	9	64
Real estate agent	9	62
Clergyman	9	52
Sales clerk	8	47
Electrician	8	44
Policeman	8	40
T.V. repairman	7	36
Plumber	7	34
Bus driver	6	24
Welder	6	25
Auto mechanic	5	19
Bartender	5	19
Operative (manufacturing)	4	17
Waiter	4	16
Cook	4	15
Laborer (metal industry)	3	14
Farm owner or tenant	3	14
Taxi driver	2	10
Janitor	2	9
Construction laborer	2	7
Porter	1	4

TABLE 5. *Mean Decile Ranks: Social Status of Caretakers and Other Adults, by Status of Origin of Adolescent Nominators*

A. Caretakers and Other Community Adult Respondents

Source of Mean Decile Ranks	Status of Nominators					
	NG	NLC	NMC	WG	WLC	WMC
Adult respondents who are caretakers	9.5(2)	9.3(12)	10.0(4)	9.4(5)	8.7(7)	9.6(14)
Other community adult respondents	3.6(21)	2.6(8)	7.9(16)	5.4(22)	5.3(15)	9.2(19)
Observed difference	+5.9	+6.7	+2.1	+4.0	+3.4	+0.4

B. All Community Adult Respondents and Adolescent Nominators

Source of Mean Decile Ranks	Status of Nominators					
	NG	NLC	NMC	WG	WLC	WMC
All community adult respondents	4.1(23)	6.7(20)	8.3(20)	6.1(27)	6.4(22)	9.4(33)
Status of origin of nominators (adolescents)	3.0(33)	3.7(15)	6.1(12)	3.9(19)	5.5(45)	9.2(34)
Observed difference	+1.1	+3.0	+2.2	+2.2	+0.9	+0.2

respondents to the status position of the families of the boys responsible for their nomination. Examining the bottom row of the table ("Observed Difference") we find in every case that the boys have nominated adults who tend, on the average, to be superior to them in terms of social status. An important part of this status differential is due to the contribution made by caretakers to the mean position of all community adult respondents. *It would seem that the presence of caretakers or their relative absence, may profoundly affect the SES characteristics of those adult roles available to youngsters in slum communities.*

ADOLESCENT–ADULT CONTACTS: GENERAL

During the course of their personal interview, each adult respondent was handed a list of all the boys in the group from which the adult's nomination had been drawn. He (or she) was asked to indicate which names identified boys that were known personally and, for each identification made, the number of times, each week, that the adult respondent saw the boy. These data appear in Table 6.

The typical adult respondent was able to recognize about six names on the group rosters. Stated differently (and taking into account the different sizes of the adolescent groups involved), this means that the average adult was able to identify about 24% of the boys in the group from which his nomination had come. Note that our "index of recognition" required each adult to know the first and last names of the boys involved.

The proportion of boys recognized on this basis (24%) strikes us as misleadingly low. Certainly among gang boys of both races, this figure could have been raised by including nicknames as part of our "index of recognition." The addition of photographs of the boys would have enhanced the probability of identification among *all* groups. Unfortunately, neither of these methods was employed and we can only recommend their future use.

Table 6 also indicates that the average adult had from two to five contacts per week with each boy identified. There is

TABLE 6. Adolescent-Adult Contacts

Status of Nominators (Adolescents)	Number of Boys in Group	When Presented with a Roster of the Names of the Boys in the Group Responsible for Nomination, the Typical Adult Respondent: Was Able to Recognize the Names of . . .	And Said that He (She) Saw Each of These Boys, During an Average Week, About . . .
NG	33	6 Boys	5 Times
NLC	15	11 Boys	3 Times
NMC	12	4 Boys	3 Times
WG	19	7 Boys	2 Times
WLC	45	4 Boys	4 Times
WMC	34	6 Boys	3 Times

no consistent pattern, by race or class or gang affiliation, in the figures given. However, substantive differences *are* revealed if we ask *where* these contacts occurred and about the *types of conversations* that these older persons have with the boys they knew. These data appear in Tables 7 and 8.

Table 7 presents the answers that adults gave to the question "Where do you generally see these boys? (Where do you generally have most of your contact with them?)." Responses categorized as "around the neighborhood" run a narrow gamut. Usually the adult has said "on the street" or something similar (for example "I see them on my way to the store," or "I only see them when I walk my dog"). We note that street-centered answers of this type are primarily characteristic of *adults nominated by gang boys*. Given what we already know of the characteristics of our adult respondents, the pattern of remaining answers is largely predictable. Thus, NLC boys have been "captured" by caretakers. The adults they nominate tend to see the boys in caretaker-dominated centers for adolescent activities (e.g., the YMCA). NMC boys nominated a large number of adults with teenagers of their own; these adults see the boys in the course of visits at the boys' home or their own. WLC adults (compared to their NLC counterparts) are less often agency-centered. They see the boys "around the neighborhood" or at home. WMC adults report an especially large number of agency contacts, and secondary encounters in the neighborhood and during home visits. What types of conversation occur when the generations meet? An answer is suggested in Table 8.

After identifying his usual place of contact with the boys, each adult was asked "What are some of the things you're likely to talk about when you see them? (What's likely to come up in conversation?)" A glance at the first category of responses ("School") shows striking differences between adults nominated by gang boys, on one hand, and all other respondents, on the other. The general issue of one's *education* almost *never* comes up in a conversation between a gang boy and the "significant" adults we interviewed. This is the

TABLE 7. *Selected Responses of Community Adults to the Question:*
"Where Do You Generally See These Boys?" by Race,
Class and Gang Status of Nominators

Settings for Adult-Adolescent Contact	Status of Nominators						
	NG	NLC	NMC	WG	WLC	WMC
Around the neighborhood	68.2	38.9	20.0	76.0	47.8	51.5
Centers for organized adolescent activities	0.0	50.0	35.0	4.0	30.4	97.0
Home of adult, or home of adolescent	22.7	11.1	85.0	28.0	56.5	48.5
At work	9.0	22.0	10.0	32.0	17.4	9.1
100% =	22	18	20	25	23	33

N   141
NA   5

Total N (Adults)

TABLE 8. Selected Responses of Adults to the Question: "What Are Some of the Things You're Likely To Talk About When You See Them?" by Race, Class, and Gang Status of Nominators

Selected Responses	Status of Nominators					
	NG	NLC	NMC	WG	WLC	WMC
School	4.5	55.6	60.0	7.7	47.8	72.7
Work	36.4	22.2	20.0	42.3	30.4	12.1
Conventional adolescent interests (cars, sports, etc.)	18.0	55.6	60.0	49.9	87.0	63.7
Neighborhood gossip, casual greetings, etc.	54.6	38.9	30.0	61.5	34.7	26.3
100% =	22	18	20	26	23	33

N 142
NA 4
146

most decisive pattern in the table, but other differences are also important:

1. There is a tendency for gang-nominated adults to report a somewhat *higher* proportion of discussions concerning the world of *work*,[17] but fewer conversations about conventional adolescent interests, such as sports and cars.
2. Gang boy–adult conversations involve chiefly neighborhood gossip and casual exchanges of greetings.

These points are worth underlining, if only because they are so obviously relevant to the general problem of structures of opportunity. In their conversations with adults, gang boys reveal themselves as relatively indifferent to more conventional adolescent interests, surely more indifferent to school; and much more likely to enter into conversations that, from a middle-class perspective, would seem to be without much content.

But are such conversations actually contentless? They do seem to lack the *instructional* quality that appears to be an important component of exchanges between the generations in middle-class communities. Middle-class adults talk to adolescents about school. In so doing it seems likely that such sentiments are conveyed as "school is important," and "you must get all the education you can." As they talk, they *teach.* When the conversation does not dwell on education, it turns on topics that are specific to middle-class images of adolescent life—sports, cars, etc. Discussions such as these would seem to stress a measure of *distance* between the age grades. That is, MC adults appear to be presenting themselves as persons who are tolerant and encouraging about adolescent interests, but they also present themselves as persons who are more expert and sophisticated than adolescents, and thus as persons who are strategically situated to offer them *advice.*

This is exactly the quality that seems to be lacking in adult conversations with gang boys. These persons exchange greetings, they gossip; occasionally they speak of the world of work. By and large they are *not* communicating in a fashion that would underline, for the youngster, any sense of dependence on the expertise of persons who are older than he is. The generations appear to interact on a basis of *equality,* sharing concerns and exchanging information in a manner that seems to *deny* that there is any special significance to their positions as adults and adolescents.

Consider the following selection of responses which gang-nominated adults gave to the question, "What are some of the things you're likely to talk about when you see them (the boys)?":

A NG adult (Case #150—Housewife): "Nothing but how do you do? How is your mother? Where are you going?"

A WG adult (Case #512—Unemployed Entertainer): "Nothing. We just bullshit around. Nothing in particular."

A NG adult (Case #125—Laborer, Poultry Market): "This depends on what they are doing when I see them. Sometimes they're shooting craps in the alley. I say What are you trying to do? Get some rest in California? That sort of stuff."[18]

A WG adult (Cast #543—Laborer, Road Maintenance): "Who's in jail? What happened to this one? How's your brother? That's about it."

Exchanges such as these are hardly likely to convince adolescents that older persons may be capable of offering entree to a more desirable way of life. If they suggest anything at all to a person familiar with these environments, they are likely to remind him of conversations that adults have with other adults.

Gang-nominated adults usually aren't *pushing* anything. Note the contrast between the answers cited above and some typical responses of middle-class respondents to the same question:

A WMC adult (Case #314—Physician): "Electronics, radio, hi-fi; how to fix things—that sort of thing. I have a complete workshop—I teach the boys how to do these things."

A NMC adult (Case #334—Housewife): "We talk about so many things—sports, different players and the schools they went to. We discuss current events. Then we talk about school."

A WMC adult (Case #730—Salesman, Electrical Equipment): "Where are you going to school? Did you get a scholarship? What are you going to major in? . . . Are you going to play baseball or football at school?"

ADOLESCENT–ADULT RELATIONS AS STRUCTURES OF OPPORTUNITY

The material in the preceding table appropriately introduces our final topic—intergenerational relations as structures of opportunity. Here we are concerned primarily with the extent to which community adults *intervene* in the lives of the younger generation to shape the life chances that they will encounter. We begin at a very basic level by asking whether "significant" adults are at all *concerned* about the eventual fate of youngsters. After some general questions about the boys in their neighborhood, each adult respondent was asked: "Have you ever wondered about the kind of life these youngsters will lead when they grow up?" The proportion of adults answering "yes" appears in Table 9.

Taking these proportions as rough indicators of adult interest, we find that interest is *highest* among adults in touch with youngsters *who are not in gangs. Interest is almost universal among LC adults.* Note that the question was phrased in terms of the adult ever *wondering* about what would happen to the boys. The choice of this term was deliberate. We could have asked, for example, if they were *interested,* or *concerned* or whether they ever *worried* about the subject at all. As it was finally phrased, the question was intended to cover *all* of these gradations—which might be seen as points along a continuum reflecting each adult's sense of *personal involvement* in the life chances of the youngsters he knew. This point is worth mentioning because the probability is high that LC adults tended to *wonder* because they were *worried.* LC adults (and NLC adults in particular) are often caretakers; LC adults tend to *dislike* the neighborhoods where they work and often live.[19] For persons such as these, wondering about the fate of adolescents will often reflect a conviction that youngsters must be *protected* from the more

TABLE 9. *Percent of Adults Responding "Yes" to the Question: "Have You Ever Wondered About the Kind of Life These Youngsters Will Lead When They Grow Up?" by Race, Class and Gang Status of Nominators*

	Status of Nominators					
	NG	NLC	NMC	WG	WLC	WMC
	65.2 (23)	95.0 (20)	85.0 (20)	55.6 (27)	95.6 (23)	84.8 (33)

N 146
NA 0

Total N 146

threatening events that exist in their environments. On the other hand, it seems likely that middle class adults *wonder* because they are *interested*. They are interested because it is "only natural" for MC adults to be interested in the life chances of adolescents, just as it is "only natural" for them when they meet, to talk of school and sports (cf. Table 8).[20]

Gang-nominated adults *wonder* less often. Perhaps they are less interested, or less concerned, or less worried. Perhaps they view the outcome of the lives of these boys as a foregone conclusion. In the absence of any follow-up items in the schedule to clarify these questions, any conclusion drawn is necessarily speculative. However, accepting the logic of the question they were asked, we are left to conclude that gang-nominated adults *less* often report a sense of *personal involvement in the life-chances of the youngsters they know.*

As we have already suggested, there may be a number of dimensions to this sense of personal involvement. Still, the entire issue might not occur to some persons if it were not *forced* upon their attention by the adolescents themselves. A relevant question then becomes: How many of these respondents have ever been *approached* by boys concerned about their performance in conventional structures of opportunity? This question was asked, and the relevant data appear in Table 10.

Looking first at Section A of the table (school problems), we note a pattern of responses similar to that observed in Table 9. Nongang boys are *most* likely to approach community adults concerning their problems at school, gang boys are *least* likely to do so. The answers are especially striking because they bear almost no relation to the number and the severity of the problems that these boys actually experience in school. Gang boys, by a large margin, are most likely to experience difficulties in school,[21] yet they are least likely to bring these problems to the attention of the older persons they know.

Section B of the table tells a similar story. More than any other group, the gang boys need jobs and need advice about finding them, yet it is mainly their LC peers who turn to

TABLE 10. *School and Work*

A. Problems at School

Percent of Adults Responding "Yes" to the Question: "Has any Boy on that List Ever Spoken to You About His Problems at School?" by Race, Class, and Gang Status of Nominators

Status of Nominator

NG	NLC	NMC	WG	WLC	WMC
39.1(23)	85.0(20)	50.0(20)	40.0(25)	78.3(23)	59.4(32)

N 143
NA 3
Total N 146

B. Finding a Job

Percent of Adults Responding "Yes" to the Question: "Has any Boy on that List Ever Spoken to You About How He Should Go About Finding a Job?" by Race, Class, and Gang Status of Nominators

Status of Nominator

NG	NLC	NMC	WG	WLC	WMC
47.8(23)	75.0(20)	50.0(20)	53.8(26)	73.9(23)	33.3(33)

N 145
NA 1
Total N 146

TABLE 11. *Percent of NG and NLC Community Adults Who Have Discussed Specific School Problems with Boys They Know*

Question: "Have You Ever Spoken to a Teenage Boy Who (Cite Specific Problem) and Advised Him About What to Do?" Problems Cited	Status of Nominators		Observed Difference
	NG	NLC	
. . hadn't learned much from his earlier school work and was finding it difficult to catch up	17.4	70.0	+52.6
. . was having difficulty getting along with his fellow students	4.3	55.0	+50.7
. . was a slow learner and having a hard time making fair grades at school	30.4	80.0	+49.6
. . felt that it cost too much money to continue with school	13.0	60.0	+47.0
. . wanted to return to school, but felt that he was too old to go back	21.7	65.0	+43.3
. . felt that he had to help out his parents financially and couldn't stay in school	21.7	65.0	+43.3
. . wanted more spending money and felt he couldn't get it if he stayed in school	21.7	65.0	+43.3
. . just didn't like the school he went to	17.4	60.0	+42.6
. . couldn't decide what to take at school	8.7	50.0	+41.3
. . was wondering about how to finance a college education	4.3	45.0	+40.7

... was wondering about the college he should apply to	4.3	45.0	+40.7
... felt that he wanted to enter the Armed Service instead of going to school	30.4	70.0	+39.6
... simply wasn't applying himself to his school work	26.1	65.0	+38.9
... felt that his teachers weren't doing a good job	21.7	60.0	+38.3
... tried hard, but just didn't sem to be lucky in school	21.7	60.0	+38.3
... just couldn't seem to get interested in his school-work	39.1	75.0	+35.9
... felt that his teachers were asking him to do too much work	30.4	65.0	+34.6
... was trying to decide whether he should go to college	8.7	40.0	+31.3
... was having difficulty getting along with his teachers and felt they didn't like him	43.5	70.0	+26.5
... wanted to return to school, but didn't know how to go about getting back in	26.1	50.0	+23.9
... felt that he wanted to get married instead of going to school	21.7	40.0	+18.3
... was a truant and spent a lot of time away from school	43.5	55.0	+11.5
100% =	23	20	

N 43
NA 0

Total N (NG & NLC Adults) 43

adults for consultation. Above we noted that gang-nominated adults less often feel subjectively involved in the life chances of these boys. One reason for this fact may well be that gang boys *less often approach adults to discuss the problems they experience in conventional structures of opportunity*.

Table 11 presents further data relevant to this point. In constructing the interview schedule we attempted to develop a list of school problems that would give adequate coverage to difficulties encountered by boys of widely divergent social backgrounds. The list was constructed on the basis of data from pretest versions of our instrument, supplemented by information from interviews with the boys and observational material concerning their adjustment to school. The list of specific school problems that was eventually handed to the respondents contained 22 items. Each adult was asked to read the list, and then to indicate the particular problems that had been mentioned in his conversations with the boys.

We were confident that a large number of these items would evoke sizeable differences in the responses of gang and LC respondents; many of the items, in fact, were aimed directly at problems that we *knew* were much more severe among members of delinquent gangs. The data in Table 11, reporting the responses of NG and NLC adults, suggest that our whole approach to this problem, however commendable it may have seemed at the time, was dead wrong. *NLC adults are more likely to report conversations with the boys regardless of the type of problem involved*.

Thus we know that gang boys get poorer grades in school, but NLC boys more often talk to adults about this problem. We know that financial problems are more likely to interrupt the schooling of gang boys, but NLC boys more often bring this issue to the attention of the older persons they know. To put it simply, *we were unable to locate any school problem at all that NG boys were more likely to discuss with adults. Yet NG boys, objectively, are much less successful in their adjustments to school.*

The decision *not* to turn to adults for assistance probably is related to a variety of factors, including the attitudes of the adults. Perhaps the boys sense that adults are less than concerned about their future. Another factor, suggested earlier, is that the generations tend to interact as *equals;* gang-nominated adults are not cast in the role of helpers for these youngsters, and the boys are able to avoid the sense of dependence that such a relationship would involve. It it no surprise, therefore, to learn that gang boys are *less* likely to define local adults as potent and effective individuals. This finding, based on interviews conducted with the boys, has been reported elsewhere.[22] Finally, we should note that gang-nominated adults less often view these boys as victims of a system of events and circumstances in which they (the adults) are a key link. If the boys do poorly in school it is *their own fault.* Gang-nominated adults, when they were asked to identify the *cause* of the school problems of gang boys, overwhelmingly laid the blame on the *personal characteristics* of the boys themselves. The youngsters were described as "stupid," "lazy," "indifferent," and so on. One WG respondent, when asked why the boys were apt to do poorly in school, phrased it this way (Case #539—Grocery Store Owner):

They just don't care about school. They're lazy bums. All they care about is running around and having fun.

This man's comment amounts to a self-fulfilling prophecy. The boys will do poorly in school and do poorly on the jobs they get. Why bother to help? So, of course, adults don't help. And the boys do poorly.

CONCLUSIONS

From the material presented above, and from other project data, it is obvious that gang boys are enmeshed in an interlocking chain of circumstances which profoundly affects their chances for mobility. Its major elements can be outlined as follows:

1. Members of delinquent gangs tend to be involved with older persons who possess few of the characteristics that might qualify an adult to improve an adolescent's performance in conventional structures of opportunity. The adults

they know tend to be low in status. Few of them are committed to the goal of "helping" adolescents as part of a formal caretaker role.

2. Compared to other respondents, the typical gang-nominated adult is simply *less concerned* with the whole problem of offering opportunities to youngsters. For gang communities, the generations do not interact in a fashion that makes this problem explicit. Adults are seldom reminded that they may have an important role to play in affecting the life chances of a younger generation.

3. NG and WG adults, as disinterested and uninvolved witnesses to the failure of gang boys in conventional structures of opportunity, pin the *blame* for these failures on the boys. The youngsters, they feel, are incompetent.

4. Perhaps the boys sense that this evaluation has been made. We do know that gang boys are less likely to describe their adult neighbors as potent and effective individuals. Thus gang-nominated adults present a negative picture of the personal qualities of the boys they know; and the boys respond in kind.

5. Finally, and inevitably, when problems *do* arise for these youngsters, especially problems affecting their life-chances, *they are less often referred to older persons for solution*. Adults (the boys seem to be saying) do not *care*. And even if they *do* care, they are *powerless* to act.

This study, like that of Kobrin and his associates,[23] suggests modification of the Cloward and Ohlin theory of delinquent gangs, and of other formulations concerning youth subcultures. The adolescent boys in this study were neither as isolated from adults nor as antagonistic toward them as some theorists would have us believe. Both Negro gang boys (the Rattlers are primarily a 'conflict' group) and white gang boys (who live in an area where criminal and conventional elements are 'integrated') do have regular contacts with older persons in their communites. Perhaps the most important contribution of this study, however, is its beginning attempt to *specify* the manner in which adult-adolescent relations operate to guide (or fail to guide) the passage of youngsters through conventional structures of opportunity. Within the *same* urban communities there are profound gang-nongang differences in the *types* of intergenerational contacts that occur. Nongang boys are given guidelines and advice that are likely to enhance their life chances; gang-nominated adults may live in the same community but they do little to prepare the boys they know to live, as adults, in a better world.

Group Process, Cohesiveness, and Delinquency

UNTIL recently, the group nature of delinquent behavior was more taken for granted than studied. The following selections represent data and interpretations from recent studies which have attempted to explore within-group processes related to the occasionally delinquent character of gang behavior—in general, and with respect to particular delinquent episodes.

A second theme of this section concerns the relation between group cohesiveness and its correlates, and delinquency. The thesis is developed elsewhere that gang boys tend to lack social assurance and other skills related to interpersonal functioning, and that the gang is less than satisfactory as a source of nurturance and fulfillment of dependency needs.[1] While these matters are not well documented, such evidence as exists suggests that cohesiveness is closely related to delinquency. Whether this linkage results from the youngsters' attempts to realize important group goals, as Jansyn suggests,[2] from forces external to the group—the thesis of Klein and Crawford—or from the delinquent's entrapment in a colossal boredom,[3] is not clear. In any case, further study of the linkage between personality, social skills, early childhood experience, and later encounters with peer groups and the larger society clearly are necessary if the behavior patterns of gangs are to be understood in all their complexity.

The third article in this section conceptualizes participation in episodes of violence, and by extension in other types of delinquency, as a function of choice behavior involving rewards and risks associated with behavior alternatives and contingent conditions.

Among the contingent conditions for the gang boy, it

should be remarked, are the vulnerabilities of the "unstable poor." S. M. Miller has characterized life among this group as "crisis-life, constantly trying to 'make do' with string where rope is needed."[4] Unskilled and subject to seasonal unemployment or other job layoffs, threatened by malnutrition, debilitating disease, or poor health generally, and by disabling injury, criminal victimization, and arrest, the unstable poor—more often than others—are confronted with situations not of their own making and beyond their control. The future, uncertain at best, is likely to be bleak indeed, unpredictable and independent of present actions. Thus, for the lower-class gang boy choices among behavior alternatives—decisions to "join the action"—"grow out of culturally patterned experiences which have failed to teach that long-run consequences are subjectively dependent on short-run decisions."[5]

The group process perspective advanced here is similar in certain respects to Matza's discussion of the "drift" into delinquency.[6] Matza sees the delinquent as responding to pressures in the immediate environment without the constraining influences of commitment either to convention or to crime. Together with Sykes, Matza has described certain inconsistencies and ambivalences of societal values, and the neutralizing mechanisms related thereto, by which delinquent behavior is rationalized.[7]

These and other recent works suggest means by which cultural and social structural factors are "translated" into behavior—not mechanistically as a robot responding to programed instructions and circuitry, but dynamically in the give and take of inter- and intrapersonal interaction.[8] In the joining of these perspectives we may hope for closer approximations to the reality each seeks to comprehend.

WHY GANGS FIGHT

James F. Short, Jr. and Fred L. Strodtbeck

> Big Jake, leader of the Potentates, had been "cooling it"
> over the fall and winter. However Guy, leader of the Vice
> Kings, with whom the Potentates were often at war,
> warned: "Better watch Big Jake—he has to do *some-
> thing*." Why? "He's *got* to build that rep again. He's been
> gone—now he's got to show everybody he's *back!*"
> —REPORT FROM A DIRECTOR OF DETACHED
> WORKERS WITH JUVENILE GANGS

LIKE Big Jake, Duke, of the King Rattlers, had also been
in jail. Before his internment he had been known for his self-
possession—for being a "cool" leader. Although a capable and
active fighter when he thought it necessary, he never lost his
head and was very effective in negotiation, conciliation, and
control. When he came out of jail his leadership and his personal future were threatened and uncertain, and he became
belligerent, aggressive, and apparently reckless—with the approval of his gang. Once things settled down for him, however, he reverted to the cool behavior that had made him such
an effective leader.

As with leaders of nations, the qualities that raise boys to
the tops of juvenile gangs are not necessarily those that best
qualify them to stay there, or to rule. "A good suitor may not
make a good husband, or a good campaigner a good president." Moreover gangs, though they may admire the fighting
campaigner, are often more difficult to control than nations;
members who feel abused can sometimes simply drop out,
as citizens cannot.

From *Trans-action*, i, No. 6 (Sept.–Oct., 1964), 25–29. Reprinted by
permission.

ON TO GLORY

These restrictions, however, do not limit fighting between gangs. Here a leader can work off his aggressions, show off his fighting prowess, and win prestige and popularity with his gang, making his position more secure. As with nations, tyrannizing outsiders is always more acceptable. A despot is someone who abuses his own people; if he attacks and tyrannizes other groups, he is a great and victorious leader, leading enthusiastic followers on to glory.

Juvenile gang leaders invest a great deal in their fighting reputations. Leadership and delinquency must therefore go together. In nearly all gangs we studied, over a three year period, we found that skill in fighting was highly valued, whether or not the gang itself had a fighting "rep." A fight often occurred because a gang, or its leaders, simply could not tolerate a real or implied threat to whatever reputation they had.

Some gangs are definitely "conflict oriented." Fighting is a major and necessary activity for them and a means of acquiring respect, admiration, and prestige within them. They must and do fight often. They have a heavy investment in—and therefore motivation toward—combat. Their leadership, reputation, and status are under constant challenge—anytime they falter some other gang will try to make them fall. They must be prepared for defense—indeed, they believe they must attack from time to time before others attack them, and to remind possible enemies to beware. "We are the mighty Vice Kings!" a leader will shout in challenge—much as Beowulf, using other names, might have done. The very titles and roles they create for themselves reflect the warlike stance —"war counselor," "armorer." These offices need not be clearly or formally defined or even performed; but they are recognized and given deference, and competition for them is fierce.

"Conflict" of course need not always involve major war— the primary purpose of battle is to prove oneself, not to capture anything. The kind of guerilla combat such gangs engage in was well illustrated in the following abstract of a detached worker's incident report:

> I was sitting talking to the Knights, re-emphasizing my stand on guns, because they told me they had collected quite a few and were waiting for the Vice Kings to start trouble. I told them flatly that it was better that I got the gun than the police. They repeated that they were tired of running from the Vice Kings and that if they gave them trouble they were fighting back.
>
> I looked out of the car and noticed two Vice Kings and two girls walking down the street. William then turned around and made the observation that there were about fifteen or twenty Vice Kings across the street in the alley, wandering up the street in ones or twos.
>
> The Vice Kings encountered Commando (the leader) Jones, and a couple of other Knights coming around the corner. The Vice Kings yelled across to Commando and his boys, and Commando yelled back. I got out to cool Commando down, since he was halfway across the street daring them to do something. I grabbed him and began to pull him back.
>
> But the Vice Kings were in a rage, and three came across the street yelling that they were mighty Vice Kings. At this point, along came Henry Brown with a revolver, shooting. Everybody ducked and the Vice Kings ran. I began to throw Knights into my car because I knew that the area was "hot."
>
> In the car the boys were extremely elated. "Baby, did you see the way I swung on that kid?" "Man, did we tell them off?" "Did you see them take off when I leveled my gun?" "You were great, baby. . . ."
>
> The tension was relieved. They had performed well and could be proud. . . .

NOBODY LOSES?

No doubt the Vice Kings too felt the thrill of having faced conflict and come off well. They had met great danger bravely, and had a good alibi for not having won unquestioned victory—the enemy had a gun. The Knights, on their part also had an alibi—the worker had intervened. Both sides therefore won, and could mutually share satisfaction and enhanced reputation. Gang combat is not necessarily a winner-take-all game. No one need be defeated. The two gangs had "played the game" according to the standards of their "community"; they had been rewarded, and law and order were now restored. The larger society too profits from a no-loser game. Of course, results are not always so harmless. Boys and gangs are often beaten and people and property often injured in this "game."

Threats to the status of a leader can result in violence to whole gangs; but the process is more complicated than it seems. Threat to leadership is merely a special case of "status management," which involves all gang boys. How can high status best be achieved and maintained in the continuing and risky give and take of gang life?

HUMBUG

Several kinds of threats to status are covered by the broad conception of status management. They are well illustrated in the elements involved in a "humbug"—a general brawl—that our workers witnessed and recorded.

Jim, the detached worker, had taken his gang, the North Side Vice Kings, to a professional basketball game at the Chicago Amphitheater. The boys were in good spirits, but restless and volatile. Duke, the strongest leader, had been drinking. He sat near a younger group, the Junior Chiefs. He was friendly to them but obnoxious to venders and others, and was generally putting on a show for the younger boys.

Duke announced that he was going to buy some beer—he had recently turned twenty-one. The worker told him that beer was out when they were on an officially sponsored activity. Duke bought it anyway, and after an argument in which Duke kept mentioning his age, Jim took the beer from him. Duke became abusive to the worker and other spectators; and the other Vice Kings also acted up. Jim then announced that the entire group had to leave immediately.

On the way out they met another group, the South Side Rattlers. As they passed, Duke "fatmouthed" one of them and blows were exchanged. The Rattlers, at first confused, retaliated and the humbug was on, while their workers, caught off guard, tried vainly to separate them.

A third group, the Cherokees, now happened on the scene. Having a grudge against the Vice Kings, they waited for no further invitation. "No one stopped to get an explanation of what was going on. The fellows just looked up, saw the fighting, and joined in." The Rattlers, apparently frightened by a couple of knives and a pistol, had started to run, and the fighting might have died had the Cherokees stayed out.

The police partially broke up the battle, but a new round of insults started it again. A fourth group, the Midget Vice Kings arrived; hearing challenge and counter-challenge, they too gave battle, siding with the Vice Kings.

After the combat, the detached workers reported that all three major groups involved talked about going home to get their "stuff" (weapons) and preparing to fight. The Rattlers, having been forced to retreat, were especially disturbed and made many threats. However, when the police came up and escorted them to their car, eliminating all possibility of further humbugs, they acted relieved and happy. On the way home they teased each other about running.

One group—the Junior Chiefs—had not been challenged, or otherwise received any "status threats." Not very surprisingly, they did not fight, and stayed and watched the basketball game.

STATUS AND MANHOOD

The other gangs, however, did feel their reputations and "manhood" threatened. Elements of threat included:

The worker publicly ignored and down-graded Duke's newly achieved adulthood.

Following this, he degraded him in the eyes of his special, younger, audience, the Junior Chiefs—and of his own gang—of which he was supposed to be a leader.

He publicly humiliated and degraded all the rest of the Vice Kings by ordering them to leave, like a bunch of kids who could not be trusted to behave in public. This too he did before the Junior Chiefs—an act which immediately downgraded them in the gang world—and before adults, who could immediately identify them as "kids."

Searching for an outlet for rage and frustration, and for a means to rebuild their shattered "reps," the Vice Kings encountered the Rattlers. They attacked them. Now the reputations of the Rattlers (and later of the Cherokees) were threatened, and *they* counter retaliated.

Yet, for all the ferocity, the fights were shortlived. Every group except the Vice Kings, who had been most threatened, were brought under control fairly quickly and stayed to see the basketball game—only the Vice Kings missed it. Moreover, despite talk of retaliation, the humbug was self-contained; in the following months there was no more humbugging between these groups. The fight served the usual purpose of upholding reputations and preserving the images of street warriors ready for combat.

Closer analysis, however, reveals more to the story. What happened to the ferocious warrior image after the fights were stopped? And why so easily stopped? Also, not all the boys fought. Except for the Vice Kings, each group contained some boys who stayed out. Careful review suggests that those most deeply involved in the fighting were the core gang-members—the leaders and those who wanted to be leaders. Not all gang members—and not all gangs—have the same investment in rep and status. Certainly no gang rules or standards, spoken or implied, require that *all* boys fight every time, even under these provocative circumstances.

Gang rules and expectations do influence the behavior of members; but that influence is not clear cut, and depends mostly on the situation. Gangs are fluid; members change; boys come and go for days or weeks at a time, and unless they are leaders, or important core members, they are hardly missed. Under such circumstances, the group leaders cannot make members—especially fringe members—conform or give obedience by threatening expulsion or withdrawal of privileges. Most of the gang leaders we studied were surprisingly conciliatory within the group. But they had a special interest in making members want to belong to a gang with a good reputation.

"KICKS," NOT BLOWS

This article is concerned primarily with juvenile gangs whose status is built around conflict. But it must be emphasized that, despite prevalent stereotypes, juvenile gangs are not all conflict oriented, and value systems may vary among them as among other human groupings. A "retreatist" gang, which built its value system around the effect of dope, provides a dramatic contrast.

Although criticized and ridiculed repeatedly by other gangs for their cowardice and lack of manhood, the retreatists seldom responded to taunts, and always retreated from combat. They did not worry about their reputations as fighters—they had none—and did not think them important—in fact, they thought the conflict oriented gangs to be "square." Directly challenged to join other white gangs in repelling Negro "wade-in" demonstrators on a beach in Chicago, they got "high" on pills and unconcernedly played cards during the entire incident.

The basis of camaraderie—what was important—to the drug users was "kicks." Past and present exploits—their legends of valor—continually recounted, concerned "high" experiences and "crazy" behavior rather than bravery or toughness. "You get the feeling," a member of the team of research observers said, "that whatever the activity of the moment, the guys will talk about it in relation to dope—how taking dope affects their participation in the activity."

Even their humor revolved around the effect of dope—the antics of friends under the influence. They laughed about the boy who kept trying to start a junked car that had no motor. Another one, beaten by a Chinese laundryman he tried to rob, "was so doped out of his mind" that he asked the arriving police to arrest the other for beating him so. Some others climbed to a bedroom window and grabbed the leg of a girlfriend to wake her, but got the wrong window and the wrong leg—both of them her father's!

Not all gangs value combat. But each will protect what it does value. When the retreatists find what they value threat-

ened, they withdraw, protectively. When a conflict oriented
gang feels its status threatened, it fights.

PRESSURES FROM OUTSIDE

"Status threat" is a special case of the general status thesis
—that people will tend to do what gives them standing and
respect in society. But with adolescent boys in a gang "what
gives them standing and respect" is contained in the limited
compass of the face-to-face relationships within the gang,
not—except indirectly—with the social class structure of
society at large. Of course, directly and indirectly, pressures
from outside do affect the gang boys. They come from at
least three levels.

Adult Sponsored and Controlled Institutions of the Larger Society

Schools, places of employment, social agencies, police, and
other officials represent adult "authority." Their orientation is
middle-class; they preach and perhaps believe that worth and
success come from hard work, deferred gratification, self control, good grades, good behavior, saving money, and becoming
a "leader" in approved organizations. Gang boys fail to
achieve according to these standards. The hypothesis that,
with legitimate channels closed to them they will choose the
illegitimate, therefore does not disagree with our findings. But
how this works precisely is not very clear, and other research
indicates that these boys may not be as alienated as many
think. Other pressures must also affect them more directly.

THE EXERCISE OF POWER

*The lower classes have their own adult community institu-
tions,* which make their own patterns and exert their own
pressures. There are poolrooms, parties, informal neighborhood gatherings, and the obvious social and political power
manifested by the adults in rackets and politics.

At this level, standards of adult behavior most appropriate
to everyday life for the boys are inferred and directly incul-
cated. Observation strongly suggests that the gang boys rec-

ognize and respect the exercise of power in their neighborhoods, whether from legitimate or illegitimate sources. But
there is no demonstration of legitimate power they know that
compares in drama and impact with the evidence of the
power of organized crime—the numerous gang slayings of
hoodlums, and even of politicians. Both Negro and white
gang boys repeat as a by-word: "You can't beat the syndicate."

But modeling behavior after adults in order to "achieve
adulthood" seems not to be as important a factor among
Negroes as among whites. Lower-class Negro communities
differ; there are fewer sharp age distinctions; all ages compete for excitement wherever it may be found—a bottle, a
battle, or a broad. Poolhalls are frequented by young and
old alike.

The adoption of adult lower-class standards therefore cannot be the only, or even the major, cause of delinquency
among adolescents. In the conflict prone gangs especially, the
next level must be the most important.

The Adolescent Gang World

The juvenile "delinquent"—especially the gang leader—is
faced with a condition, not a theory. He must daily act out
his role under the eyes of his fellow gang members, and the
members and leaders of other gangs. Almost by definition,
the destiny of a warlike gang is controlled by the actions, real
or expected, of other gangs. How a gang defends or enhances
its status depends on its judgment of the whole fluid situation. What is the state of peace or war with rival gangs?
What old gangs are feuding? What new gangs are trying to
carve out niches for themselves?

Even a group organized for criminal purposes, as one of
ours was, will shift its goals to fighting if under threat or
attack from outside—even though this might, for a criminal
gang, bring on risk of exposure.

BRANCH GANGS

The interrelationships in the gang world are extensive. A
gang will have "branches" across neighborhood lines (East

Side Cobras and West Side Cobras); it will have Senior, Junior, and Midget divisions within a neighborhood, with the younger members modeling themselves on the older, and expecting model behavior from them.

Even where pressures from outside make themselves manifest, they must filter down into and be expressed within the values of the gang itself. In fact the gang owes much of its reason for existence to its need to face and cope with such pressures, not losing status in the process—as would certainly happen if the adolescents had to face, nakedly, the censures, criticisms, and punishments of a middle-class or adult world they do not understand, and which does not understand them.

Each outside level represents forces which affect status within the gang—a boy can acquire "rep" by defiance of police, by vandalism of a neighborhood institution, or by showing "heart" in a gang fight. Whether or not the threat originated inside or outside the group, recognizing the existence of the gang and its internal dynamics is crucial to understanding how gang boys maintain status. The larger society is remote and abstract; even the neighborhood has indirect contact; the gang provides the face-to-face audience, the most direct and meaningful rewards and punishments.

Problems of status management are not confined to adolescent gangs. They affect us all—they rain on the just and the unjust alike, on parents, on delinquents, on corporation vice-presidents. And they rouse many besides juvenile gangs to violence.

In our work we noted that often merely assigning a worker to a gang, even before he had a chance to do anything, made the gang more docile, because being important enough to rate your own worker was such a mark of prestige that more energetic proof was not as necessary. Learning the techniques of status management—understanding the dynamics and importance of status considerations within juvenile gangs—provides a powerful lever by which gang behavior and delinquency can be grasped—and, perhaps, controlled.

GROUPS, GANGS, AND COHESIVENESS

Malcolm W. Klein and Lois Y. Crawford

". . . if a group lacks a task, purpose, or mission as a result of not being integrated into a demanding external system— as may in fact be the case for street-corner gangs—then it would fail to generate a major part of the rewards and sentiments which its members might expect to gain from it."[1]

This statement by Gordon, quoted by Short and Strodtbeck, derives from experience and data in the context of the Chicago juvenile gang world. It also is the nub of the position we have taken on the basis of independently collected data and experience with Los Angeles gangs. This paper is concerned with selected, and presumably important, *qualitative differences* between juvenile gangs and other groups which have been the more traditional subject of empirical research. Our emphasis will be upon group cohesiveness and the differential nature and function of this concept when the distinctions between gangs and other groups are taken into account.

The Sherifs[2] have adopted the position, in very strong terms, that separating gang phenomena from the more generic peer group context does violence to one's perspective on gangs. We agree with the *intent* of the Sherifs' argument, believing that the understanding of gang dynamics must

An earlier version of this paper was presented at the annual meeting of the Pacific Sociological Association in Vancouver, B. C., April, 1966. It reports one aspect of a larger project funded by the Ford Foundation and carried out in collaboration with the Los Angeles County Probation Department. The authors are grateful for their constructive criticisms of an earlier draft to LaMar Empey, Solomon Kobrin, Barbara Myerhoff, and George Newland. This version previously appeared in the *Journal of Research in Crime and Delinquency*, Vol. 4 (January, 1967).

come in the conceptual context of general group concepts and findings. We hope to demonstrate, however, that the rather extreme position taken by the Sherifs commits one to the opposite error of emasculating the juvenile gang of just those characteristics which make it stand out as a social problem.

SOCIAL GROUPS

Laboratory groups, T-groups, fraternities, and the other group targets of most empirical research are frequently studied in terms of the interpersonal attraction of the members and derive their cohesiveness (whether natural or experimentally induced) from such factors as common goals, explicitness of goals, shared norms and values, and stability of membership. They further tend to be characterized by behaviors and goals which are acceptable to society. Our understanding of group process and cohesiveness is understandably colored by these facts.

It is a major thesis of this report that the existing literature on cohesiveness is less directly applicable to gangs because of qualitative factors which distinguish gangs from most other groups previously studied. As Lott and Lott observe in their review of the empirical literature, while most researchers have subscribed to the position that group cohesiveness is contributed to by a number of independent forces, most investigations have focused on intermember attraction. Thus, they "assume that interpersonal attraction, liking, or positive attitudes among group members is central to the cohesiveness of small groups."[3]

JUVENILE GANGS

It is our contention that gang cohesiveness is based not only on these normal group processes, but, to an even greater extent, on the interaction of these processes with negatively sanctioned behavior and attitudes. In the gang setting, cohesiveness and delinquent behavior are mutual interactors and reinforcers.[4] Indeed, the currently available literature on gangs bifurcates into these two major emphases or concerns with group variables.

One group of writers lays stress on group structure and cohesiveness *per se*. Thrasher,[5] for example, recognized great variation in the size and structure of the gangs under his purview. He distinguished between "diffuse" and "solidified" gangs, with any one group's position along this dimension being a function of the amount of conflict with neighboring groups. In the same vein, Yablonsky has emphasized that gang cohesiveness varies as a function of conflict, or—more accurately—of shared sociopathic withdrawal from perceived environmental threat.[6]

The other major emphasis in the current literature has to do more specifically with the modal behavior patterns of gangs. As examples, one can cite Cloward and Ohlin's[7] conception of criminal, conflict, and retreatist groups; Spergel's[8] analysis of the relationship between neighborhood characteristics and conflict, racket, theft, and drug subcultures; the Short *et al.*[9] report of five behavior factors characterizing the activities of gang members.

Thus, variations in gang cohesiveness and in gang-related behavior patterns are well established. It would appear, in addition, that group cohesiveness and group product are interdependent. The importance of this interdependence to the practitioner has been underscored by Bernstein.[10] It seems especially important at this point to investigate systematically the relationships between these two sets of variables. This paper presents preliminary analyses of the gang cohesiveness problem.

SOURCES OF COHESIVENESS

As noted above, most groups may be said to derive their cohesion primarily from "internal" sources with respect to both origination and perpetuation of the group. In identifying these sources of cohesion as "internal," we recognize a certain semantic looseness, but our meaning may become clear when major sources of gang cohesiveness are examined.

It is our contention that internal sources operate with far less impact among gangs than among most groups, and that, in contrast, gang cohesiveness derives from and is perpetuated by sources primarily external to the group. This contention is not new; most of the writers referred to above would be in sympathy with it. Cohen's[11] "reaction formation" analysis and Yinger's[12] discussion of "contraculture" are in the same tradition. We believe in addition, however, that elimination of external sources of cohesiveness of gangs would in most cases be followed by dissolution of a relatively large proportion of gang membership. That is, only rarely does a gang develop a sufficient number of internally oriented systems to perpetuate itself in the absence of external pressures. This position is the result of two concomitant observations: (a) that internal sources of gang cohesion are weak, and (b) that strong external pressures are present. These two characteristics of delinquent groups provide an explanation for what Gerrard has described as "the intense but fragile quality of gang cohesion."[13]

To be more specific about the weak aspects of internal sources of cohesiveness:

1. *Group qua group goals* are usually minimal. The most commonly expressed group goal is the protection of members against rival gangs. Clearly this falls under what we have termed an *external* source of cohesion. Gangs assigned a detached worker sometimes learn to verbalize goals such as self-betterment, improving their group image, and "holding their cool." However, such goals are far more easily verbalized than internalized, and their general acceptance, when it does take place, is more often associated with gang dissolution than with solidification.

2. *Membership stability* in gangs is relatively low. We have observed large groups in which the combined subgroup memberships have totalled upwards of 200 over a two to three year period. Yet at any given point of time, there may be only 30 or 40 active members. In other words, turnover is high; many members affiliate with the group for brief periods of from a few days to a few months, while others move out

of the neighborhood or are incarcerated for periods sometimes exceeding a full year. The bonds of member relationships are rendered even more transitory by the existence of
intragang suspicions. Under these circumstances, it is hard
to *conceive* of, much less observe, a continuing cohesive
group. Even within gangs which have existed over several
generations, the mobility factors mentioned above operate to
reduce the stability of active membership, in spite of the fact
that allegiance to a given group may persist for many years.

3. *Group norms* among gang members have received much
attention in the literature, but few have been found which
are distinguishable in kind from those of the social class
from which gang members generally are drawn. Group *qua*
group norms are relatively nonexistent in the gang world
except as myths which are exploded upon test. Loyalty, for
instance—it is often said that gang members will not inform
("fink") on each other and will come to each other's aid in
time of threat, attack, or retaliation. Yet most gang researchers report numerous occasions in which such behavior
fails to materialize, or does so only among selected members.
The one norm that does seem to be shared is that of acceptance of a wide variety of illegal acts. Again, however,
this may be more class or subculture related than specifically
group related.

4. *Role differentiation* is difficult to observe in gangs.
There are often official positions such as president, vice-presi-
dent, or war counselor, but the influence of the position incumbents is nebulous at best. Functional leadership related
to different categories of activity is often present, but this
leadership is unstable and tends to shift from one person to
another during various phases of group development. A most
illuminating experience in this regard is to question several
members of a group about the respective roles which they
expect others to assume during various anticipated future
activities. Uniformity of expectation is *not* the standard finding of such an endeavor. The major agreement is upon status,
not role. In fact, the boys can seldom differentiate beyond the
status dimension.

5. *Group names*—Gladiators, Vice Lords, Egyptian Kings —are assumed by many to indicate a common "we-feeling" among gang members. In fact, however, these names often change within a group, and derive their greatest effect during conflict periods when cohesion is increased by external threat. Many gang names, on the other hand, derive from street or neighborhood labels—Ochenta, Parks, White Fence —suggesting again an external rather than internal base for identification.

Thus, minimal group goals, membership instability, a paucity of unique group norms, little group role differentiation, and a lack of lasting identity with group names all militate against the formation of delinquent gangs based on internal sources of cohesion.

An exception is to be found among gangs with a long history, for gang tradition does seem to be a major internal source of cohesiveness. These traditions in Los Angeles extend over 30 or 40 years. A boy growing up in the Clover, Hazard, or White Fence areas of East Los Angeles knows at an early age that gang membership is a highly salient opportunity open to him. This perception is continually reinforced on the street, in school, and even in his home. In this sense, a boy living in such a neighborhood is initiated into the gang culture before he has an opportunity to make an independent decision.

In contrast with internal sources, strong external sources of cohesion are everywhere apparent. Any informed layman can discourse upon the perils of poverty, low educational performance, job skills, disrupted family relations, "social disability,"[14] and so on. It needs to be added only that these facts of urban life lead to withdrawal symptoms, as documented by Cohen and Hodges.[15] When a number of boys in a neighborhood withdraw from similar sets of environmental frustrations and interact with one another enough to recognize, and perhaps generate, common attitudes, the seeds of the group are sown. Added to threats of rival groups are the many ways in which society reinforces this tendency—police behavior, teacher reactions, lack of acceptance by adults on playgrounds and in local business establishments, etc. Adolescent behavior, adult and rival group reactions thus reinforce each other, and the range of alternatives open to these youngsters is decidedly restricted. The result is delinquent group cohesiveness, however tenuous.

THE DELINQUENT PRODUCT

Thus far little reference has been made to the deviant behavior associated with the gang. But, the *delinquent product* of gang interaction is the second factor which distinguishes the juvenile gang from groups that have provided the bulk of social science knowledge of group behavior.

Society does not disapprove of gangs because they are groups, or because their membership is adolescent, or because they are urban, or because of their normal, urban, adolescent, group behavior. For gangs share all of these attributes in common with many nondelinquent youth groups. In addition, many other youth groups originate as expressions of opposition to adult expectations concerning their behavior. And while all the activities of these spontaneous adolescent groups may not be condoned by society, such groups are not likely to engage in behavior which will result in social rejection. On the other hand, society does disapprove of juvenile gangs specifically because of that small portion of member behavior labeled as delinquent. It is this delinquent product of the group that causes the reaction. Society knows this, its agents know it, and so do the boys.[16]

We have tried thus far to indicate that gangs are distinguishable from most groups on the basis of (a) a disproportionate measure of external sources of cohesion and (b) a societally disapproved group "product." Gangs are not the only such groups in existence. Consider for example political extremist groups, motorcycle clubs, Beatniks, the Black Muslims, the KKK, and some inmate cultures. But in most of these cases there are specifiable common goals from which the groups originated. They have this, and sometimes other internal sources of cohesion which distinguish them from the gang. The best juvenile gang parallels may in fact be to

inmate cultures and to San Francisco's now defunct North
Beach Beatnik colony.[17]

TRADITIONAL APPROACHES TO COHESIVENESS

In relating gang cohesiveness to gang-connected delinquency, one must choose among available conceptions and
measures of cohesiveness, or create new ones. A review of the
literature strongly suggests that one should create new measures of cohesiveness to fit this particular problem (as have
so many others in the past).

Cohesiveness, like patient care in medical sociology or
morale in industrial psychology, proves upon examination to
be a complex concept. It has been used as independent variable,[18] dependent variable,[19] intervening variable[20] and
hypothetical construct.[21] It has been used as an experimental
gimmick, induced so that relationships between other variables might be illuminated.[22]

Cohesiveness, nominally, has referred to mutual liking or
acceptance,[23] attraction to group,[24] degree of shared norms
or values,[25] and resistance to disruptive forces.[26] Operation-
ally, it has been measured by coordination of efforts,[27] sum-
mated attractiveness scores,[28] reaction to threat,[29] choice of
group over other alternatives,[30] ratio of in-group to out-group
choices or contacts,[31] and so on.

So many dimensions of cohesiveness run through the
literature that cohesiveness can hardly be considered a definitive concept. Resolution of this problem is perhaps best
achieved by reference to one's own particular interests based
on relevant theoretical concerns.

We have said that the delinquent product of the gang
makes it a special case. Further, it is generally acknowledged
that gang membership increases delinquency involvement.
The question is, how much and why? The "why," we suggest,
is in part a function of cohesiveness, the "how much" ultimately an empirical question.

Why should high cohesiveness lead to high delinquency in
the gang? It's not just the external sources of cohesiveness
that bring this about—these have to do with gang formation

first, reinforcement second. Most gang theorists presently concur that, if offenses are affected by mutual gang membership, it is because the antecedent deviant values, the requisite skills, and the opportunities for misbehavior are learned and reinforced through association with other members. Status forces are operative here also. We would add, only, that these processes can occur and persist because the external sources of cohesion continually throw the gang members together, forcing the kinds of interactions which are preliminary to increased gang-related offenses. These interactions become secondary sources of cohesion in conjunction with offense behavior, each reinforcing the other as the members mingle and verbalize the deviance which labels them as different.

Some of the jargon, the "tough" talk, and recounting of delinquent exploits engaged in by gang members probably serves the function of reinforcing the weak affiliative bonds within the group. Several writers have analyzed both individual and group offenses at critical points in gang development—points of low status and low cohesiveness—to indicate how these offenses revitalize failing group patterns.[32]

Thus a measure of cohesiveness which might most directly relate to gang delinquency must involve *member interaction.* It should not rely on members' verbal responses to an investigator, however, since those willing to respond are not likely to constitute a representative sample of the membership. Interviewing and questionnaire responses thus are of limited value for the task at hand.

Group *qua* group measures are also inappropriate for they reflect only *indirectly* a presumed summation of member interaction. This eliminates retaliations against rival groups as a measure, an infrequent occurrence in any case.

Index measures which are based upon the attractiveness of gang participation as the numerator and other alternatives as the denominator are suspect because the researcher cannot adequately assess these other alternatives. We have attempted one such analysis, using average distance from member homes to evening meeting sites as representing a summation of barriers overcome to join in group activities.

This measure yields findings which are highly gang-specific, rather than generalizable. In some groups it is related to attendance figures, in others it is not. The variance seems more a function of core than fringe members when analyzing between-gang differences, and variance is far greater between gang clusters than within subgroups of the same cluster.[33] All in all, we see little advantage in continuing this approach.

A SUGGESTED APPROACH

Another approach currently seems more promising. This approach is not dependent upon member responses, presents fewer sampling problems, and is a direct measure of member interaction, our primary criterion. It requires the presence of an observer, in our case, a "detached worker."

For the past four years, the authors and their colleagues have been conducting studies of gang intervention practices employed by detached workers with Negro juvenile gangs in Los Angeles. As part of this project, we have received daily "Contact Reports" from the gang workers assigned to *four large Negro gang clusters* (involving 16 separate gang groups). These Contact Reports give an accounting of all individuals seen by the workers in the course of each day. The reporting form lists the names of the persons seen and indicates the site, duration, and mode of initiation in each case, as well as the content of the conversation between the worker and the person contacted. There is also an indication of the grouping of persons involved in each interaction situation. Thus for any given gang member it can be determined not only how often he has been seen by the worker during a specified time period, but also with which other members he is seen most frequently.

Approximately 600 male and 200 female gang members have been identified through these Contact Reports in combination with other data collecting procedures. Most of these members have interacted with the detached workers numerous times.

Figure 1 is a model of the intragroup companionship patterns as summarized for one gang over a six-month period

Group Members

	1	2	3	4	5	6	7	8	9	10	11	12	13	14	15	16	17	18	19	20	21	22	23	24	25	26	27	28	29	30	31	32	
1	2	2	0	12	1	5	0	0	4	0	0	0	17	0	18	1	2	0	5	0	4	17	5	0	1	9	0	0	5	0	0	0	108
2	0	0	0	3	0	2	0	0	2	0	0	2	4	2	2	0	2	0	2	0	6	4	2	0	0	2	0	0	2	0	0	0	39
3	0	0	0	0	0	0	0	0	0	0	0	0	0	0	0	0	0	0	0	0	0	0	0	0	0	0	0	0	0	0	1	0	1
4	12	3	0	0	1	9	3	0	11	1	0	0	18	0	11	1	7	0	4	1	2	16	6	0	1	7	1	0	5	0	0	0	114
5	1	0	0	1	0	0	1	0	0	1	0	0	0	0	1	1	4	0	4	0	0	16	6	14	1	7	1	0	4	0	0	0	66
6	5	2	0	9	0	0	1	0	6	0	0	0	3	0	7	5	3	0	0	0	2	1	0	0	2	1	1	0	4	0	0	0	74
7	0	0	0	3	1	0	0	0	0	2	0	0	0	0	0	0	0	0	0	0	0	0	0	0	0	0	0	0	0	0	0	0	10
8	0	0	0	0	0	0	0	0	1	0	0	0	2	0	2	0	0	0	0	0	0	0	0	0	0	0	0	0	0	0	0	0	7
9	4	2	0	11	0	6	0	1	0	0	0	0	18	0	14	0	3	0	6	0	2	15	5	0	0	9	0	0	5	0	0	0	102
10	0	0	0	1	0	2	0	0	1	0	0	0	0	0	1	0	1	0	1	0	0	0	0	0	0	0	0	0	0	0	0	0	8
11	0	0	0	0	0	0	0	1	0	0	0	0	0	0	0	1	0	0	0	0	0	0	0	0	0	0	0	0	0	0	0	0	3
12	2	2	0	0	0	0	0	0	0	1	0	0	0	0	0	0	0	0	0	0	2	1	0	0	0	0	0	0	0	0	0	0	11
13	17	4	0	18	0	7	0	2	8	2	0	3	0	2	37	0	5	0	5	0	6	40	6	0	0	11	0	0	4	0	4	2	202
14	0	2	0	0	0	0	0	0	0	0	0	2	2	0	0	0	0	0	0	0	2	0	0	0	0	0	0	0	0	0	0	0	10
15	2	2	0	11	3	0	0	2	14	0	1	3	37	0	0	1	0	0	5	0	4	34	5	0	0	12	1	0	4	0	0	0	162
16	1	2	0	1	0	0	0	0	0	1	0	0	0	0	1	0	3	0	3	0	0	2	0	0	0	1	0	0	0	0	0	0	23
17	2	2	0	7	1	6	0	2	14	0	1	2	37	0	0	1	0	0	3	0	0	10	0	0	0	3	1	0	0	0	3	0	57
18	0	0	0	0	0	0	0	0	0	0	0	0	0	0	0	0	0	0	1	0	0	0	0	0	0	0	0	0	0	0	0	0	1
19	5	2	0	4	0	4	0	0	3	0	0	0	5	0	3	0	0	0	0	0	4	6	2	0	1	5	0	0	5	0	0	0	57
20	0	0	0	0	0	0	0	0	0	0	1	0	0	0	0	0	1	1	0	0	0	0	0	0	0	0	0	0	0	0	0	0	3
21	4	6	1	16	1	2	0	1	6	2	0	2	6	2	4	0	3	0	2	0	0	4	2	0	0	3	0	0	5	0	0	0	44
22	17	4	0	6	1	11	0	1	15	0	1	2	40	2	34	2	0	0	6	0	4	0	6	0	1	11	0	0	5	0	0	0	189
23	5	2	0	6	0	6	0	0	5	0	0	0	6	0	5	0	3	0	2	0	2	6	0	2	0	5	0	0	4	0	0	0	58
24	0	0	0	0	14	0	0	0	0	0	0	0	0	0	0	0	0	0	0	0	0	0	0	0	0	0	0	0	0	0	0	0	16
25	1	0	0	0	21	0	0	0	0	0	0	0	0	0	0	0	0	0	0	0	2	0	2	2	0	2	0	0	0	0	3	0	33
26	9	2	0	7	1	5	0	1	5	0	0	0	11	0	12	1	3	0	5	0	0	11	5	0	1	0	0	0	4	0	0	0	88
27	0	0	0	1	1	0	0	0	0	0	0	0	0	0	1	0	1	0	0	0	2	0	0	0	0	0	0	1	0	0	0	0	19
28	0	2	0	0	1	0	0	1	0	0	0	0	0	0	0	0	0	0	0	0	0	0	0	0	1	0	1	0	0	0	0	0	1
29	5	2	0	0	1	4	0	0	5	0	0	0	5	0	4	0	2	0	4	0	2	5	4	0	0	4	0	0	0	0	0	0	52
30	0	0	0	0	0	0	0	0	0	0	0	0	0	0	0	0	0	0	0	1	0	0	0	0	0	0	0	0	0	0	0	0	1
31	0	0	0	0	10	0	3	0	0	0	0	0	4	0	0	3	5	0	0	0	0	0	0	3	3	0	13	0	0	1	0	2	45
32	0	0	0	0	1	0	0	0	0	0	0	0	3	0	0	0	0	0	0	0	0	0	0	0	0	0	0	0	0	0	2	0	12
																																	1616

Group Members

Figure 1. Illustrative Model of Contact Data.

and indicates how often each member contacted each of the other members in the presence of the worker. For example, member #1 was seen most often with members #13, 15, and 22, and he was never seen in the company of fifteen of the thirty-two members contacted by the worker during this time period.

Using data such as those illustrated in the model in Figure 1, we explored the ability of various combinations of the data to differentiate one group from another. The indexes explored are summarized below, using the data in Figure 1 for illustrative purposes. The first five indexes are measures of subgroup or clique cohesiveness.

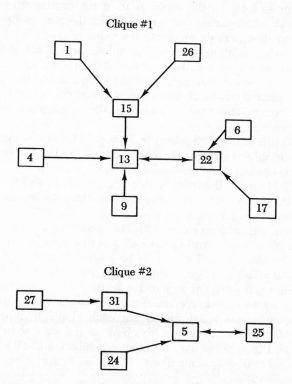

Figure 2. Cliques Within Members of Figure 1.

1. *Number of cliques:* Any approach to analysis based upon a factor analytic model can be used to reveal subgroupings among the members. For instance, if one applies the first steps of McQuitty's Elementary Linkage Analysis[34] to Figure 1, two cliques emerge. The first involves members #1, 4, 6, 9, 13, 15, 17, 22 and 26 and the second involves members #5, 24, 25, 27, and 31. The relationships within each group are shown in Figure 2, following McQuitty's procedure.

In this illustration, we have *arbitrarily* limited potential clique members to those who have at least 10 contacts with one other member. The arbitrariness thus introduced has no theoretical or statistical justification, but this represents no problem so long as the index is used for *comparative* purposes, i.e., comparing one group to another, or comparing different time periods involving the same group.

One other cautionary note is required here. This analysis employs only those members contacted during the time period selected. In other situations, it might be preferable to include in the contact matrix all known gang members, whether contacted or not. This choice applies equally to the other indices cited below.

2. *Percentage of members in cliques:* This index consists of the number of clique members divided by the total membership (however defined—see previous paragraph). In the case of Figure 1, the index yields a figure of .44 (14/32).

3. *Percentage of clique members with 50% or more of their contacts within their own cliques* (the 50% figure is obviously an arbitrary choice): This provides a measure of clique cohesiveness rather than of overall gang cohesiveness, although the two will obviously be positively related. In our illustration, all 14 clique members fall above the 50% figure, ranging from 58% for #31 to 100% for #24.

4. *Average within-clique over all-contacts ratio:* In this index, one merely determines for each clique member the ratio of his contacts within his clique to the sum of his contacts and then sums over all clique members and divides by the number of clique members. The index figure in our illustration is 77%.

5. *Percentage of clique membership with core status:* Most

gang workers make a gross distinction between two classes of gang membership, core and fringe. Using the worker's designation as the operational definition of core and fringe status, this index merely states the ratio of core to fringe members within identifiable cliques.

The first five possible indexes of gang cohesiveness have all dealt with clique membership. The potential importance of such indexes is that the clique members clearly constitute friendship groups within a much larger and somewhat amorphous collection of individuals. From a practical viewpoint, the practitioner concerned with decreasing the cohesive bonds of a juvenile gang must understand the nature and intensity of these bonds where they are the most binding, that is, within the natural friendship groups. A suitable index of the relative extent and intensity of clique relationships is thus the first order of business.

The remaining indexes refer to the entire matrix of contacts, thus representing an attempt at measuring total gang cohesiveness rather than the tightness of selected subgroups.

6. *Number of contacts per cell:* Referring again to Figure 1, it can be seen that a total of 808 mutual contacts was made (1616 contact notations in the two symmetric halves of the matrix). There are (32 x 31)/2 or 496 possible combinations of individuals who might have made mutual contacts. This index merely divides the first figure by the second to arrive at an overall measure of the relative frequency of gang interaction (in the illustration, this figure is 1.63).

7. *Percentage of empty cells:* It is one of the interesting facets of our obtained matrices that a number of gang members are never seen together, with the result that many of the matrix cells are empty. Much of this lack of contact is due to age differentials among the members. Ages range from twelve to the early twenties and, as with all adolescents, friendship patterns are strongly related to the age dimension. Younger boys are seldom seen in the company of older boys within the gang. Another contributing factor here is the inclusion of many fringe members, boys who have fewer contacts "across the board." This index provides a measure of these factors as they and others affect behavioral interactions. In the

illustration, 68% of the matrix, cells are empty, indicating no observed contact between the individuals concerned.

8. *Percentage of single-contact cells out of all contact cells:* Given the relatively high index figures resulting from index #7, percentage of empty cells, it was felt that we should obtain a similar measure among those boys who *were* in contact with each other. The index is derived by dividing the number of cells with only one entry by all cells containing one or more entries. In Figure 1, the result is 78/322 or 24%.

9. *Percentage of empty and single cells:* This is a combination of the numerators of the 7th and 8th indexes, using the total number of cells as the denominator. For our example, the index percentage is 75%.

Results: No doubt other combinations may occur to the reader, but the foregoing is sufficient to illustrate the general approach taken. We have been unashamedly exploratory in the absence of consistent theoretical guidelines to be derived from the existing literature on group cohesiveness. It was hoped that some of the above indexes, along with meeting attendance and average residential "spread" as reported on page [264] of this report, might evidence a differential relationship to the current status of the four gang clusters involved in our Los Angeles study. From many sources we know that gang Clusters A and B have continued the gang pattern far longer than have Clusters C and D. Further, we know from structural premises that cohesiveness declines with age beyond a certain point. In comparing the indexes of cohesiveness taken from the workers' contact reports, we have found the following (see Table 1):

a. The number of identifiable subcliques within a cluster seems unrelated to overall cluster patterns, but the proportion of boys identifiable as clique members *is* related. These proportions in Clusters A, B, C, and D are .42, .43, .16, and .15, respectively. Remember throughout these items that Clusters C and D are the ones with lower delinquency involvement.

b. The index based upon the number of mutual contacts

between members divided by the number of boys contacted, squared (actually n × [n − 1]) clearly differentiates between clusters. In the same order as in (a) above, the index figures for Clusters A, B, C, and D are .81, .72, .20, and .32.

c. Similarly, the number of single mutual contact situations (2 boys see each other just once during a standard period of time) over the number of all mutual contact situations yields indexes of .54 for Cluster A, .35 for B, .73 for C, and .77 for D.

d. Among clique members, the proportion of in-clique contacts to all clique member contacts is related in a fashion similar to the above. In the same order to Clusters A, B, C, and D, the figures are .82, .73, .47, and .40.

e. The remaining indexes failed to differentiate between the four groups.

That the indexes listed in a through d above refer to more than differences between clusters is revealed by a pilot analysis carried out on Cluster A. The older and younger members were compared on two indexes over three, consecutive, 6-month periods, with the results shown in Table 2.

Preliminary data indicate that the increase in cohesiveness among the younger boys and the decrease among the older boys parallels similar trends in recorded offense rates. In any case, it is clear from both tables that we are employing indices of some sensitivity. It remains to be shown just how directly they are related to gang offense patterns, but our hopes are high.

The development of these indexes of cohesiveness is an effort to assess this group variable as it is found in delinquent gangs. Our concurrent development of offense measures endeavors to ascertain the seriousness of the delinquent product.[35] The interaction patterns of these measures of gang cohesiveness and juvenile offenses, we believe, represent a sorely needed investigation in our understanding of group delinquency phenomena. If our investigation adds to the placement of these phenomena within the larger context of group process and outcome relationships, we shall be doubly rewarded.

TABLE 1. *Cohesiveness Measures in Four Gang Clusters*

	Higher Delinquency Clusters		Lower Delinquency Clusters	
	A	B	C	D
a. Clique members/all members	.42	.43	.16	.15
b. Mutual contacts/n × [n − 1]	.81	.72	.20	.32
c. Single contacts/all contacts	.54	.35	.73	.77
d. In-clique contacts/all clique contacts	.82	.73	.47	.40

TABLE 2. *Cohesiveness Index Changes Among Older and Younger Members of Cluster A*

Index	Age Group	July–Dec. '63	Jan.–June '64	July–Dec. '64
# Contacts/ n(n − 1)	Older	.25	.25	.16
	Younger	.21	.25	.29
# Nonsingle contacts/ Total contacts	Older	.65	.54	.51
	Younger	.60	.57	.70

*aleatory - pertaining to chance or con
tingency*

ALEATORY RISKS VERSUS
SHORT-RUN HEDONISM IN
EXPLANATION OF GANG ACTION

Fred L. Strodtbeck and James F. Short, Jr.

THE CENTRAL question raised in this paper relates to the motivation of gang boys to expose themselves to the risks of serious incidents arising from delinquent activity. We can conceptualize their action as a game played for small reward with little risk of loss, save that when the loss does occur it involves great costs. The argument suggests that the participation is rational, rather than impulsive, and that the critical element in the understanding of the motivation involves the recognition of the chance or aleatory process by which consequences—both good and bad—are allocated.

In a critique of "near-group theory," in this journal, Harold Pfautz makes reference to a report from the Chicago study of "street corner groups and patterns of delinquency" which conceptualizes certain factors in delinquency episodes as "aleatory" in nature.[1] Pfautz incorrectly identifies our position as referring to "those aspects 'which are beyond understanding or, potentially, prediction.'" He goes on to say that our "formulation only emphasizes the contingent, episodic, and non-routinized nature of this 'collective behavior.'" While the report in question specifically stated that we did *not* refer

Reprinted from *Social Problems*, 12 (Fall, 1964), 127–140, by permission of the Society for the Study of Social Problems.

The research reported in this paper is made possible by grants from the National Institute of Mental Health (Research Grant M-3301), the Ford Foundation, the President's Committee on Juvenile Delinquency and Youth Crime. We wish to acknowledge critical, and helpful, comments by Howard Becker, Meda White, and Richard Ogles.

to factors "beyond understanding or potentially, prediction," we recognize that we had not written, nor thought, as clearly as we should have. It was our intention to suggest that understanding could be greatly deepened by a conceptualization of delinquent behavior which stressed the joint relevance of motivated and aleatory considerations.

This paper carries the early argument further. We shall first review how we encountered the problem and then present a utility-risk paradigm proposed as a solution. In separate supporting sections, the role of cultural responses to potential violence and the absence of satisfying interpersonal peer group relations will be introduced as factors which predispose one to play at the utility-risk game.

This perspective has implications for a definition of delinquency and leads to predictions concerning subsequent movements to the rackets or away from the corner. In contrast with Merton's deviance paradigm, the present model postulates striving for status within the group rather than class mobility and explains continued participation in incidents of group action rather than distribution of delinquency in the social order.

RISK AND ILLEGITIMACY

We first encountered the problem of assessing the rational in contrast with chance elements in corner boy behavior in an analysis of parenthood among the Chiefs.[2] Illegitimate fatherhood was conceptualized as an "outcome" of several distinct components of behavior.[3]

A kind of two-step stochastic process is involved. First there is the probability that a given boy will engage in extramarital intercourse with a given frequency. Secondly, there is the probability that these actions will eventuate in illegitimate parenthood. The term "aleatory" refers to the independence between the first and second probabilities.

The first probability is dependent upon the cultural tolerance of intercourse, the intrinsic pleasures of intercourse, etc. However the full matrix of costs of payoffs is conceptualized, it is clear that, for the class of actions involved in the first step of this process, the outcome of the second step has little consequence. It makes little difference whether or not the boys become fathers, and for this reason, the outcome probabilities of the second stage are given little thought at the time of the first action. In this way, the incidence of illegitimacy becomes a function of the amount of time spent "at risk," and the explanations of variance among individuals is, so far as we can tell, independent of intentions or expectations about parenthood.

This explanation evolved in the course of two years' observations during which the number of illegitimate fathers among core members in the group increased from three to nine out of twelve boys. Almost without exception, the Chiefs individually expressed attitudes supporting the virtues of fidelity in marriage, small families, hard work and thrift, and keeping one's sons in school. Despite these verbal attitudes, the boys became school dropouts, job failures, and fathered illegitimate children for whom they assumed little if any responsibility.

The Chiefs' "area" was characterized by high physical deterioration, illegitimacy, juvenile and adult crime, and was a known center of drug traffic and use. The attitude of the adult community toward illegitimacy was in general permissive, and ample evidence of sexually unconventional role models among adults of both sexes could be found. Group norms placed a high value on sexual exploits and treated with derision the stable attitudes and expectations expressed in individual interviews. Yet illegitimate paternity did *not* confer status in the gang, and there was no indication that the boys actively sought to become fathers.

Even in this first conceptualization, our use of the term "aleatory" did not restrict it to events which are independent of the actions of the persons involved. It was incidentally true that the events in question were not, for this stratum, punished by society. However, we now wish to go beyond this feature and direct the argument to instances of serious aggression in which the outcome is not desired either by the boys or the community, and for which serious consequence, like imprisonment, may result from the response by the larger society. We do not say that all cases of serious aggression result from action with such an aleatory element, but that, etiologically, those which do should be distinguished from cases in which serious injury is the clear intent of the actor.

Specifically, it is our hypothesis that much of what has previously been described as short-run hedonism may, under closer scrutiny, be revealed to be a rational balancing, from the actor's perspective, of the near certainty of *immediate* loss of status in the group against the remote possibility of punishment by the larger society *if* the most serious outcome eventuates. Viewed this way, one does not hold that punishable behavior occurs because the youngsters are blind to the possibility of unfortunate consequences. We assume they realize that intercourse may result in paternity and that the bluff of an enemy may fail. Nor is it necessarily the case that delinquents generally value violent outcomes which society views with alarm. They risk these undesired outcomes because, from their perspective, the rewards and probabilities associated with risk taking appear to outweigh the disadvantages. In a very special way they gamble and, sometimes, lose.

STATUS AND SUDDEN VIOLENCE

To make clearer how involvement comes about, we call attention first to the way in which seeking leadership in a gang provides certain and immediate gratification if one is successful but, in the process, confers a heightened exposure to risks at times of violence. To illustrate this process, we include a brief account of Duke and the King Rattlers.[4] This case also indicates the existence of important background considerations which are otherwise unacknowledged but, as will be shown, should be recognized as preconditions for the general explanation.

Duke's gang had a well deserved "rep" for conflict, and also engaged in systematic strong-arming and other illegal means of acquiring money (some of which involved cooperation with the girls in a local house of prostitution—to the extent of not rolling their customers until after the girls had made the mark), some pot smoking and a good deal of heavy drinking. Though small in stature, Duke was a powerful leader in the rough and tumble of street corner life. He was "cool" in his relations with other gangs and with adults in the community. He exercised a strong influence on other boys in the group who respected his organizational ability, his coolness in crisis situations, and his ability to take quick, decisive action when the occasion demanded it.

Close to Duke in the leadership clique was Harry, a hard drinking, quick to fight, expert strong-armer, who effectively restrained any tendency toward aggressive dominance within the gang but could always be counted on for assistance in outgroup encounters. Duke and Harry thus complemented each other in their differing leadership styles. Duke, the stronger leader, was cool and cunning. He spent fewer hours on the street with the boys than did Harry, partially because of his attachment to one steady and several part-time girl friends, and at times seemed standoffish in his relations with the gang. Harry, by contrast, was forever with the gang and more "one of the boys." He was less cautious in involving himself in episodes of violence and often in trouble with the police.

Duke, Harry, and a few other boys constituted a leadership clique among the Rattlers. These boys supported one another in a loose sort of way. When there was no trouble, these boys were hardly distinguishable from the remainder of the group. Their worker commented:[5]

Just to see them [the officers] on the street you wouldn't think there were any [leaders]. . . . This stuff of officers don't go on the street. *Everybody's* body punching, from the Duke on down . . . [but] it's like [when] these guys are all on the street, they won't make a move unless Duke tells them.

The incident to be examined involved a fight between Harry and another boy and his brothers, not members of the Rattlers. We do not know the circumstances which led to the altercation, but we do know that it took place in the middle of the crowded main street in King Rattler territory, and Duke was a spectator. The detached worker with the Rattlers tells the story:[6]

A: . . . He [Duke] wasn't directly involved in the fight. He said that Harry had a fair fist fight with one of the brothers . . . [but] then another brother jumped in to two-time Harry. Then Billy [another Rattler] took on this other brother and they were going to it. When the third brother jumped in, the other two Rattlers stood back, and Duke came on with the revolver. Now the revolver [wasn't Duke's, it had] passed through everybody's hands—all the Rattlers' hands. The revolver was brought to this fight by this boy who isn't even in the King Rattlers. But the gun didn't belong to this boy. It belonged to his friend who again isn't in the Rattlers. The revolver passed all the hands and Duke ended with it. He jumped in the middle of the street and fired one shot up in the air, and no one responded. He told me they started closing in on him so he fired low. He wasn't firing at any particular person, but he wanted to keep the brothers off of him, and he didn't know he shot anybody other than a woman, and he felt real bad about it. But he said that he just got excited. This is the first time that he's ever put himself in that position. He said, "They just closed in on me all of a sudden." And he just started firing away.

Q: Did he hit more than one person?

A: He hit three. The youngest brother is 19 and the other ones are 20 and in the 20's. One was on crutches. I think he broke his left leg. Duke shot him in the right leg below the kneecap, and the other brother got shot in the arm. The woman got shot in the arm.

Q: Was he actually aiming to hit any of these people?

A: I don't know. He did say that he shot a warning shot.

Q: That just doesn't sound like Duke.

A: No, it doesn't, and none of the policemen can understand that. Why Duke? 'Cause Duke usually won't get himself involved; he'll direct everything from the outside. The gun was knocked out of Duke's hand by the fellow with the crutch. Now Duke says he doesn't believe he shot anybody but the woman. [He maintains] the gun fired after it hit the ground.

Q: Does he know how many times he shot?

A: He said he shot three times. The gun was fired five times. But no one wanted to admit anything else. Duke will admit that he fired the gun three times. He says he shot one warning shot and then he just blasted away until the gun was knocked out of his hands.

Duke's leadership role was not originally achieved by being recklessly disposed to use a gun, but by standing up to aggression directed toward him by members of the King Rattlers before he became a member of the gang. Once in power, he proved to be cool in crisis situations, *up to the point when action was required.* Then, he struck hard and fast. Under these circumstances he was fearless and effective. He possessed, in addition, other valued skills and characteristics which fitted him for a leadership role in this kind of group. He could dance well enough to "turn out" most anyone in the neighborhood—other dancers typically cleared an area for him and his partner. He dressed "sharp" and "made out" with the girls. He did not needlessly cause other boys to lose face when he directed decisions within the gang. For these qualities he was rewarded with deference, both within the gang and within the larger neighborhood, by adults and young people alike.

Unlike our earlier analysis of outgroup aggression in response to leadership threats,[7] there is no evidence that Duke precipitated this incident to deal with a challenge to his rank, or that status threats of any sort were involved in Duke's initial action. Once the situation crystallized, however, there was a clear expectation that Duke would take charge. Duke did not "just happen" to get the gun; it was passed to him. Once it was in his hands, it seems likely that Duke's perception of the norms of the group, along with the exigencies of the violence he faced, strongly determined that he use the gun. In this sense, his actions arose "in line of duty," as part of the leadership role.

THE UTILITY-RISK PARADIGM

Once the incident has occurred, so much is lost relative to possible gain that one is tempted to regard Duke's behavior as a conditioned response elicited by the stimulus situation rather than as a cognitively mediated response arising after rational assessment of choices. Only after the incident is formulated into a utility-risk paradigm in which Duke's actions coincide with the rational choice does the probability of

cognitive mediation seem clear. Consider the matrix in Figure
1. The Figure conceptualizes the situation as a two-person
game, the actor against the environment, with columns representing options available to the actor. Rows represent the
occurrence or nonoccurrence of a violent event after the

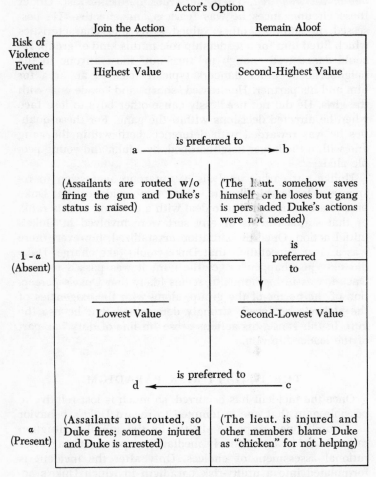

Figure 1. Matrix of Behavior Options and Outcomes.

actor makes his choice. Each cell contains a description of the outcome and the value placed on it by the actor.

Figure 1 shows four alternatives (a, b, c, and d) as Duke might have defined them in terms of his experience. The alternatives do not, of course, exhaust the courses of action or the outcomes which were possible in this incident, nor do they necessarily represent those which actually occurred to Duke. The paradigm does not represent the freezing of alternatives such that decision making and action processes become locked into discreet units. It is known that, under pressure, individuals narrow the range of alternatives which they consider in reaching decisions, but it is our belief that in on-going activities such as occur on the street, behavior is a continuing process of adjustment to elements in the situation such as those being described. The paradigm simplifies exposition of the process. Returning to it, therefore, we assume that an actor will be able to rank the utilities associated with the four alternatives in a set, $V(a)$, $V(b)$, $V(c)$, $V(d)$, where V refers to values assigned various outcomes, and that an alternative will be chosen only when the associated utility is larger than that for any other alternative in the set. The utility of an outcome is, however, not solely a function of its subjective preferability.

To describe the subjective utility (μ) one must associate with each alternative not only a preference value (V) but also a subjective estimate of the likelihood of the event occurring. The subjective probabilities, like ordinary objective ones, can be symbolically represented by a number (ψ) between zero and one. Subjective expected utility involves, therefore, a combination of preference and probability.

$$\mu(a) = V(a)\psi(1 - \alpha)$$
$$\mu(b) = V(b)\psi(1 - \alpha)$$
$$\mu(c) = V(c)\psi(\alpha)$$
$$\mu(d) = V(d)\psi(\alpha)$$

To denote the alternatives of joining or not joining the action, we will write $a_\alpha d$ and $b_\alpha c$. The expression $a_\alpha d$ indicates that the highly desired outcome "a" materializes if risky alternative α does not occur, and that "d" materializes if α does occur. With these conventions we may now write a description of the two alternatives open to Duke as in Figure 1.

Join:

$$\mu(a_\alpha d) = V(a)\ [1 - \psi(\alpha)] + V(d)\psi(\alpha)$$

Remain Aloof:

$$\mu(b_\alpha c) = V(b)\ [1 - \psi(\alpha)] + V(c)\psi(\alpha)$$

From these equations, in which it is assumed that the preference ordering, i.e., a > b > c > d is independent of the judgment of the likelihood of the outcome,[8] one can deduce a series of empirically testable statements.

For example, if α were an event which never occurred, then one would always choose the first column, the option to join the action. On the other hand, if α always occurred, one would always choose the second column, the option to stay aloof. Stated in somewhat more general terms, if the risk of violence or *some other undesirable outcome* were not present, then boys would always join the action because this makes possible the most highly valued outcome. If serious violence or some other extremely undesirable outcome always resulted when the action was joined, boys presumably would always remain aloof. Thus, as the probability of undesirable outcome (α) moves from zero to one, the probability of joining the action moves from one to zero.

Under conditions of the model here utilized, the sole assumption necessary for the prediction of choice is that a > b > c > d strictly hold. The absolute magnitude of the differences are immaterial, so long as "a" is more preferred than "b," etc. This contrasts with other game theoretic models in which the play is directly influenced by the magnitude of the difference of the preferences.

More conventional decision making experiments by Luce suggest that, in a situation of this sort, the probability of α and the probability of choosing the first column do not define a continuous ogive curve,[9] as one might expect from psychophysical data, but will show a step-wise, discontinuous relationship (see Table 1). Luce's analysis would lead one to conclude that, when the probability of α was perhaps as high as 0.4, the actor would consistently join the action and expose himself to the risk of "d." If Duke makes his decisions as subjects do in laboratory experiments, he would routinely be expected to decide to join the action.

TABLE I. *Probability Step Function for the Paradigm Matrix*

Probability of Consequences Being Avoided $(1-\alpha)$	Luce's Empirical Estimates of Probability of Joining the Action
0.00 ≈ 0.20	0.00
0.28 ≈ 0.41	0.18
0.41 ≈ 0.46	0.59
0.46 ≈ 0.58	0.89
0.58 ≈ 1.00	1.00

THE CULTURE AND THE (α) CONSEQUENCE

The selected lower class values to which street corner gangs give heightened emphasis increase the destructive potential of gang behavior. In Chicago, particularly in the Negro slums, guns are valued as defensive weapons, and sometimes for offensive purposes. The boys are afraid of guns, and Duke, in the incident described, might well have expected that the combatants would respond immediately to his demand to stop the action when he brandished the gun. Characteristically, when one gang has guns and another does not, the gang without guns flees the scene of the battle, and with good reason. Among adults in these neighborhoods, parents are known to tell their children to "keep the gun handy" when they are home alone; at other times a child may be told to bring a gun along when meeting a parent at a bus stop after dark. Guns are not perceived as objects of sport, as in hunting or target shooting, and there is little support in middle class society or in the mass media for their use in active defense. The rationale appears to arise from widespread fear that sudden violence may be perpetrated—at almost any time—and that the police power will not be effective to stop it. The fear is not wholly unrealistic; women are assaulted near train stations, unoccupied apartments are broken into and, by official estimate, there are more armed robberies in Chicago than anywhere else in the United States. Ownership of a gun (or control to the degree that it can be produced for a rumble) is both sought and, if attained, status conferring. Having guns available in turn increases the possibility that others will feel them necessary and that they will, eventually, be used.

Public drinking on the street, in the pool halls, taverns, and at "quarter parties," complicated by the interpersonal strains of a frequent succession of sex partners, produces episodes of violence where short-lived demonstrations of toughness are appropriate. The toughness of lower class urban Negroes[10] is quite unlike the Yamato Damashi of Japanese culture which places emphasis upon the ability to withstand pain and work hard no matter what the challenge. In the culture of the gang, themes which suggest superego elements associated with patrilineality are absent. There is little emphasis upon being able to suffer and endure.[11] For the most part, the emphasis is upon being able to avoid all pain, and to injure and dominate without risk through superior weapons and numbers. Hence the seriousness and irreversibility of certain actions which arise in inner-city gang delinquency are in this way related to the availability of guns, but not this alone. There is a pervasive sense of threat, an emphasis upon aggressivity, and the absence of heroic or masochistic battle ethics.

Our conservative estimate is that not more than one in five instances of potential violence actually result in serious consequences. When serious consequences arise, these are discovered by the authorities in only approximately one-fifth of the cases, and this figure is less than one in ten when the injury is inflicted in individual and group fighting. For average Negro gang boys the probability of arrest for involvement in instances of potential violence is probably no greater than .04, and for the very skillful this figure might fall to .02.[12] However estimated, the probability of avoiding serious outcome appears to be sufficiently large to make the option of joining the action quite attractive.

More than this, once the decision to join the action has been made and rewarded a few times, the actors are not assumed to be motivated to alternate in the way subjects guessing which of two lights will be lighted are reported to do. In such experiments it has been demonstrated that the naive subject in a sequence rewarded seven-tenths of the time tends to converge toward giving the rewarded option seven-tenths of the time—a strategy which is inferior to taking the more frequently rewarded option all of the time.[13] For the case in question, we assume that while one or two episodes of violence with serious injury (α) might take a boy out of circulation, it would not materially reduce his selection of the option to play once he were back with the gang. The source of the motivation to join the action becomes more intelligible when one views the role of the gang action in reducing the isolation of the individual boy.

STREET CORNER PEER RELATIONS AND BEHAVIOR OPTIONS

To the extent that predictable friendship networks exist, we assume that threats of corner life are reduced. Field observation and other data from the present research program suggest, however, that the search for satisfying friendships often is thwarted and the uneven quality of corner relationships gives rise to uneasy tension between unmet needs to affiliate and fear of involvement. The result is an uncertainty about identification which is periodically resolved by a precipitate "joining" in group action.[14]

We note the tendency to distrust all "outsiders" beyond one's own intimate associates. There is a common disposition to exploit each situation to one's personal advantage and, as is characteristic of many persons at the bottom of the social and economic ladder in a variety of cultures, to assume that others are similarly motivated.[15] For inner-city Negro gang boys in particular, the exploitative skills which is part of a trickster-trader easy money tradition is poorly developed. As a result, the fearfulness of being conned or exploited is reinforced by a projection of desires which they lack the ability to carry out. Torn between needs for affiliation and suspicion, the youngsters alternate between gullibility and suspiciousness of others with regard to long-term involvement.

While the desire to avoid involvement with strangers loses out very easily to a gregarious need for friendship, friends often make demands which at times cannot be met or, if met, cannot be repaid. There is a rapid shift of residences in dwelling units in which fear of actual injury at the hands of newcomers motivates the avoidance of overinvolvement. The tensions with usurious landlords and the defensiveness before bill collectors, A.D.C. investigators, police, and other agency representatives creates an atmosphere in which other potentially legitimate sources of support, as well as neighbors, are defined as part of a hostile outgroup. The result is that, for the adolescents, a liaison which is as informal as standing on the corner with other boys comes to be sought precisely because it requires so little formal commitment or exposure. The sociability pattern turns on being near, but not being a part of—a kind of adjacency to events which can be easily transformed to active milling when a crisis arises.

It would be inconsistent for this "adjacency" pattern to be observed and for there to be, at the same time, a tight organization. When a crisis is brewing or a decision is being made about a trip or a ball game, the centrality of boys with leadership roles becomes visible and activated. But most of the day-to-day interaction seems to arise more from transfer to the corner of emphases upon drinking, dancing, food, sex, and money from the parent lower class culture than from any distinctive norms or special discipline of the group. So far as standing in the group is concerned there is so little formal apparatus of institutionalized leadership that the day's gains evaporate with the passage of time. As a result, all boys are in jeopardy of radically changing their standing if they elect to "stand aloof" in an incident such as that described above. If a leader does play it "cool" and others choose not to follow, he loses control over the action even though he would be touched by the negative consequences if matters turned out badly. Taken together, we view these considerations as creating the social basis for the vulnerability which leads to electing the "join the action" option.

THE PERSONALITY AND SITUATION PARADOX

One implication of the inclusion of risk factors in the delinquency sequence concerns a theoretically adequate definition of the delinquent. Can one say a boy is transformed from a nondelinquent to a delinquent by the aleatory outcome of his action, or does the essential delinquency begin at the earlier point when he elects to join the action? A long tradition in criminology cautions against generalizations about crime which are based solely upon persons who have been apprehended and incarcerated.[16] The point at issue here is similar. It underlines the need for knowledge about those who join the action without regard for the aleatory play of circumstances which bring a particular boy to the attention of the larger society.

At a superficial level this distinction only calls attention to the fact that "a"-type careers of joiners who have not been hit (as in "d") by the play of chance are included among nondelinquents in many research designs. While this is unfortunate it is less fundamental than decisions concerning relative contributions of, on the one hand, the delinquent's personality and, on the other, the payoff paradigm which, by its operation, at least in some percentage of cases, produces delinquency.

Since the subjective probability that event "α" will occur if the actor joins is influenced in part by the objective probability of "α" and in part by the actor's personality, and since the subjective preference is influenced in part by the actor's personality and in part by how those around him respond, both personality and the process represented by the payoff paradigm inevitably are implicated. More generally, the role of personality factors should be greatest when (1) the objective possibility is obscure or unknown; (2) the value of an event is *not* affected by reactions of other people; and (3) when there are many events (courses to action) to evaluate and choose from. The role of personality factors is reduced when (1) the objective probability is clear, evident, and cannot be ignored; (2) the value of an event depends on reactions of others; and (3) there are few choices open.

The conditions for conflict delinquency give little latitude for differential response due to personality once it is established that an actor attributes a given degree of legitimacy to the payoff paradigm. In general, the situation will be one in which personality makes little difference save when the personality factor at issue relates to the capacity to become "involved." For example, we have found that boys with "scoutish" self-descriptions are more involved in conflict than are boys who describe themselves as "cool aggressive," and boys who are "clean" are more involved than those who are "athletic." We have suggested in previous work[17] that this is the case because "cleans" among the latter must compensate for the lack of status-rewarding athletic skills, and because the characteristically responsible interpersonal relations which are the mark of the "scouts" place them in positions of group centrality and influence and, therefore, of vulnerability to joining the utility-risk game. The imperfect correlation of self-concept and behavior arises because boys with widely differing self-concepts seek to at least maintain, and perhaps increase their status in the group.

RACKETS AND RISK ELEMENTS

The utility and risk paradigm can also be associated with more deliberately chosen options which are to a greater degree coerced by the larger society, rather than peers. This can be illustrated by the later career of Duke, whose role in the street shooting was previously described.

Shortly after he secured a job as messenger boy with a large department store, Duke married the girl who had borne him two children out of wedlock. He liked the job from the start, and he performed well. Despite the fact that he had less than an elementary education, the position gave him a good deal of personal responsibility which he accepted easily. He became very much involved in the firm's employee profit-sharing plan. He was buying new clothes and furniture, and making payments on an automobile. After nearly a year of successful employment, Duke was promoted to another job with more pay. He was reluctant to make the change to the other department, and almost immediately began to be late for work and to miss entire days. He was fired after only a few days on the new job.

Shortly thereafter, while he was also collecting unemployment compensation, he made a connection with "policy" operators in the area and became a "runner" for the organization. With these two sources of income he was, of course, making a good deal more money than his department store job had paid him. At last report he was still working in "policy" and his wife had secured a job. He had expressed some interest in legitimate employment, but with his limited education and skills it seems unlikely that he can ever obtain a job which would provide as much income as does policy.

We view Duke's decision to join the action, i.e., push numbers, as determined in part by the fact that his legitimate job had given him the "opportunity" to get so deeply into debt that he would not be able to meet his payments even with the increased pay of the promotion (b). Without the messenger's uniform and opportunity for shifting, pleasant but peripheral contacts which his messenger job had involved, it is likely that he feared that his lack of education would be more unequivocally known. He might well have reasoned that he would have little chance for further promotion (c).

The rackets option had the immediate bonus of unemployment compensation plus earnings, a chance to float and be personable with many different contacts a day (a), but with the possibility that at sometime he would be picked up by the law (d). Here, however, the "d" outcome no longer has its place in the a > b > c > d order of the model. It is now preferred to "b" and "c" because the penalties for pushing numbers are small in contrast with the rewards and, in the event of arrest, Duke could possibly expect some legal help from those in control of policy operations.

For the Negro gang boys who drift away from the gang into lower class jobs, the "stay aloof" option is in part determined by the decrease in the importance of maintaining his rank in the group of what eventually becomes younger peers (i.e., b α c $>$ a α d). Since the average gang boy doesn't have the opportunities for racket jobs which Duke's personal skills had won for him, the legitimate rewards of steady work such as spending money and credit become determinatively important. Thus while leave-taking from the gang via both the rackets and lower class occupations is describable by different utility and risk states of the basic model, it is important to note that, with leave-taking, the original ordering, a $>$ b $>$ c $>$ d, is necessarily broken.[18]

DISCUSSION

In concluding this paper, we return to the related questions of what we mean by the term "aleatory" and what we suggest as an explanation of the disposition of gang boys to join the action in instances in which serious delinquency results. For our data in particular, we conclude that the disposition to join the action is not satisfactorily explained by the degree of deviance in values or neurotic or irrational tendencies of gang boys. We argue that the disposition to expose oneself to the risk of serious trouble should not be described as short-run hedonism, for we believe that the abandon in actions suggested by the term *hedonism* is misleading.

The alternative explanation recognizes the role of three parties in the action situation: the gang, the society, and the actor. We view the status-maintaining mechanisms of the gang as working continuously. The culture of the gang concentrates energies in activities which are outside the level of awareness of the larger society except in those instances in which serious consequences result. The possibility of serious consequences is increased by the easy availability in lower class culture of offensive weapons, widespread feelings of threat, and the absence of codes of honor surrounding aggressive behavior. The typical delinquent gang is not perceived as highly integrated and the most serious outcomes of gang action are viewed with concern by both the gang and by the larger society.

The dynamic mechanism by which these elements are related involves the collective effects of a narrowing of attention at times of heightened in-group interaction and out-group conflict. At the moment of truth, the field of potential responses becomes narrowed to joining the action or staying aloof. For any given incident a good proportion of the boys do stay aloof, but those who are leaders, or are within striking distance of leadership roles, are particularly responsive to the immediacy and implication of the group response for their status.

The paradigm represents an intersection of two fields of influence: the group and the larger society. Both are essential. The implications for status in the gang reinforce the involvement in activities which, on occasion, lead to serious consequences. The capacity of the larger society to strike back after serious incidents creates the tension. To maintain the conditions under which rational choice to join the action can occur, two conditions must be met: (1) the aleatory play of circumstance by which an action leads to serious consequences should not be subjectively perceived as too frequent (say, less than about four in ten); and (2) joining must be relevant to status within the gang sought by the actor, or required of him by virtue of role expectations.

In this framework, the term *aleatory* is narrowly restricted to the risk that an action, which in itself is below the threshold of concern of the larger society, will result in an outcome of such severity as to bring about punishment of the actor by agents of the larger society. So long as the utilities are ordered $a>b>c>d$ and the $P(\alpha)$ is low, the actor will elect to join the action. If the action is not joined, rank, which flows through familiar social exchanges of the group, will in some degree be sacrificed. Against this near certain loss of rank in the group the actor assumes the low risk of serious trouble with society and gambles to win the group reward.

Postscript

It is clear from these selections and from a much larger research literature that "not all the data are in" which would permit assessment of theoretical notions concerning the etiology of delinquent subcultures and gang behavior.[1] Equally clearly, however, none of the existing formulations are adequate. The difficulties are several.

There is great need, first of all, for better and more relevant data concerning existing formulations. Far too little research has focused primarily and specifically on theory testing. This is due, in part, to demands by society which often force research effort into channels which are less than central to the primary mission of the social sciences—i.e., the generation of knowledge about social phenomena—in the interests, for example, of social accounting related to a great variety of social control agencies, such as police, courts, and detached-worker programs. It is due, also, to the great need in the behavior sciences for descriptive studies, i.e., studies which describe and, hopefully, delineate phenomena to be explained. This, in turn, is related to a primary theoretical problem, viz., the need for greater specification of theories and greater rigor in formulation. So elementary a matter as delineation of the "dependent variable," for example, whether *the* delinquent subculture, a variant thereof, or this or that conflict, criminal, or retreatist gang has lagged behind theoretical explanation. Concepts are inadequately specified to permit clear-cut tests of theoretical formulations—what precisely, for example, is meant by "status discontent" or "position discontent," "status threat" or "status management"; what by "lower" or "middle" class, or their associated values? Theories utilizing these terms have not stood up well when subjected to empirical examination, or they have not been specified in detail sufficient to permit systematic examination. The notion of status threat, for example, requires theoretical specification and extension. Neither of these is likely to be successful without a good deal more empirical work. What are the conditions under which status threat provokes aggressive behavior? How are these related to structural and cultural properties of the group, and to skill levels of individuals comprising the group? Many such questions remain to be specified and examined critically.

These are, of course, neither "simply" theoretical nor empirical problems. There is no clear line of responsibility, no mutually exclusive division of labor between theorist and researcher in this domain though some behavior scientists tend to concentrate on only one of these activities; each must do those things for which he is best equipped by disposition and training. We close this section, therefore, with a decidedly unoriginal but fervent plea for more and better research which is theoretically focused and relevant, and for patience on the part of the society which must support these activities and wait for answers and solutions.

Notes

INTRODUCTION: ON GANG DELINQUENCY AND THE NATURE OF SUBCULTURES

James F. Short, Jr.

1 For a review of these studies see LaMar Empey, "Delinquency Theory and Recent Research," *Journal of Research in Crime and Delinquency*, 4 (January, 1967), 28–42.

2 Frederic M. Thrasher, *The Gang*, abridged ed. (Chicago: University of Chicago Press, 1963), p. 222.

3 James F. Short, Jr., Ray A. Tennyson, and Kenneth I. Howard, "Behavior Dimensions of Gang Delinquency," *American Sociological Review*, 28 (June, 1963), 411-428.

4 See Leon Jansyn, "Solidarity and Delinquency in a Street Corner Group: A Study of the Relationship between Changes in Specified Aspects of Group Structure and Variations in the Frequency of Delinquent Activity," unpublished M.S. thesis, University of Chicago, 1960, and Leon Jansyn, "Solidarity and Delinquency in a Street Corner Group, "*American Sociological Review*, 31 (October, 1966), 600–614.

5 Lewis Yablonsky, *The Violent Gang* (New York: Macmillan, 1962).

6 James F. Short, Jr., and Fred L. Strodtbeck, *Group Process and Gang Delinquency* (Chicago: University of Chicago Press, 1965).

7 See, for example, Andrew Greeley and James Carey, "An Upper Middle Class Deviant Gang," *American Catholic Sociological Review* (Spring, 1963), 33–41; also LaMar T. Empey and Maynard L. Erickson, "Hidden Delinquency and Social Status," *Social Forces*, 44 (June, 1966), 546–554. In this article delinquency is shown to occur among middle-class quite as much as among lower-class youngsters, and it is overwhelmingly of a group nature.

8 See, for example, Robert Shellow and Derek V. Roemer, "No Heaven for 'Hell's Angels,'" *Trans-Action*, 3 (July–August, 1966), 12–19, and Ned Polsky, *Hustlers, Beats, and Others* (Chicago: Aldine, 1965).

9 Wolf Middendorf, "New Forms of Juvenile Delinquency: Their Origin, Prevention, and Treatment" (New York: UN Department of Economic and Social Affairs, 1960).

10 William F. Whyte, *Street Corner Society*, 2nd ed. (Chicago: University of Chicago Press, 1955).

11 Albert K. Cohen, *Delinquent Boys* (New York: Free Press, 1955).

12 Harrison E. Salisbury, *The Shook-Up Generation* (New York: Harper & Row, 1958), pp. 66–67.

13 See, for example, Laura Thomasson Fishman, "Aspirations and Delinquency: The Case of Negro Girls," unpublished M.S. thesis, University of Chicago, 1966; Robert Rice, "The Persian Queens," *The New Yorker* (October 19, 1963), pp. 153 ff.; K. Hanson, *Rebels in the Streets: The Story of New York's Girl Gangs* (New York:

Prentice-Hall, 1964); and D. James, *Girls and Gangs* (New York: Monarch, 1963).

14 See Helen MacGill Hughes, ed., *The Fantastic Lodge* (New York: Macmillan, 1961); see also Albert K. Cohen and James F. Short, Jr., "Research in Delinquent Subcultures," *Journal of Social Issues*, 14 (Summer, 1958), 20–37.

15 Ernest W. Burgess, "The Growth of the City: An Introduction to a Research Project," in Robert E. Park, E. W. Burgess, and Roderick D. McKenzie, *The City* (Chicago: University of Chicago Press, 1925).

16 Roland J. Chilton, "Delinquency Area Research in Baltimore, Detroit, and Indianapolis," *American Sociological Review*, 29 (February, 1964), 71–83.

17 Christen T. Jonassen, "A Re-evaluation and Critique of the Logic and Some Methods of Shaw and McKay," *American Sociological Review*, 14 (October, 1949), 608–617.

18 From personal communication by kind permission of Henry D. McKay.

19 William Foote Whyte, *op. cit.*

20 Short and Strodtbeck, *op. cit.*

21 Gary Schwartz and Donald Merton, "The Language of Adolescence: An Anthropological Approach to the Youth Culture," *American Journal of Sociology*, 72 (March, 1967), 453–468.

22 Yablonsky, *op. cit.*; Jansyn, *op. cit.*

23 Paul Lerman, "Gangs, Networks, and Subcultural Delinquency," *American Journal of Sociology*, 73 (July, 1967), 63–72; Paul Lerman, "Argat, Symbolic Deviance and Subcultural Delinquency," *American Sociological Review*, 32 (April, 1967), 209–224.

24 See, for example, Solomon Kobrin, "Sociological Aspects of the Development of a Street Corner Group: An Exploratory Study," *American Journal of Orthopsychiatry*, XXXI (October, 1961), 685–702, also, Muzafer Sherif and Carolyn Sherif, "The Adolescent in His Group in Its Setting," in *Problems of Youth: Transition to Adulthood in a Changing World*, edited by the Sherifs (Chicago: Aldine, 1965), pp. 325–327; and Richard A. Cloward and Lloyd E. Ohlin, *Delinquency and Opportunity*, (New York, Free Press, 1960).

25 Cohen, *op. cit.*

26 Edwin H. Sutherland and Donald R. Cressey, *Principles of Criminology*, 6th ed. (Philadelphia: Lippincott, 1960).

27 Federal Bureau of Investigation, *Crime in the United States*, Uniform Crime Reports—1965 (Washington, D.C., 1966).

28 H. A. Bloch and Arthur Niederhoffer, *The Gang: A Study in Adolescent Behavior* (New York: Philosophical Library, 1958).

29 George Grosser, "Juvenile Delinquency and Contemporary American Sex Roles," unpublished Ph.D. dissertation, Harvard University, 1952.

30 Short and Strodtbeck, *op. cit.*

31 Ivan Nye, James F. Short, Jr., and Virgil Olson, "Socio-economic

Status and Delinquent Behavior," *American Journal of Sociology*, 63 (January, 1958), 381–389; Jerome Himelhoch, "Socioeconomic Status and Delinquency in Rural New England," paper read at the annual meeting of the American Sociological Association, 1964; Empey and Erickson, *op. cit.*; and Kenneth Polk, "An Exploration of Rural Juvenile Delinquency," mimeographed paper from Lane County Youth Study Project, University of Oregon, 1963.

32 As set forth in Albert K. Cohen and James F. Short, Jr., "Juvenile Delinquency," Chap. 2, in Robert K. Merton and Robert A. Nisbet (eds.), *Contemporary Social Problems*, rev. ed., (New York: Harcourt-Brace, & World, 1966).

33 See Robert A. Gordon, James F. Short, Jr., Desmond S. Cartwright, and Fred L. Strodtbeck, "Values and Gang Delinquency: A Study of Street Corner Groups," *American Journal of Sociology*, 69 (September, 1963), 109–128; James F. Short, Jr., Ramon Rivera, and Harvey Marshall, "Adult-Adolescent Relations and Gang Delinquency," *Pacific Sociological Review*, 7 (Fall, 1964), 59–65; see also Martin Gold, *Status Forces in Delinquent Boys* (Ann Arbor: Institute for Social Research, 1963).

1. CONFLICT GANGS AND SUBCULTURES

1 New York City Youth Board, *Reaching the Fighting Gang* (New York, 1960); Thomas M. Gannon, S. J., "Dimension of Current Gang Delinquency," *Journal of Research in Crime and Delinquency*, 4 (January, 1967), pp. 119–131.

2 Roger E. Rice and Rex B. Christensen, "The Juvenile Gang: Its Structure, Function, and Treatment," Los Angeles County Probation Department, Research Office Report #24.

3 James F. Short, Jr., and Fred L. Strodtbeck, *Group Process and Gang Delinquency* (Chicago: University of Chicago Press, 1965). See also the selection in this book, "Why Gangs Fight," by these authors.

4 Jerome Himelhoch, "Socioeconomic Status and Delinquency in Rural New England," paper read at the annual meeting of the American Sociological Association, 1964. Research in small cities and towns by Empey and Polk (unpublished), and this editor's boyhood in such a community (also unpublished—fortunately) provide further testimony in this regard.

5 From research conducted by this editor and his associates. See articles and references to this research throughout this book.

6 James F. Short, Jr., "Street Corner Groups and Patterns of Delinquency," *American Catholic Sociological Review*, 24 (Spring 1963), 13–33.

7 Thus, a gang's "rep" may be important even when the gang has forsaken active gang fighting for some time. Members of the Egyptian Cobras did not want to go back to fighting. They gathered at the home of their old gang leader, however, and were ready to fight

because their old "rep" was at stake. The leader in this case held the boys off until a detached worker arrived, and together they dissuaded the remnants of the gang from retaliatory action.

8 James F. Short. Jr., "Gang Delinquency and Anomie," in Marshall B. Clinard (ed.), *Anomie and Deviant Behavior* (New York: Free Press, 1964).

AGGRESSION IN A BOYS' STREET-CORNER GROUP

Walter B. Miller, Hildred Geertz, and Henry S. G. Cutter

1 The following quotations represent prevalent modes of characterizing gang delinquency: "The gang exhibits . . . gratuitous hostility toward nongang peers as well as adults. . . . There is an element of active spite and malice, contempt and ridicule, challenge and defiance . . ." (Albert K. Cohen, *Delinquent Boys;* Glencoe, Ill. Free Press, 1955; p. 28). "Groups of frustrated, confused youths direct their hostility toward institutions they see as symbols of the society" (Mary E. Blake, *Youth Groups in Conflict;* Washington, D. C., U. S. Dept of Health, Education, and Welfare, Social Security Administration, Children's Bureau, 1958; p. 8). Psychologists and psychiatrists often add the attribute of "primitiveness" to the characterization of gangs as aggressive and antisocial: "Youngsters who increasingly participate in tribal warfare in . . . [gang activities] and acts of violence, are primitive. They . . . have no concern about survival" (Cornelius Beukencamp, Jr., address to the Association for Group Psychoanalysis, reported in *The New York Times,* February 22, 1959).

2 Delinquent activity is defined here as "behavior by nonadults which violates specific legal norms or the norms of a particular societal institution with sufficient frequency and/or seriousness so as to provide a firm basis for legal action against the behaving individual or group" (Walter B. Miller, "Some Characteristics of Present-Day Delinquency of Relevance to Educators," address to the American Association of School Administrators, Atlantic City, February 18, 1959). Data from the Roxbury Project indicate that about 5 percent of all recorded "behaviors" engaged in by 200 members of 7 groups designated as "delinquent gangs" over a period of 12 observation years were specifically law-violating.

3 Further description of the structure, values, and relational patterns of Roxbury corner groups is contained in the following articles by Walter B. Miller: "The Impact of A Community Group Work Program on Delinquent Corner Groups," *Social Service Review* (1957) 31: 390–406; "Lower Class Culture as a Generating Milieu of Gang Delinquency," *J. Social Issues* (1958) 14(3): 5–19; "Preventive Work with Street-Corner Groups: Boston Delinquency Project," *Annals Amer. Acad. Political and Social Science* (1959) 322:97–106.

4 The observational situation was affected by the observer to some extent, since he was, in fact, attempting to change some forms of the group's behavior. However, since this was his first year with the group, his main effort was directed toward establishing good rapport with the boys. He observed the group in its indigenous milieu, rather than in the more artificial settings of school, clinic, or settlement house, and he was a frequent participant in its main activities. Once he overcame initial suspicion and was accepted, he was for the most part perceived not as a supervisory or critical adult but as a peer in whose presence one could act normally and unself-consciously.

In accordance with the worker's training, his records, rather than giving evaluative comments or personal reactions, consist of extensive direct quotation of conversations and detailed descriptions of observed behavior. The records were checked for accuracy by comparison with tape recordings and simultaneous field observations by the senior author, and comparability was high. During the year selected for analysis, the worker contacted the Junior Outlaws an average of 4.8 times a week, with contacts ranging from 2 to 6 hours, and recorded 644 typescript pages of data.

From this material 2,174 aggressive acts were identified—1,490 performed by the Junior Outlaws. A conceptual distinction was made between the external form of an action and the subjective state of the actor, since an act may be culturally defined as aggressive but entail little or no hostile intent, and vice versa. Care was taken not to impute hostile intent without good behavioral evidence; yet ambiguous acts, accompanied by clues indicating an aggressive component, were not arbitrarily eliminated. Acts meeting any of the following three combinations of conditions were characterized as aggressive: (1) formally aggressive with observable hostile intent; (2) formally aggressive without observable hostile intent or with cues indicating friendly intent; (3) formally nonaggressive but with discernible hostile intent.

The demarcation of a single act from a sequence of ongoing activity varied according to both the nature of the activity and the level or recording—that is, from a case involving one actor, one act, and one object (Joe hit Pete) to a whole sequence of events including multiple actors, multiple actions, and multiple objects (some of the boys engaged in a heated argument with others over who should be allowed to wear club jackets). While the differing specificity of unit acts imposes certain limitations, the proportion of specific to general acts in different parts of the records was relatively constant, creating an averaging-out effect.

There were 26 coding categories for aggressive acts, each containing from two to 100 variable designations. Each act was coded by two independent coders and often checked by a third, and the few differences were reconciled.

5 The present paper is a condensed version of "Patterns of Aggressive

Behavior in a Male Adolescent Street-Corner Group" (on file, National Institute of Mental Health, Washington, D.C., M-1342; Special Youth Program Research, Roxbury, Massachusetts), in which the social context of aggression is examined.

6 To test the possibility that the extremely low proportion of aggression toward adults might have been the result of a sampling accident whereby such situations were underrepresented, the year's target-distribution figures were compared with those obtained for two duly recorded episodes: (1) a three-day camping trip during which a peak of internally and externally directed aggression was reached, and which concluded abruptly when three boys were arrested by State Police on charges of molesting a teen-age girl; (2) a series of crises during which police forbade the boys to congregate on several of their usual corners. During both these episodes the same type of distribution prevailed; aggressive orientations toward adults and authority figures were as infrequent proportionately during these two occasions as in the entire record.

7 Each aggressive act was assigned an "emotional intensity" rating by the coder, utilizing a six-point scale, as follows: (1) No anger or "charge," very slight anger. (2) Mild anger, pique, irritation. (3) Some anger, moderate anger. (4) Genuine anger, intense anger. (5) Uncontrollable fury, rage. (6) Difficult or impossible to estimate. While these ratings were of necessity estimates, a coder familiar with the material was able to base his appraisal on a variety of contextual cues; for example, if immediately following an ostensibly acute verbal exchange participants engaged in friendly interaction, a condition of "mild anger" could be assumed. The form and style of the record also furnished direct cues.

8 See footnote 5.

9 Comparing the proportion of "object-present" to "object-absent" verbal acts shows that backbiting or hostile gossip—a prevalent form of verbal aggression in many groups—was rare among the Junior Outlaws. Of all aggressive statements, 82 percent were made in the presence of the object. This proportion was even higher (85 percent) in the case of peers. A substantially higher proportion of object-absent remarks was noted in the case of adults (45 percent); this probably relates to the facts that most adult targets were less frequently present in the neighborhood, and that the direct expression of aggression toward adults was less "safe."

10 The method employed for analyzing the content of verbal statements was as follows: A tentative listing was made of some 20 or 30 personal qualities or traits presumed to be of concern to group members. These were phrased in standard literary English and set up as quality dimensions—for example, bravery-cowardice was conceived of as referring to one general order or area of quality, with separate terms applicable to the generally valued and generally devalued aspects of the quality dimension. Four modes of orientation could then be subsumed under a single quality dimension—

for example, for bravery-cowardice a person could be characterized as (1) possessing the valued aspect of the quality, (2) possessing its opposite, (3) lacking the quality, and (4) lacking its opposite.

An attempt was then made to code a large number of verbal acts using these categories, and to construct equivalencies between standard literary English and corner-boy English. For example, cowardice could be rendered as "He's a square," stupidity as "What a meathead." It was found that several of the categories on the original list were not relevant, and that a large number of qualities of concern to the boys had not been included on the list.

A second listing was constructed which contained 89 quality dimensions and necessitated 308 words to characterize their nature and associated nuances. This process revealed that literary English very frequently lacked adequate equivalencies for corner-boy concepts, and awkward back formations and neologisms, such as nonbossiness, troublemakingness, and nonhipness, were needed. Of 1,047 verbal aggressive acts directed by Junior Outlaws at one another, 454 contained evaluative content sufficiently explicit to permit assignment to content categories. In the analysis of these data, it was necessary to make even finer distinctions than the 89 allowed for in the coding system, in order to group data according to perceptual categories of the boys themselves, rather than those dictated by the lexical forms. These empirical groupings were then reduced to Table 3's 34 content categories, which were still quite directly indicative of specific events in the data.

11 A Scout is trustworthy, loyal, helpful, friendly, courteous, kind, obedient, cheerful, thrifty, brave, clean, and reverent.

12 See Walter B. Miller, "A System for Describing and Analyzing the Regulation of Coordinated Activity," pp. 175–182, in *Selected Papers of the Fifth International Congress of Anthropological and Ethnological Sciences:* Philadelphia, Univ. of Pennsylvania Press, 1956.

13 While there is reason to believe that the pattern is both more pronounced and more prevalent in lower-class groups, it is impossible to be certain of this in the absence of equivalent research studies with higher social class groups. It would be most profitable, in fact, to analyze a range of group types—manifesting different combinations of age, sex, class, and ethnic characteristics—using the categories of this study. Many of the patterns emerging from this analysis—such as the high ratio of in-group to out-group aggression, low incidence of behind-the-back aggression, and virtual absence of abstract or impersonal aggression targets—provoke speculation as to the patterning of other types of groups in these areas.

14 Several theories as to the nature and sources of aggressive behavior of lower-class adolescents are presented by Cohen (see footnote 1); by Richard A. Cloward and Lloyd E. Ohlin, *Delinquency and Opportunity;* Glencoe, Ill., Free Press, 1960; by S. N. Eisenstadt, *From Generation to Generation: Age Groups and Social Structure;*

Glencoe, Ill., Free Press, 1956; and by Herbert A. Bloch and Arthur Niederhoffer, *The Gang: A Study in Adolescent Behavior;* New York, Philosophical Library, 1958.

15 See Walter B. Miller, "Lower Class Culture as a Generating Milieu of Gang Delinquency," footnote 3; "Implications of Urban Lower Class Culture for Social Work," *Social Service Review* (1959) 33:219–236; "Preliminary Generalized Theoretical Orientations to the Study of Gang Delinquency Developed from the Boston Delinquency Program," *Internat. Research Newsletter in Mental Health* (1959) 1:3–4.

2. ON PROPERTY CRIMES AND DELINQUENT SUBCULTURES

1 Richard A. Cloward and Lloyd E. Ohlin, *Delinquency and Opportunity* (New York: Free Press, 1960).

2 Albert K. Cohen and James F. Short, Jr., "Research in Delinquent Subcultures," *Journal of Social Issues,* 14 (Summer, 1958), 20–37.

3 James F. Short, Jr., Ray A. Tennyson, and Kenneth I. Howard, "Behavior Dimensions of Gang Delinquency," *American Sociological Review,* 28 (June, 1963), 412–428.

4 James F. Short, Jr., and Fred L. Strodtbeck, *Group Process and Gang Delinquency* (Chicago: University of Chicago Press, 1965).

5 Irving Spergel, *Racketville, Slumtown, Haulberg* (Chicago: University of Chicago Press, 1964).

JUVENILE DELINQUENCY: A GROUP TRADITION
Clifford Shaw

1 C. R. Shaw and H. D. McKay, *Social Factors in Juvenile Delinquency: Report on the Causes of Crime for the National Commission on Law Observance and Enforcement,* Vol. II (Washington, D. C.: U. S. Government Printing Office, 1931).

LEADERSHIP AND THE POWER SITUATION
Herbert A. Bloch and Arthur Niederhoffer

1 Czelaw Milosz, *The Captive Mind* (New York: Alfred A. Knopf, 1953), pp. 54–81.

3. ON DRUG USE AND DELINQUENT SUBCULTURES

1 For more extensive treatment of what is known concerning drug use and its control, see John A. O'Donnell and John C. Ball (eds.), *Narcotic Addiction* (New York: Harper & Row, 1966).

2 Richard A. Cloward and Lloyd E. Ohlin, *Delinquency and Opportunity* (New York: Free Press, 1960).

3 Isidor Chein and Eva Rosenfeld, "Juvenile Narcotics Use," *Law and Contemporary Problems*, 22 (1957), 52–68.
4 James F. Short, Jr., and Fred L. Strodtbeck, *Group Process and Gang Delinquency* (Chicago: University of Chicago Press, 1965).
5 See *ibid.*, pp. 207–209.
6 See this volume,"Why Gangs Fight."
7 See Harold Finestone, "Cats, Kicks, and Color," *Social Problems*, 5 (July, 1957), 3–13.

DRUG ADDICTION AMONG YOUNG PERSONS IN CHICAGO

Solomon Kobrin and Harold Finestone

1 Contacts with young addicts were initially established through field workers on the staff of the Chicago Area Project and the Institute for Juvenile Research Sociology Department, who had close and continuing contacts with delinquents. Addicts were paid in cash for interviews on a per interview basis. The initial sample obtained was systematically expanded in order to increase its representativeness by offering payment for referral of addict associates selected for age, sex, duration of addiction, social class background, and similar variables. The sample focused on the non-institutionalized young addict functioning in his natural social habitat. So far as could be determined, payment for interviews did not affect adversely the value of the material elicited. The validity of information regarding addict practices and experience provided by informants does not come into question, as the volume of material available was large enough to enable detection of the relatively rare instances of attempts to practice gross deception.

2 Further confirmation of the completeness of the police records was obtained when even those few persons in the interview series who had not yet acquired a police record did so shortly after they became known to us.

3 The evidence on the problem of an increase in the number of drug users provided by police records alone is admittedly not conclusive. However, further evidence suggesting that such an increase did actually occur is furnished by the observations of social agency workers in close and continuous contact with the activities of young persons in these neighborhoods most seriously affected by the heroin use problem.

4 These figures are based upon the Annual Reports of the Chicago Police Department. It is assumed that the frequency with which arrested individuals were re-arrested for violation of narcotic drug laws was the same for all age groups during the period covered.

5 Based on data furnished by the United States Public Health Hospital at Lexington, Kentucky.

6 Evidence in police, hospital, or agency records of regular, self-administered dosage of an opiate over a period of several weeks was regarded as grounds for assuming the person to have an established addiction.

7 See E. G. Williams et al., "Studies on Marijuana and Pyrahexyl Compound," *Public Health Reports*, Vol. 61, No. 29, pp. 1059–1083.

8 The designation of a drug as addicting appears to be a matter of definition. Some uncertainty exists as to whether only those drugs qualify as addicting which produce both physical and emotional dependence in the user. While some students of the problem regard the recognition of physical dependence as the essential factor in addiction, others tend to assimilate to the definition of addiction the element of harmfulness to the user and to the community which may result from emotional dependence alone. Since the term "addiction" seems to be variously defined, depending upon the commitment of the student to a particular frame of value reference, it appears necessary to state explicitly the sense in which this term is used. Cf. A. R. Lindesmith, *Opiate Addiction* (Bloomington: Principia Press, 1947); and Harris Isbell and H. F. Fraser, "Addiction to Analgesics and Barbiturates," *The Journal of Pharmacology and Experimental Therapeutics*, Part II, Vol. 99, No. 4 (August, 1950), pp. 355–397.

9 These groupings of community areas are those which rank highest in rates of Police Narcotics Bureau cases, Boys' Court narcotics cases, and Juvenile Court narcotics cases.

10 Length of time addicted was an item derived mainly from the police records and is based on addicts' statements to police in the course of interrogation. In the nature of the situation addicts arrested for the first time expect more lenient treatment if they understate the duration of addiction. Since the estimate presented here is based so largely on police records, it should probably be revised upward. On the other hand, statements of persons in the interview series regarding length of time addicted, made under circumstances in which they had little or nothing to gain by deliberate falsification, tallied almost exactly with the same information in their police records.

11 See Table 1 for distribution of average median income when community areas are ranked by rates of Police Narcotics Bureau offenders. In American cities the areas of low economic status are those in which social problems tend to be concentrated. Shaw and McKay, *Juvenile Delinquency and Urban Areas* (Chicago: University of Chicago Press, 1942), p. 141.

12 The social characteristics of these areas are described in an extensive literature. The most systematic and rigorous analysis of these features of low-income urban areas was made by Clifford R. Shaw and Henry D. McKay, "Social Factors in Juvenile Delinquency," Vol. II, *Report on the Causes of Crime, National Commission on Law Observance and Enforcement*, Washington, D.C.,

1931; and *Delinquency and Urban Areas* (Chicago: University of Chicago Press, 1943).

13 This term was coined by W. F. Whyte in his *Street Corner Society* (Chicago: University of Chicago Press, 1943), a decade ago. Whyte described the social organization of a representative group of young males in a Boston slum area around their leisure time activities which included racketeering and politics. While the groups examined in the course of the present study differed from Whyte's group in a number of important respects, it was felt that the term "street corner society" was appropriately denotative of the essential fact that young males in the urban milieu in which drug use is prominent assimilate important elements of their value orientation from sources outside the social institutions established for the purpose of socializing the rising generation. However, unlike Whyte's street corner "boys," some of whom were super-annuated youths in the late twenties and early thirties, the street groups examined in the present study were in their late teens and early twenties, tended to reject school and work as inconsistent with the dominant model of the successful delinquent, and spent virtually all of their time in activities centered around delinquency, sex, and intoxicants.

14 The absence of drug use in the delinquency pattern several decades ago in the same areas of the city from which the present interview sample was drawn is indicated in documentary studies of the problem in C. R. Shaw's *The Jack-Roller* (Chicago: University of Chicago Press, 1929) and *Natural History of a Delinquent Career* (Chicago: University of Chicago Press, 1932); and in C. R. Shaw and H. D. McKay's "Social Factors in Juvenile Delinquency," in *op. cit.*

15 Herbert Blumer, "Collective Behavior," in Alfred McC. Lee (ed.) *Outline of the Principles of Sociology* (New York: Barnes and Noble, 1946).

16 Outside the street society here described instances of youthful heroin use were found among a small number of middle-class adolescents and young adults who had been drawn into the unconventional *avant garde* of the jazz music world. They are not, however, in any way representative of the overwhelming majority of young heroin users in the street gangs of the city.

CULTURAL AND SOCIAL STRUCTURAL EXPLANATIONS

1 See, especially, Robert A. Gordon, James F. Short, Jr., Desmond S. Cartwright, and Fred L. Strodtbeck, "Values and Gang Delinquency: A Study of Street Corner Groups," *American Journal of Sociology*, 69 (September, 1963), 109–28; James F. Short, Jr., Ramon Rivera, and Harvey Marshall, "Adult-Adolescent Relations and Gang Delinquency," *Pacific Sociological Review*, 7 (Fall, 1964),

59–65; see also Martin Gold, *Status Forces in Delinquent Boys* (Ann Arbor: Institute for Social Research, 1963).

LOWER CLASS CULTURE AS A GENERATING MILIEU OF GANG DELINQUENCY

Walter B. Miller

1 The complex issues involved in deriving a definition of "delinquency" cannot be discussed here. The term "delinquent" is used in this paper to characterize behavior or acts committed by individuals within specified age limits which if known to official authorities could result in legal action. The concept of a "delinquent" individual has little or no utility in the approach used here; rather, specified types of *acts* which may be committed rarely or frequently by few or many individuals are characterized as "delinquent."

2 A three year research project is being financed under National Institutes of Health Grant M—1414, and administered through the Boston University School of Social Work. The primary research effort has subjected all collected material to a uniform data-coding process. All information bearing on some seventy areas of behavior in reference to school, police, theft, assault, sex, collective athletics, etc.) is extracted from the records, recorded on coded data cards, and filed under relevant categories. Analysis of these data aims to ascertain the actual nature of customary behavior in these areas, and the extent to which the social work effort was able to effect behavioral changes.

3 Between 40 and 60 per cent of all Americans are directly influenced by lower class culture, with about 15 per cent, or twenty-five million, comprising the "hard core" lower class group—defined primarily by its use of the "female-based" household as the basic form of child-rearing unit and of the "serial monogamy" mating pattern as the primary form of marriage. The term "lower class culture" as used here refers most specifically to the way of life of the "hard core" group; systematic research in this area would probably reveal at least four to six major subtypes of lower class culture, for some of which the "concerns" presented here would be differently weighted, especially for those subtypes in which "law-abiding" behavior has a high overt valuation. It is impossible within the compass of this short paper to make the finer intracultural distinctions which a more accurate presentation would require.

4 The "brains-brawn" set of capacities are often paired in lower class folk lore or accounts of lower class life, e.g., "Brer Fox" and "Brer Bear" in the Uncle Remus stories, or George and Lennie in "Of Mice and Men."

5 Further data on the female-based household unit (estimated as

comprising about 15 per cent of all American "families") and the role of one-sex groupings in lower class culture are contained in Walter B. Miller, Implications of Urban Lower Class Culture for Social Work. *Social Service Review*, 1959, 33, No. 3.

ILLEGITIMATE MEANS, ANOMIE, AND DEVIANT BEHAVIOR

Richard A. Cloward

1 This paper is based on research conducted in a penal setting. For a more detailed statement see Richard A. Cloward *Social Control and Anomies: A Study of a Prison Community* (to be published by The Free Press).

2 See especially Emile Durkheim, *Suicide*, translated by J. A. Spaulding and George Simpson, Glencoe, Ill.: Free Press, 1951; and Robert K. Merton, *Social Theory and Social Structure*, Glencoe, Ill.: Free Press, 1957, Chapters 4 and 5.

3 See especially the following: Clifford R. Shaw, *The Jack-Roller*, Chicago: The University of Chicago Press, 1930; Clifford R. Shaw, *The Natural History of a Delinquent Career*, Chicago: The University of Chicago Press, 1931; Clifford R. Shaw et al., *Delinquency Areas*, Chicago: The University of Chicago Press, 1940; Clifford R. Shaw and Henry D. McKay, *Juvenile Delinquency and Urban Areas*, Chicago: The University of Chicago Press, 1942; Edwin H. Sutherland, *Principles of Criminology*, 4th edition, Philadelphia: Lippincott, 1947; Edwin H. Sutherland, *White Collar Crime*, New York: Dryden, 1949.

4 "Illegitimate means" are those proscribed by the mores. The concept therefore includes "illegal means" as a special case but is not coterminous with illegal behavior, which refers only to the violation of legal norms. In several parts of this paper, I refer to particular forms of deviant behavior which entail violation of the law and there use the more restricted term, "illegal means." But the more general concept of illegitimate means is needed to cover the wider gamut of deviant behavior and to relate the theories under review here to the evolving theory of "legitimacy" in sociology.

5 All of the excerpts in this section are from Durkheim, *op. cit.*, pp. 247–257.

6 For this excerpt and those which follow immediately, see Merton, *op. cit.* pp. 131–194.

7 See, e.g., Seldon D. Bacon, "Social Settings Conducive to Alcoholism —A Sociological Approach to a Medical Problem," *Journal of the American Medical Association*, 16 (May, 1957), pp. 177–181; Robert F. Bales, "Cultural Differences in Rates of Alcoholism," *Quarterly Journal of Studies on Alcohol*, 16 (March, 1946), pp. 480–499; Jerome H. Skolnick, "A Study of the Relation of Ethnic Background

   to Arrests for Inebriety," *Quarterly Journal of Studies on Alcohol,*
   15 (December, 1954), pp. 451–474.

8 See Isidor T. Thorner, "Ascetic Protestantism and Alcoholism"
   Psychiatry, 16 (May, 1953), pp. 167–176; and Nathan Glazer,
   "Why Jews Stay Sober," *Commentary,* 13 (February, 1952), pp.
   181–186.

9 See Bales, *op. cit.*

10 Merton, *op. cit.,* p. 151.

11 For this excerpt and those which follow immediately, see Sutherland, *The Professional Thief,* pp. 211–213.

12 For this excerpt and those which follow immediately, see Albert
   Cohen, Alfred Lindesmith and Karl Schuessler, editors, *The Sutherland Papers,* Bloomington: Indiana University Press, 1956, pp.
   31–35.

13 See especially *Delinquency Areas,* Chapter 16.

14 Shaw, *The Jack-Roller,* p. 54.

15 We are referring here, and throughout the paper, to stable criminal
   roles to which persons may orient themselves on a career basis,
   as in the case of racketeers, professional thieves, and the like. The
   point is that access to stable roles depends in the first instance upon
   the availability of learning structures. As Frank Tannenbaum says,
   "it must be insisted on that unless there were older criminals in
   the neighborhood who provided a moral judgement in favor of the
   delinquent and to whom the delinquents could look for commenda-
   tion, the careers of the younger ones could not develop at all."
   Crime and the Community, New York: Ginn, 1938, p. 60

16 Shaw, *The Natural History of a Delinquent Career,* p. 229.

17 Cohen, Lindesmith and Schuessler, *op. cit.,* p. 21.

18 It is interesting to note that the concept of differentials in access
   to *legitimate* means did not attain explicit recognition in Sutherland's work, nor in the work of many others in the "subculture"
   tradition. This attests to the independent development of the two
   traditions being discussed. Thus the ninth proposition in the differential association theory is stated as follows:
     (9) *Though criminal behavior is an expression of general needs
     and values, it is not explained by those general needs and values
     since noncriminal behavior is an expression of the same needs
     and values.* Thieves generally steal in order to secure money, but
   likewise honest laborers work in order to secure money. The
   attempts by many scholars to explain criminal behavior by general drives and values, such as the happiness principle, striving
   for social status, the money motive, or frustration, have been and
   must continue to be futile since they explain lawful behavior as
   completely as they explain criminal behavior.
     Of course, it is perfectly true that "striving for status," the
   "money motive" and similar modes of socially approved goal-
   oriented behavior do not as such account for both deviant and

conformist behavior. But if goal-oriented behavior occurs under conditions of socially structured obstacles to fulfillment by legitimate means, the resulting pressures might then lead to deviance. In other words, Sutherland appears to assume that the distribution of access to success-goals by legitimate means is uniform rather than variable, irrespective of location in the social structure. See his *Principles of Criminology,* 4th edition, pp. 7–8.

19 William F. Whyte, *Street Corner Society* (original edition, 1943). (Chicago: The University of Chicago Press, 1955), p. viii.

20 *Ibid.,* p. xviii.

21 *American Sociological Review,* 16 (October, 1951), pp. 657–658, which includes the excerpts which follow immediately.

22 The excellent work by Albert K. Cohen has been omitted from this discussion because it is dealt with in a second article, "Types of Delinquent Subcultures," prepared jointly with Lloyd E. Ohlin (mimeographed, December, 1958, New York School of Social Work, Columbia University). It may be noted that although Cohen does not explicitly affirm continuity with either the Durkheim-Merton or the Shaw-McKay-Sutherland traditions, we believe that he clearly belongs in the former. He does not deal with what appears to be the essence of the Shaw-McKay-Sutherland tradition, namely, the crucial social functions performed by the integration of adult carriers of criminal and conventional values. Rather, he is concerned primarily with the way in which discrepancies between status aspirations and possibilities for achievement generate pressures for delinquent behavior. The latter notion is a central feature in the anomie tradition.

23 Daniel Bell, "Crime as an American Way of Life," *The Antioch Review* (Summer, 1953), pp. 131–154.

24 For a discussion of kinship relationships among top racketeers, see Stanley Frank, "The Rap Gangsters Fear Most," *The Saturday Evening Post* (August 9, 1958), pp. 26 ff. This article is based on a review of the files of the United States Immigration and Naturalization Service.

25 See David W. Maurer, *Whiz Mob: A Correlation of the Technical Argot of Pickpockets with Their Behavior Pattern,* Publication of the American Dialect Society, No. 24, 1955.

26 For a discussion of racial, nationality, and sex differentials governing access to a stable criminal role, see *ibid.,* Chapter 6.

27 Training in conventional, specialized occupational skills is often a prerequisite for the commission of white collar crimes, since the individual must have these skills in hand before he can secure a position entailing "trust." As Cressey says, "it may be observed that persons trained to carry on the routine duties of a position of trust have at the same time been trained in whatever skills are necessary for the violation of that position, and the technical skill necessary to trust violation is simply the technical skill necessary

to holding the position in the first place." (Donald R. Cressey, *Other People's Money*, Glencoe, Ill.: Free Press, 1953, pp. 81–82.) Thus skills required in certain crimes need not be learned in association with criminals; they can be acquired through conventional learning.

28 Merton, *op. cit.*, p. 132.

29 *Ibid.*, pp. 144–145.

30 Retreatist behavior is but one of many types of deviant adaptations which might be re-analyzed in terms of this consolidated theoretical approach. In subsequent papers, being prepared jointly with Lloyd E. Ohlin, other cases of deviant behavior—e.g., collective disturbances in prisons and subcultural adaptations among juvenile delinquents—will be examined. In this connection, see footnote 22.

31 Merton, *op. cit.*, pp. 153–154.

32 The processes of "double failure" being specified here may be of value in re-analyzing the correlation between alcoholism and petty crime. Investigation of the *careers* of petty criminals who are alcoholic may reveal that after being actively oriented toward stable criminal careers they then lost out in the competitive struggle. See, e.g., Irwin Deutscher, "The Petty Offender: A Sociological Alien," *The Journal of Criminal Law, Criminology and Police Science*, 44 (January–February, 1954), pp. 592–595; Albert D. Ullman *et al.*, "Some Social Characteristics of Misdemeanants," *The Journal of Criminal Law, Criminology and Police Science*, 48 (May–June, 1957), pp. 44–53.

33 Merton, *op. cit.*, pp. 188-189.

CRITERIA OF STATUS AMONG STREET GROUPS

Solomon Kobrin, Joseph Puntil, and Emil Peluso

1 Albert K. Cohen, *Delinquent Boys: The Culture of the Gang* (New York, The Free Press, 1955).

2 Richard A. Cloward and Lloyd E. Ohlin, *Delinquency and Opportunity.* (New York, The Free Press, 1960).

3 Cohen, *op. cit.*, pp. 109–119, 121.

4 Cloward and Ohlin, *op. cit.*, pp. 19–20.

5 Albert K. Cohen and James F. Short, Jr., "Research in Delinquent Subcultures," *Journal of Social Issues*, 14, No. 3 (1958), 20–37.

6 Cloward and Ohlin, *op. cit.*, pp. 173–184.

7 *Ibid.*, pp. 194–202.

8 For a description and appraisal of the program see Solomon Kobrin, "The Chicago Area Project—A 25-Year Assessment," *The Annals*, 322 (March, 1959), 19–29.

9 The extent of agreement between the two panels regarding group norms was difficult to measure. It was the interviewers' judgments

that the descriptions coincided with only minor discrepancies. No effort was made to ascertain the precise degree of agreement respecting prestige rankings as between the two panels since only those of the group member informants were deemed relevant.

10 The structural grounds of the egalitarian bias among adolescent peer groups have been set forth in S. Eisenstadt, *From Generation to Generation* (New York, The Free Press, 1956).

11 Ideally, information regarding status criteria should have been obtained from a panel of gang members similarly challenged to justify their prestige rankings. This procedure was avoided for two reasons. First, disclosure of the actual grounds for attributions of prestige seems to require a situation of group discussion in order to develop consensual support for acknowledging sources of status that persons who do not possess them are inclined defensively to deny when polled individually. The same persons, when confronted with the interviewer's assertion respecting a given criterion of status and requested to rate a group on that criterion is inclined to comply, since the interview situation relieves him of responsibility in acknowledging its existence. Second, it was our judgment that opening the question of status criteria to discussion by the twelve group member informants would tend to embarrass the participants and yield distorted information. The decision was consequently made to accept as valid for the street groups the criteria of status defined by the agency staff panel. The fact that all its members were local residents, of whom two were themselves alumni of street gangs, reduced the hazards of the decision.

12 Group rank on either achieved or ascribed status is not necessarily the arithmetic average of rank on items specific for each of these status categories. Cumulated scores over all items constituting either achieved or ascribed status do not always yield a total score whose rank is identical with that based on the score for any given status item. Moreover, cumulated scores produced no tied ranks, as was true for scores on individual items.

13 The authors concede the elementary point that given the small number of groups no case can be made for the statistical significance of any of the differences in the rank order correlations. It was none the less deemed useful to present them for whatever suggestive value they might have for theory (e.g., perhaps the reputation of conflict gangs is not based solely on their fighting ability, but on their use of violence as symbolic support of community values), and for their descriptive utility in characterizing the study sample. In general, the data of this study are intended to serve the purpose of discovery rather than of proof.

14 The involvement of adults in the orientation of adolescents to athletic competition is emphasized in Coleman's finding that "the athlete gains . . . status in . . . schools" because "he is doing something for the *school* and the *community* in leading his team

to victory." James S. Coleman, *The Adolescent Society* (New York, The Free Press, 1961), p. 309. That sports competence represents an adult as much as it does an adolescent value is attested to by the wide audience for the sports pages of the metropolitan press, most of which is probably adult. Adult endorsement and sponsorship of athletic proficiency is perhaps most dramatically evident in the involvement of parents in Little League baseball.

15 Cloward and Ohlin, *op. cit.*, pp. 204–206. An additional feature of the transformation, germane in the present case, is the tendency on the part of organized crime to divert substantial capital resources into legitimate business enterprise, with a consequent enlargement of access to the legitimate opportunity structure for the younger members of racketeering family and kinship groups.

16 Cf. R. K. Merton, *Social Theory and Social Structure* (New York, The Free Press, 1957), pp. 225–280. Merton observes that "some similarity in status attributes between the individual and the reference group must be perceived or imagined in order for the comparison [with members of the reference group] to occur at all." *Ibid.*, p. 242.

17 The importance of exploiting reference group theory in accounting for variation in delinquent subcultures was first suggested to us by Harold Finestone.

18 Cloward and Ohlin limit their use of reference group concepts to the problem of differentiating lower class boys who are not assimilated into local delinquent subcultures from those who are. Thus, they state that lower class boys may seek membership in the middle class, in which case they reject the lower class status goal, which is limited solely to the possession of money. Boys who are content to retain their membership in the lower class are, however, faced with the two aspirational possibilities of improving or of accepting their economic position. Thus, the two dichotomized variables of orientation toward membership in the middle class and orientation toward improvement in economic position yield in their possible combinations a typology of four categories of lower class youth. They do not extend their use of reference group theory to suggest, however, the mechanisms that determine the actual choice of reference group on the part of specified segments of lower class youth. *Op. cit.*, pp. 90–97.

19 Cohen and Short, *op. cit.*

20 This view is in general supported by the Short and Strodtbeck finding that, with both race and class controlled for, delinquents were differentially subject to what they termed "social disability." While their data and observations related to the special case of disability imposed by membership in the delinquent gang, in the general case disability is likely to be found to involve family background as well. James F. Short, Jr. and Fred L. Strodtbeck, *Group Process and Gang Delinquency* (Chicago, University of Chicago Press, 1965), pp. 243–247.

SIGNIFICANT ADULTS, CARETAKERS, AND STRUCTURES
OF OPPORTUNITY: AN EXPLORATORY STUDY

Ramon J. Rivera and James F. Short, Jr.

1 The most comprehensive discussion of the design of this study
is found in James F. Short, Jr., and Fred L. Strodtbeck, *Group
Process and Gang Delinquency* (Chicago: University of Chicago
Press, 1965), pp. 1–26.

2 Edward Reuter, "The Sociology of Adolescence," *American Journal
of Sociology*, 43 (November, 1937), 421.

3 Ernest Smith, *American Youth Culture* (New York: Free Press,
1962), p. 26.

4 *Ibid*, p. 19.

5 See, for example, Ruth Benedict, "Continuities and Discontinuities
in Cultural Conditioning," *Psychiatry*, 1 (May, 1938), 161–167;
Kingsley Davis, "Adolescence and the Social Structure," *Annals
of the American Academy of Political and Social Science*, 236
(November, 1944), 8–16; Kingsley Davis, "The Sociology of Parent-
Youth Conflict," *American Sociological Review*, 5 (August, 1940),
523–535; Talcott Parsons, "Age and Sex in the Social Structure
of the United States," *Personality in Nature, Society, and Culture*,
edited by Clyde Kluckhohn and H. A. Murray, (New York: Alfred
A. Knopf, 1949), pp. 269–281; James S. Coleman, *The Adolescent
Society* (New York: The Free Press, 1961).

6 Ivan Nye, "Adolescent Parent Adjustment: Socio-Economic Level
as a Variable," *American Sociological Review*, 16 (June, 1951),
341–349; S. B. Withey and E. Douvan, *A Study of Adolescent Boys*
(Ann Arbor: University of Michigan, Survey Research Center,
1955) (mimeographed); E. Douvan and E. Kaye, *Adolescent Girls*
(Ann Arbor: University of Michigan, Survey Research Center,
1957) (mimeographed); Frederick Elkin and William Westley,
"The Myth of Adolescent Culture," *American Sociological Review*,
20 (1955), 680–684; Frederick Elkin and William Westley, "The
Protective Environment and Adolescent Socialization," *Social
Forces*, 35 (March, 1957), 243–249.

The implications of these works, and others, for the "theory of
youth culture" are discussed in Ramon J. Rivera, *The Sociology of
Adolescence: A Selective Review of the Literature* (Chicago: University of Chicago, National Opinion Reasearch Center, 1963),
pp. 5–29.

7 Richard A. Cloward and Lloyd E. Ohlin, *Delinquency and Opportunity: A Theory of Delinquent Gangs* (New York: The Free Press,
1960).

8 See, for example, James F. Short, Jr., Ramon Rivera, and Ray A.
Tennyson, "Perceived Opportunities, Gang Membership, and Delin-

quency," *American Sociological Review*, 30 (February, 1965), pp. 56–67.

9 For an analysis of the behavior of Negro gang boys which relies heavily on qualitative material describing adult-adolescent integration, see Short and Strodtbeck, *op. cit.*, pp. 102–116.

10 The New York School of Social Work, in conjunction with Mobilization for Youth, Inc. interviewed a stratified random sample of the adult residents of Manhattan's Lower East Side. Several of the questionnaire items employed in the New York survey were adapted for use in the Chicago study, but in sample design, and in intent, the two studies seem to be quite different. For an early report on the New York findings, see Richard A. Cloward and James A. Jones, "Social Class: Educational Attitudes and Participation", *Education in Depressed Areas.* Edited by A. Harry Passow (New York: Bureau of Publications, Teachers College, Columbia University, 1963), 190–216.

11 The Negro gang (Rattlers) was highly involved in conflict activities. The delinquent behavior of boys in the white gang (Pizza Grill Boys) was less specialized. The WG (and WLC) area however, showed evidence of being an "integrated community," i.e., an area with stable relationships between carriers of conventional and criminal values.

12 See E. Franklin Frazier, *The Negro Family in the United States* (Chicago: University of Chicago Press, 1930), and Charles E. King, "The Negro Maternal Family: A Product of an Economic and a Culture System," *Social Forces*, 24 (October, 1945), 100–104.

13 Herbert Gans, *The Urban Villagers* (New York: The Free Press, 1962), pp. 142–145.

14 Elkin and Westley (1957), *op. cit.*

15 Duncan's scale is presented in Albert J. Reiss Jr., *Occupations and Social Status* (New York: The Free Press, 1962), pp. 263–275. Table 4 is adapted from Duncan's list of occupations.

16 It should be noted that not *all* caretakers will receive a rank of 9 or 10. Thus one adult in the NLC group is a porter. Adults who worked as caretakers on a *volunteer* basis received an SES score reflecting the way they made a living, and not on the basis of their caretaker activities. Finally, female caretakers, if they were married, were coded in terms of their husband's occupation; the assumption being that the husband's position determines the SES location of the family.

17 It is interesting to note that adult-gang boy conversations involving *work* infrequently touch upon the problem of *finding* a job for the adolescent. In almost two-thirds (63%) of the work conversations described in the gang adult interviews, the boys and the adult respondents were simply comparing notes on the jobs that each held. This finding is consistent with our interpretation of other differences in the table.

18 The term "get some rest in California" is a lower class Negro

slang expression that refers to serving a sentence in the Cook County Jail. This facility is located on California Avenue in Chicago's South Side.

19 Data relevant to this point were obtained. Middle-class adults are most likely to "like" the communities where the boys were found. NLC adults have the most negative attitudes concerning their neighborhood.

20 According to this line of reasoning, the small proportion of MC adults who do *not* wonder about the fate of adolescents (about 15% in both the NMC and WMC groups) do not wonder about the problem because the outcome is a foregone conclusion—the boys will do very well for themselves when they grow up.

21 For a discussion of the school adjustments of the boys in the Chicago study, see Jonathan Freedman and Ramon Rivera, "Education, Social Class, and Patterns of Delinquency," paper read at the annual meetings of the American Sociological Association, 1962. Within each race, middle-class boys are most successful in school, followed by LC boys. Gang boys make the poorest adjustments to school.

22 See Short, Rivera and Tennyson *op. cit.*, for the relevant data (esp. Tables 1 and 2).

23 See Kobrin *et al.*, "Criteria of Status Among Street Gangs," this issue.

GROUP PROCESS, COHESIVENESS, AND DELINQUENCY

1 James F. Short, Jr., and Fred L. Strodtbeck, *Group Process and Gang Delinquency* (Chicago: University of Chicago Press, 1965), Chapter 11; Robert A. Gordon, "Social Level, Social Disability, and Gang Interaction," *American Journal of Sociology*, 73 (July, 1967), pp. 42–62; see also William Foote Whyte, *Street Corner Society*, 2nd ed. (Chicago: University of Chicago Press, 1955), p. 256.

2 See, also, reports of the Sherif's extensive research on reference groups in laboratory and "natural" settings. Muzafer and Carolyn Sherif, *Reference Groups: Exploration into Conformity and Deviation of Adolescents* (New York: Harper & Row, 1964); and Chapters 12 and 13 in *Problems of Youths Transition to Adulthood in a Changing World*, edited by the Sherifs (Chicago: Aldine, 1965). See Jansyn's excellent article, Leon R. Jansyn, Jr., "Solidarity and Delinquency in a Street Corner Group," *American Sociological Review*, 31 (October, 1966), pp. 600–614.

3 See Arthur Miller, "The Bored and the Violent," *Harper's Magazine*, 225 (November, 1962), pp. 50–56.

4 S. M. Miller, "The American Lower Class: A Typological Approach," *Social Research* (Spring, 1964). Republished in the Syracuse University Youth Development Reprint Series, pp. 1–22.

5 Short and Strodtbeck, *op. cit.*, p. 281.

6 David Matza, *Delinquency and Drift* (New York: John Wiley and Sons, Inc., 1964).

7 David Matza and Gresham M. Sykes, "Delinquency and Subterranean Values," *American Sociological Review* (October, 1961), pp. 712–719; and Gresham M. Sykes and David Matza, "Techniques of Neutralization: A Theory of Delinquency," *American Sociological Review* (December, 1957), pp. 664–670.

8 See, e.g., Scott Briar and Irving Piliavin, "Delinquency, Situational Inducements, and Commitment to Conformity," *Social Problems* (Summer, 1965), pp. 35–45.

GROUPS, GANGS, AND COHESIVENESS

Malcolm W. Klein and Lois Y. Crawford

1 Robert A. Gordon "Social Level, Social Disability, and Gang Interaction," unpublished paper quoted in James F. Short, Jr. and Fred L. Strodtbeck, *Group Process and Gang Delinquency*. Chicago: University of Chicago Press, 1965, pp, 272–273.

2 Muzafer and Carolyn Sherif, *Reference Groups*. New York: Harper & Row, 1964, pp. 48–49.

3 Albert J. and Bernice E. Lott, "Group Cohesiveness as Interpersonal Attraction: A review of relationships with antecedent and consequent variables," *Psychological Bulletin*, 1965, 64, #4, pp. 259–309.

4 This point—the interaction of normal group processes with delinquency involvement and the consequent impact on group structure—is overlooked by the Sherifs in their argument, although they quote Polsky on just this issue; Sherif and Sherif, *op. cit.*, p. 129.

5 Frederic M. Thrasher, *The Gang: A Study of 1,313 Gangs in Chicago*, abridged and with a new introduction by James F. Short, Jr. Chicago: University of Chicago Press, 1963, particularly Chapters 4 and 14.

6 Lewis Yablonsky, *The Violent Gang*, New York: MacMillan, 1962, particularly Chapter 13. Yablonsky's seemingly overstated interest in violence, paranoia, and sociopathic characteristics should not blind one to his legitimate contribution to the placement of gangs in the group-structure tradition.

7 Richard A. Cloward and Lloyd E. Ohlin, *Delinquency and Opportunity: A Theory of Delinquent Gangs*. Glencoe: The Free Press, 1960.

8 Irving Spergel, *Racketville, Slumtown, Haulburg: An Exploratory Study of Delinquent Subcultures*. Chicago: University of Chicago Press, 1964.

9 Short and Strodtbeck, *op. cit.*, Chapter 4.

10 Saul Bernstein, *Youth on the Streets: Work with Alienated Youth Groups.* New York: Association Press, 1964, pp. 98–100.

11 Albert K. Cohen, *Delinquent Boys.* Glencoe: The Free Press, 1955.

12 J. Milton Yinger, "Contraculture and Subculture," *American Sociological* Review, October 1960, 25 #5, pp. 625–635.

13 Nathan L. Gerrard, "The Core Member of the Gang," *British Journal of Criminology*, April 1964, 4, #4, pp. 361–371.

14 Short and Strodtbeck. *op. cit.*, Chapter 10.

15 Albert K. Cohen and Harold M. Hodges, "Lower-Blue-Collar-Class Characteristics," *Social Problems*, Spring 1963, 10, #4, pp. 303–334.

16 Parenthetically, it is often the failure to separate specific delinquent acts from the offender which makes for the inefficiency of many of our delinquency prevention programs. For, perhaps due to stimulus generalization, it is the whole boy and the whole group which is condemned, and not their delinquent product alone.

17 Francis J. Rigney and L. Douglas Smith, *The Real Bohemia: A Sociological and Psychological Study of the "Beats."* New York: Basic Books, 1961.

18 J. Downing, "Cohesiveness, Perception, and Values," *Human Relations*, 1958, 11, 157–166; A. Pepitone and G. Reichling, "Group Cohesiveness and the Expression of Hostility," *Human Relations*, 1955, 8, 327–337; S. Schacter, N. Ellertson, Dorothy McBride, and Doris Gregory, "An Experimental Study of Cohesiveness and Productivity," *Human Relations*, 1951, 4, 229–238.

19 B. N. Phillips and L. A. D'Amico, "Effects of Cooperation and Competition on the Cohesiveness of Small Face-to-Face Groups," *Journal of Educational Psychology*, 1956, 47, 65-70; H. P. Shelley, "Focused Leadership and Cohesiveness in Small Groups," *Sociometry*, 1960, 23, 209–216; J. W. Thibaut, "An Experimental Study of the Cohesiveness of Underprivileged Groups," *Human Relations*, 1950, 3, 251–278.

20 R. S. Albert, "Comments on the Scientific Function of the Concept of Cohesiveness," *American Journal of Sociology*, 1953, 59, 231–234.

21 A. J. Lott and Bernice E. Lott, "Group Cohesiveness, Communication Level and Conformity," *Journal of Abnormal and Social Psychology*, 1961, 62, 408–412.

22 L. Berkowitz, "Group Standards, Cohesiveness, and Productivity," *Human Relations*, 1954, 7, 509–519.

23 B. N. Phillips and L. A. D'Amico, *op. cit.*; Bernice Eisman, "Some Operational Measures of Cohesiveness and their Interrelations," *Human Relations*, 1959, 12, 183–189; Warren O. Hagstrom and Hanan C. Selvin, "Two Dimensions of Cohesiveness in Small Groups," *Sociometry*, 28, 1, 30–43

24 Leon Festinger, "Group Attraction and Membership," in *Group Dynamics, Research and Theory*, edited by Dorwin Cartwright and Alvin Zander. Evanston, Illinois: Row, Peterson and Company

1953, pp. 92–101; Annie Van Bergen and J. Koskebakker, "Group Cohesiveness in Laboratory Experiments," *Acta Psychologica*, 1959, 16, 81–98; Warren O. Hagstrom and Hanan C. Selvin, *op. cit.;* Bernice Eisman, *op. cit.*

25 Bernice Eisman, *op. cit.;* Warren O. Hagstrom and Hanan C. Selvin, *op. cit.*

26 Neal Gross and William E. Martin, "On Group Cohesiveness," *American Journal of Sociology*, 57, May 1952, 546–554.

27 Dorwin Cartwright and Alvin Zander, *op. cit.*, p. 76.

28 A. J. Lott and Bernice E. Lott, *op. cit.*

29 A. Pepitone and R. Kleiner, "The Effects of Threat and Frustration on Group Cohesiveness," *Journal of Abnormal and Social Psychology*, 1957, 54, 192–199.

30 Muzafer and Carolyn Sherif, *op. cit.*, p. 242.

31 Neal Gross and William E. Martin, *op. cit.;* Muzafer and Carolyn Sherif, *op. cit.;* Leon Festinger, Stanley Schacter and Kurt Back, *Social Pressures in Informal Groups.* New York: Harper, 1950; P. R. Hofstaetter, "A Note on Group Cohesiveness," *American Journal of Sociology*, 58, Sept. 1952, 198–200.

32 Short and Strodtbeck, *op. cit.*, especially Chapters 8 and 9; also see Leon Jansyn, *Solidarity and Delinquency in a Street Corner Group*, unpublished Master's thesis, University of Chicago, 1960.

33 A gang "cluster" refers to a pattern of inter-gang affiliations commonly observed among traditional gangs in Los Angeles. Typically, a cluster consists of three or four age-graded male subgroups plus a girls' group. Each subgroup maintains its own self-identity, yet clearly affiliates with the overall cluster and its "generic" name. See Malcolm W. Klein, "Internal Structures and Age Distributions in Four Delinquent Negro Gangs," paper presented at the annual meetings of the California State Psychological Association, Los Angeles, 1964. Youth Studies Center, University of Southern California, mimeo.

34 Louis L. McQuitty, "Elementary Linkage Analysis for Isolating Orthogonal and Oblique Types and Typal Relevancies," *Educational and Psychological Measurement*, 1957, 17.

35 Richard I. Martin and Malcolm W. Klein, "A Comparative Analysis of Four Measures of Delinquency Seriousness," paper presented at the annual meeting of the Pacific Sociological Association, Salt Lake City, April 1965. Youth Studies Center, University of Southern California, mimeo.

ALEATORY RISKS VERSUS SHORT-RUN HEDONISM IN EXPLANATION OF GANG ACTION

Fred L. Strodtbeck and James F. Short, Jr.

1 See Harold W. Pfautz, "Near-Group Theory and Collective Behavior: A Critical Reformulation," *Social Problems*, 9 (Fall, 1961), p. 173. The report referred to is "Street Corner Groups and Patterns of

Notes

Delinquency," a Progress Report on research grant M–3301 to the National Institute of Mental Health, March, 1961. For a revised edition of this paper, see James F. Short, Jr., same title, *The American Catholic Sociological Review* (March, 1963), particularly on pp. 20–21. The language in the latter publication conforms more closely to this analysis than does the original paper. The authors owe a debt for the original use of the terms to Edwin Sutherland, with whom FLS studied, and for the stochastic phrasing to marginal comments by Albert K. Cohen on an earlier manuscript. Appreciation is also expressed to the Program for Detached Workers of the YMCA of Metropolitan Chicago, whose dedicated cooperation has made possible the entire research program.

James F. Short, Jr., Fred L. Strodtbeck, and Desmond S. Cartwright, "A Case from the Study of Parenthood in a Street Corner Gang," *Sociological Inquiry*, 32 (Spring, 1962), pp. 185–202.

Ibid., pp. 200–201.

Case materials are taken from interviews with detached workers of the YMCA who were in contact with the gangs, or from field notes by research team members who reported on their contacts with boys or workers. Detached workers are young men who meet gang boys on the street, on their own terms, and very rapidly become their confidants. See Ray A. Tennyson, "Detached Workers as Sources of Data," paper read at the annual meeting of the Society for the Study of Social Problems, 1960 (mimeographed).

Interview, 9/17/59.

Interview, 10/1/59.

James F. Short, Jr., and Fred L. Strodtbeck, "The Response of Gang Leaders to Status Threats: An Observation on Group Process and Delinquent Behavior," *American Journal of Sociology*, 68 (March, 1963), pp. 571–579.

R. Duncan Luce, *Individual Choice Behavior*, New York: John Wiley, 1959, pp. 78–90.

R. Duncan Luce, in *Social Science Approaches to Business Behavior*, George B. Strother and Richard D. Irwin, editors, Homewood, Illinois: Dorsey Press, 1962.

10 See Walter P. Miller, "Lower Class Culture as a Generating Milieu of Gang Delinquency," *Journal of Social Issues*, 14 (1958), pp. 5–19.

11 The only significant exception to this is the tendency among retreatist gangs to engage competitively in apparently self-destructive activities. Members of such a gang included in the present study took drugs to the point literally of "knocking themselves out" and engaged in delinquent episodes which inevitably led to incarceration, embarrassment, or personal injury. Their "folklore" revolved around discussion of kicks, and of "way out" behavior under the influence or in pursuit of drugs. This group is discussed at greater length in James F. Short, Jr., and Fred L. Strodtbeck, *Group Process and Gang Delinquency* (Chicago: University of Chicago Press, 1965).

12 See John M. Wise, "A Comparison of Sources of Data as Indexes of Delinquent Behavior," unpublished M.A. thesis, University of Chicago, 1962.

13 David G. Hays and Robert R. Bush, "A Study of Group Action," *American Sociological Review*, 19 (December, 1954), pp. 693–701.

14 Evidence on this point is discussed in Robert A. Gordon and James F. Short, Jr., "Social Level, Social Disability, and Gang Interaction," unpublished manuscript, 1962; and in Short and Strodtbeck, *Group Process, ibid.*

15 Edward Banfield, *The Moral Basis of a Backward Society*, New York: Free Press of Glencoe, 1958.

16 Cf. Frank Tannebaum's classic discussion of this issue in *Crime and the Community*, Boston: Ginn and Co., 1938, pp. 17th ff.

17 Fred L. Strodtbeck, James F. Short, Jr., and Ellen Kolegar, "The Analysis of Self-Descriptions by Members of Delinquent Gangs," *Sociological Quarterly* (October, 1962), pp. 331–356; and "Self-Description and Delinquent Behavior," by the present authors, Chapter 7 in *Group Process, op. cit.*

18 Cases in which a young man is employed to engage in violent activity, e.g., a "hired gun," would *not* break the $a > b > c > d$ chain.

POSTSCRIPT

1 See, for example, Martin Gold, *Status Forces in Delinquent Boys*, Ann Arbor: Institute for Social Research, 1963; Larry Karacki and Jackson Toby, "The Uncommitted Adolescent: Candidate for Gang Socialization," *Sociological Inquiry*, 32 (Spring, 1962), 203-215; James F. Short, Jr., "Gang Delinquency and Anomie," in Marshall B. Clinard (ed.), *Anomie and Deviant Behavior* (New York: Free Press, 1964); Ramon Rivera and James F. Short, Jr., "Occupational Goals: A Comparative Analysis," in Malcolm Klein and Barbara Myerhoff (eds.), *Juvenile Gangs in Context: Theory, Research, and Action*, (Englewood Cliffs, N.J.: Prentice-Hall, forthcoming).

INDEX